Islam Between East and West

ISLAM BETWEEN EAST and WEST

الإسلام بين الشرق والغرب

'Alija 'Ali Izetbegovic

American Trust Publications

1412 A.H. - 1991 A.D.

First Edition 1984
Second Edition 1989

American Trust Publications
10900 W. Washington Street
Indianapolis, Indiana 46231

Copyright© American Trust Publications

This book is copyright under the Berne Convention
No reproduction without permission
All rights reserved

Library of Congress Cataloguing in Publication Data
84-045552
ISBN 0-89259-057-2

Sole Distributor In The Middle East, Asia, Africa and Australia
INTERNATIONAL ISLAMIC PUBLISHING HOUSE
P.O. Box 55195, Riyadh 11534 - Saudi Arabia - Tel. 4650818 - 4647213 - Fax 4633489

الموزع الوحيد في الشرق الأوسط وآسيا وأفريقيا واستراليا
الدار العالمية للكتاب الاسلامي
ص.ب: ٥٥١٩٥ ـ الرياض ١١٥٣٤ ـ هاتف: ٤٦٥٠٨١٨ ـ ٤٦٤٧٢١٣ ـ فاكس: ٤٦٣٣٤٨٩

PUBLISHER'S NOTE

This is the revised edition of *Islam Between East and West*. We have tried to provide additional footnotes to the text as needed. We have also supplemented the fragmented footnotes of the first edition published in 1984. It is hoped that this edition will enhance the book's value.

Until this date, we have not heard about the author's release from the prison in Sarajevo (Yugoslavia). Mr. Izetbegovic predicted the fall of communism well before the current tide of change in Eastern Europe. His assessment of the situation there was based on his thesis that life, like Islam, is bipolar, and any effort to undo its bipolarity will therefore lead to an unstable state of existence. What bothers us is the irony in his case: the man who strove for this change and predicted it remains incarcerated while his countrymen celebrate life in freedom.

December 25, 1989

"Though it is from the East that the sun rises,
showing itself bold and bright,
without a veil, it burns and blazes with inward fire
only when it escapes from the shackles of East and West.
Drunk with the splendor it springs up out of its East
that it may subject all horizons to its mastery,
its nature is innocent of both East and West,
though in origin, true, it is an Easterner."

Muhammad Iqbal, *Javīd Nāma*

CONTENTS

Chapter 3
THE PHENOMENON OF ART

Chapter 4
MORALITY

Chapter 5
CULTURE AND HISTORY

Chapter 6
DRAMA AND UTOPIA

PART II
ISLAM — BIPOLAR UNITY

Chapter 7
MOSES — JESUS — MUHAMMAD

Chapter 8
ISLAM AND RELIGION

Chapter 9
THE ISLAMIC NATURE OF LAW

Chapter 10
IDEAS AND REALITY

Chapter 11
"THE THIRD WAY" OUTSIDE ISLAM

PREFACE

Islam Between East and West is the result of a comprehensive multidisciplinary study of the leading world views in the contemporary history of mankind. The phenomenon of self-forgetfulness which characterizes the modern history of the Islamic world puts both the Eastern and Western intellectual in the same position in relation to this book.

Through comparative studies of the basic premises and consequences — social, legal, political, cultural, psychological, and so on — of two ideologies which have defined the destiny of mankind for several of the last centuries, the author reveals the symptoms of the increasingly dramatic perspective of Christianization and atheization of the world. Chrisitanity as a paradigmatic cultural-religious phenomenon — that is, religion in its Occidental meaning, alienated from the act of revelation — is a generic idea of creation, culture, art, and morality. As such, it has aspired to spiritualization of history. Atheization, however, based on a materialistic approach with socialism being its practical and historical perspective, is a common denominator of evolutionistic, civilizational, political, and utopian elements which take care of the physical nature of man and his history.

Modern man has found himself on a historical razor edge, dramatically divided into spirit in the vision of Christianization and into matter in the praxis of atheization. The Islamic teaching of synthesis has proven to be the only possible model for coping with this situation. As such, Islam is more a need than a question of choice. Some elements similar to the original Islamic teaching discovered by the author in the Anglo-Saxon world are not the sign of conscious conversion of that world but an imperative of inner logic which the modern world will have to understand more.

Symptoms such as family disintegration, the increase of social vices, crime, prostitution, neuroses, and general hopelessness appear in both of the previously mentioned leading systems and point to the same etiology of the disease, though with different signs. Neglecting the act of God's creation, the atheistic teaching reduces man to a perfectly drilled member of society, depersonalized and despiritualized, and thus deprived of any wish to rebel. On the other hand, the Christian man, spiritualized but bodiless, has turned his rebellion into an almost aesthetic act, sublime in art but futile and inhuman in practice and everyday life.

Through restitution of Islamic thought as the bipolar thought, the author has pointed to the fatigue existing in the minds of both materialistic and religious provenance who are increasingly ready to admit the one-sidedness of their approaches, but who, nevertheless, keep on closing their eyes even when the latest historical events warn us in a most evident way. However, the "Islamic fever" is a historical fact, and the submission to God which semantically explains the notion of Islam, is the only dignified human choice in the destiny of an individual, this destiny being but a reflection of the cosmic destiny.

Hasan Karachi

AUTHOR'S NOTE

Islam Between East and West is not a book of theology. It deals with dogmas, institutions, and teachings of Islam with the aim of establishing the place of Islam in the general spectrum of ideas. It is a look at Islam not from within but rather from without. In this sense, the topic of the book is not primarily Islam as a teacher but Islam as an outlook on the world.

The book consists of two parts. The first part entitled PREMISES deals with religion in general. The second part is dedicated to Islam or more precisely to one of its aspects — bipolarity.

The PREMISES are in fact polemics on atheism and materialism. The respective positions held by religion and atheism in facing the question of man's origin and related issues of evolution and creation are discussed through the following six chapters of this part:

Chapter 1: Creation and Evolution, Chapter 2: Culture and Civilization, Chapter 3: The Phenomenon of Art, Chapter 4: Morality, Chapter 5: Culture and History, and Chapter 6: Culture and History.

The thesis is that by an inherent logic, evolution, civilization, science and utopia are parallel to atheism, whereas creation, culture, arts and morals are parallel to religion.

Evolution by its very nature and regardless of complexity and duration could not "produce" man but only a perfect or perfected animal as a future member of society. Socialism, as a practical and social consequence of materialism, does not deal with man but rather with the organization of the life of the social animal. Man is primarily a spiritual and not a biological or social factor and could originate only by the act of divine creation. Thus, if there were no God, there could be no man, and if there were no man, there would be no culture, only the needs and their satisfaction — that is, only civilization. Atheism accepts science and progress; yet, in its essence, it implies the negation of man and by the same token a refutation of humanism, freedom, and human rights. Behind the contradiction between culture and civilization stands in fact the basic contrast between conscience /mind and being/ nature, or on the practical plane, between religion and science.

Every culture is theistic in its essence; every civilization is atheistic. Therefore, in the same way as science does not lead to humanism and in principle has nothing in common with culture, religion by itself does not lead to progress. By widening and deepening this analysis, the first part of the book establishes this all-encompassing dualism of the human world, exemplified by the "insurmountable" conflicts between spirit and body, religion and science, and culture and civilization. This view of the world reflects the so-called Christian level of humanity consciousness.

Socialism is an expression of the same level of consciousness. The same dilemma is in question, only the choice is different and anti-Christian Socialism is inverse Christianity. Socialistic values are Christian values with negative signs; in fact, they are inverted equivalents: instead of religion science; instead of individuality, society; instead of humanism, progress; instead of upbringing, drill; instead of love, violence; instead of freedom, social security; instead of human rights, social rights; instead of civitas dei, civitas solis.

Is man able to overcome this contradiction, this either or between heaven and earth, or is he condemned forever to this stretching between the two? Is there a way by which science can serve religion, hygiene, piety, progress, and humanism? Could the utopia of civitas solis be inhabited with human beings instead of anonymous and faceless individuals and have the features of "God's kingdom" on earth?

The second part of the book is dedicated to this question. The answer is yes, in Islam. Islam is not only a religion or a way of life but primarily the principle of the organization of the universe. Islam existed before man and it is, as the Qur'ān explicity states, a principle by which man was created.[1] Hence, one finds an inherent

[1]The Qur'ān 30:30.

harmony between man and Islam or, as the book calls it, the "man-likeness" of Islam. In the same way as man is a unity of spirit and body, Islam is a unity of religion and social order, and just as the body in prayer (*salāh*) can follow the movement of the soul, the social order can serve the ideals of religion and ethics. This unity, foreign both to Christianity and materialism, is basic and the "most Islamic" characteristic of Islam.

The concept in question is examined in the second part of the book by discussing a series of topics in the field of religion, law, and cultural and political history. This part of the book begins with a parallel of Moses, Jesus, and Muhammad (upon them be peace) who represent three primeval answers to mankind's encounter with history, while the Qur'ān is a unique synthesis of the realism of the Old Testament and the idealism of the New Testament.

In Chapter VIII an analysis of the five basic pillars of Islam is given, with *salāh* (Islamic prayer) holding the central position.

Salāh is in fact an abbreviation of Islam as a whole, its "code" or "cipher." It originated from bringing together two principles which in the viewpoint of Christianity are contradictory and unlinkable, namely that of *wuḍū'* (ritual ablution) and that of prayer. These two principles are in the very foundation of Islam. Rationalism that rejects mysticism and mysticism that excludes a rationalistic approach violate this "*salāh* balance principle." Any one-sided radicalism in this regard is a descent to the Christian level of consciousness — a violation of the axis of Islam. In the same way, if Islam represents man's natural potential, it must be found be it in imperfect form or in fragments wherever religious people think and work, that is, wherever religious people "...do not forget their part in this world."[2] The author finds the symptoms of this phenomenon, especially in the Anglo-Saxon world.

The book ends with the essay *Submission to God* as the soul of Islam.

[2]The Qur'ān 28:77.

INTRODUCTION

The writer of this book, 'Alija 'Ali Izetbegovic, a lawyer from Sarajevo, Yugoslavia, comes from South Slav which for more than 500 years belonged to Islam. He views his environment, therefore, with an Islamic frame of mind. Nevertheless, he charts his own course — daring but fascinating.

Closest to his heart appears to be a desire to offer the younger generation of Muslims of the world implements for orientation.

'Ali Izetbegovic has meanwhile entered into the history of Islam in Bosnia. In August 1983, he, together with eleven Bosnian intellectuals (among them one poetess) was sentenced to fourteen years in jail for his "fundamentalist digressions" by a court in Sarajevo. Evidently, the communist rulers in Yugoslavia see in the philosophy of our writer a great threat to their current order.

As a Bosnian Muslim who has been struggling for several decades to preserve Islamic faith under the strenuous conditions of secularized society, I accept with great pleasure this opportunity to point to an intensive concept of Islam in the hearts and minds of Bosnian Muslims.

Neither 'Ali Izetbegovic nor any other of the defendants from the 1983 Sarajevo's trial have any political goals or interest in politics in their life's circle. None of them can be accused of any intentions against the state or against the people as was wrongfully stated by the court.

For the clarification of some key issues and possible criticism of the book's content what follows are the views of a group of enlightened Muslims as these were expressed in the publication "Islam and West," printed in Vienna. It should be noted that this publication is, in fact, the only organ of Bosnian Muslims in the free world. It is printed mainly in the German, Bosnian, and Serbo-Croatian languages.

These views are presented without any pretense to systematization or completeness:

In secularized Europe, the cry "back to our origins," which is shaking the Islamic world in our days, can only be interpreted as a challenge to us to carefully examine our Islamic and cultural heritage and to jettison the accumulated historical ballast of centuries which is a hindrance to progress. If undertaken in a realistic and independent way, this return to our origins is not likely to give rise to reactionary movements. On the contrary, it can be expected to lead to a purer understanding of Islam.

Islam cannot mean submission to the tyranny of history; on the contrary, it means a continuing obligation to order life in any given situation in accordance with the needs of the time and *in total submission to God.* This calls for a greater emphasis on the universal dimension of Islam which actually regards Judaism and Christianity as its earlier manifestations.

The innate propensity of Eastern people to cling to long-established thought patterns, a charge already brought against the Arabs by the Qur'ān itself, is a hindrance to a modern Islamic education based on scientific knowledge — an essential element for Muslims in their witnessing to God. A change has long been overdue here. Only if we grow out of *blind* submission to the doctrinal authority of our ancestors can new perspectives be opened up.

Even in secularized Europe, Islam will hardly let itself be persuaded to regard God as primarily the "Lord of History." In the view of Islam, and thus not only of history but also of prehistory and "posthistory," the restricted view of God from a human standpoint alone is obviously a source of anthropocentrism which has led in the end to a distorted view of humankind itself. As a consequence, humankind is dangerously far from the order willed by God.

Islam offers its adherents many ways of coping with life in secularized society. Mention may be made, for example, of the absence of sacraments, of a priesthood, and of baptism; the civil nature of marriage; the natural approach to sexuality; the rejection of the idea of excommunication; the positive attitude to knowledge and scientific research; the relative toleration of mixed marriages; and the long-standing readiness for dialogue with the monotheistic religions.

Blind progress that does not take its bearing on any firm valuational framework risks leading to decultivation and loss of personality. The effects of such dedication to the *Zeitgeist* manifests itself, for example, in the case of the Jews. That is why Martin Buber has already warned: "If you become like other peoples, you no longer deserve to be."[1]

Taking into account the undeniably existing will of Islam toward improvement of the world, it becomes evident that it is a fallacy to attribute fatalism to Islam. Fatalism is more likely to be met in the view of life shaped by modern psychology and based on a fatal reductionism of all human dimensions to environmental influences. This reductionism does not ask what the meaning of life is and does not encourage man to develop the will to give life meaning; it tells man that he is the victim of circumstances. "That is grist to the mill of mass neurosis because fatalism is part of the symptomatology of mass neurosis," a reputed scholar holds.

As is known, the zenith and ultimate act of the spiritual side in Muhammad's life was his visionary flight into the heavenly spheres mentioned in the Qur'ān under the name of *mi'rāj*. This example of the spirituality of Muhammad (upon whom be peace) indicates the direction in which the life of a Muslim should move. This direction clearly is vertical.

Religiousness that understands its culmination to be in the heavenly ascent — the *mi'rāj* can be but bent toward God. It is dynamic, uplifting, and open-minded because it is not bound by tradition and custom. In Islamic philosophy which flourished until the end of the thirteenth century and sporadically even later, the thought persisted that science had to be in accord with revelation — a view firmly held by ibn-Rushd / Averroes (died in 1198). The course of Islamic cultural history shows convincingly that religion and science can in fact be in accord.

The writer of this book, who also wrote the Islamic Declaration — the subject of frequent publicity in the international media and the main argument against the defendants at the Sarajevo trial —

---

[1]Martin Buber, *Gesammelte Werke*, ed. Richard Beer — Hofmann (Frankfurt am Main: Fischer, 1963).

attempts to build on its inherited spiritual ground an alternative to capitalism and dialectical materialism. That is, however, nothing new for the Islamic world. 'Ali Izetbegovic brings a refereshingly new approach to this tradition.

The treatment as well as the methodology of problematics is the legitimate and rightful property of the writer. Within the framework of these two elements, approach and method, the author's specific life philosophy has found its form. This specific philosophy appears also in the pages of this book.

Because of the sudden and unexpected arrest of the author, the academic apparatus of the book (bibliography and references) have remained unfinished. The sources and sometimes even titles of the quoted books are incomplete ... and it is not clear whether the author quotes the original or the translation of some book. These cases are indicated with the abbreviation "n.p.d." (no publication data).

Considering the extraordinary circumstances under which this book is published, it is hoped that the reader will pardon these weaknesses. I am sure this will not detract from its immense appeal.

Dr. S. Balic
Institut für Geschichte der Arabisch - Islamischen Wissenschaften
Ander Johann Wolfgang Goethe — Universitat
Frankfurt Am Main

ABOUT THE THEME

The modern world is characterized by a sharp ideological encounter. All of us are involved in it, whether as its partakers or as its victims. What is the place of Islam in this gigantic confrontation? Does it have a part in the shaping of the present world? This book tries in part to answer the question.

There are only three integral views of the world: the religious, the materialistic, and the Islamic.[1] They reflect three elemental possibilities (conscience, nature, and man), each of them manifesting itself as Christianity, materialism, and Islam. All variety of ideologies, philosophies, and teachings from the oldest time up to now can be reduced to one of these three basic world views. The first takes as its starting point the existence of the spirit, the second the existence of matter, and the third the simultaneous existence of spirit and matter. If only matter exists, materialism would be the only consequent philosophy. On the contrary, if the spirit exists, then man also exists, and man's life would be senseless without a kind of religion and morality. Islam is the name for the unity of spirit and matter, the highest form of which is man himself. The human life is complete only if it includes both the physical and the spiritual desires of the human being. All man's failures are either because of the religious denial of man's biological needs or the materialistic denial of man's spiritual desires.

Our forefathers used to say that there existed two substances: mind and matter, under which they understood two elements, two orders, two worlds, with different origins and different natures, which

[1]In this book, the term religion has the meaning it has in Europe — that is, faith as an esoteric experience which does not go beyond a personal relationship with God and as such expresses itself only in dogmas and rituals. Accordingly, Islam cannot be classified as a religion. Islam is more than a religion for it embraces life.

do not emerge from one another and which cannot be reduced one to another. Even the greatest spirits of the world could not avoid this differentiation; however, their approach was different. We could imagine these two worlds as separated in time, two successive worlds ("the present and the next"), or look at them as two simultaneous worlds different by nature and meaning, which is nearer to the truth.

Dualism is the closest human feeling, but it is not necessarily the highest human philosophy. On the contrary, all great philosophies have been monistic. Man experiences the world dualistically, but monism is in the essence of all human thinking. Philosophy disagrees with dualism. However, this fact does not mean too much, because life, being superior to thought, may not be judged by it. In reality, since we are human beings, we are living two realities. We can deny these two worlds, but we cannot escape from them. Life does not depend too much on our understanding of it.

Therefore, the question is not if we live two lives, but only if we live so with understanding. In this lies the ultimate meaning of Islam. Life is dual. It became technically impossible for man to live one life, from the moment he ceased to be plant or animal, from the time of *qalu balā* (the Qur'ān, 7:172), when the moral norms were established, or when man was "thrown out into the world."

We have no rational evidence that there exists another world, but we have a clear feeling that man does not exist only to produce and to consume. Scientists or thinkers who try to discover the truth cannot find that higher life by thinking alone, but their own life, spent in search for the truth and neglecting the physical living, is just that higher form of human existence.

The two discussed lines of thinking in human history are parallel and can be easily drawn. In spite of their ceaseless mutual antagonism, they continue to date showing no essential progress. The first starts with Plato and runs through the Christian thinkers of the Middle Ages, followed by al-Ghazāli, Descartes, Malenbranche, Leibnitz, Berkeley, Fitche, Cudworth, Kant, Hegel, Mach, and Bergson in our day. The materialistic line could be represented as follows: Thales, Anaximander, Heraclitus, Lucretius, Hobbes, Gassendi, Helvetius, Holbach, Diderot, Spencer, and Marx. In the field of practical human objectives, these two extremes of man's thinking are represented by humanism and progress. Religion, as it is understood in the West, does not lead toward progress, and science does not lead toward humanism.

However, in reality, there is neither pure religion nor pure science; for example, there is no religion without some elements of science in it and no science without some religious hope in it. This fact creates a mixture in which it is difficult to find the true origin or true place of an idea or tendency. By discussing them, our aim is to reach their pure forms, with their ultimate and logical but sometimes practically absurd conclusions. We will find the two systems as two inwardly logical and closed orders, but for many of us the picture will seem surprising. They even explain each other in terms of a mosaic, in which an empty place can be filled using the inverse argument. When, for example, materialism claims that only objective factors, independent of men, are the prime movers of all historical events, then in antithesis a quite opposite opinion should be expected. Indeed, after short searching we find the so-called "heroic" interpretation of history, for example Carlyle's, in which all historical events are explained as having been influenced by some strong characters — heroes. According to materialists, "history does not walk on its head,"[2] and according to the others, quite the contrary: geniuses make history.

In the same fashion as in the preceding example, historical materialism is against Christian personalism, and by the same logic, creation is against evolution, ideal against interest, freedom against uniformity, personality against society, and so forth. The religious demand "destroy the wishes," had to have its opposite equivalent in civilization's imperative "create constantly the new wishes." In the table in the appendix at the end of this work, the reader will find a more detailed attempt to classify the ideas and views according to the said model. The result, although quite incomplete, can show that religion and materialism are the two elementary views of the world, neither of which can be split anymore, nor one fused into the other — to use a figure from the Qur'ān — the two seas "...which cannot prevail one over another."[3]

It is impossible to find rational arguments for either of these world views. Both of them are within themselves logical systems, and there is no other logic that could stand above them and judge them. In principle and in practice, only human life is above them. To live — and above all to live completely and righteously

---

[2]Karl Marx, *The Karl Marx Library*, trans. Saul K. Padower (New York: McGraw-Hill, 1972).
[3]The Qur'ān 55:19-20.

— is more than any religion or socialism. Christianity offers salvation, but only inner salvation. Socialism offers only external salvation. Faced with these two parallel worlds in a logically unsolvable clash, we feel we have to accept both of them, trying to find their new natural balance. The two opposed teachings divide life, truth, and man's fate between them.

There are some essential facts on which everyone counts in life, regardless of one's own philosophy. Man learned them owing to his common sense or to his successes and failures. These facts are the family, material security, happiness, righteousness, veracity, health, education, freedom, interest, power, responsibility, and the like. If we analyze these facts, we will see that they group around a common axis and form a realistic system, maybe heterogeneous and incomplete, but reminding us very much of Islam.

The differences between the said basic teachings seem unbridgeable, but only so in theory. In practical life, the situation is different. What they were fighting against yesterday is today approved, and some very dear ideas remain only as a decoration of theory.

Marxism rejected the family and the state, but in practice it kept these institutions. Every pure religion disapproved of man's worrying about this world, but as the ideology of living people, it accepted the struggle for social justice and a better world. Marxism has had to accept some degree of individual freedom and religion some use of force. It is obvious in real life that man cannot live according to a consistent philosophy.

The question is whether they can find a way out and remain what they are. To adapt themselves to real life, they borrow from each other. Christianity, which has become a church, began to talk about work, wealth, power, education, science, marriage, laws, social justice, and so forth. And Materialism, on the other hand, which became socialism or an order, a state, speaks about humanism, morality, art, creation, justice, responsibility, freedom, and so forth.

Instead of pure doctrines, we are offered their interpretations for everyday use. The deformation of both religion and materialism has been happening according to a kind of law. In both cases the problem was the same: how can something that is only one aspect of life be implemented in real life which is more complex?

In theory, one can be a Christian or a materialist, more or less radical, but in reality no one is consistent, neither Christian nor materialist.

Modern utopias in China, Korea and Vietnam, which held themselves as the most consistent forms of Marxist teaching, are good examples of the compromise and inconsistency in practice. Instead of allowing time to form the new morals reflecting new relations in the economic base, they have simply taken over the traditional moral norms, especially two of them: modesty and respect for elders.[4] So, on the side of radical Marxism, we find also the two most known principles of the existing religion. The authors of the system unwillingly admit this fact, but facts remain what they are, regardless of our recognition of them.

In some socialist states well-performed work is rewarded with moral stimulants instead of material ones. However, the moral stimulants cannot be explained by materialistic philosophy. It is the same case with the appeals for humanism, justice, equality, freedom, human rights, and so forth, which are all of religious origin. Certainly, everybody has the right to live as he thinks best, including the right not to be consistent with his own pattern. Still, to understand the world correctly, it is important to know the true origin and meaning of the ideas ruling the world.

In research of this kind, the dangers lie in different "obviousnesses" and so-called generally accepted opinions. The sun is not turning around the earth, although it is evident. The whale is not a fish, regardless of the fact that most people believe so. Socialism and freedom are not compatible, regardless of repeated convincings. In spite of the general confusion, ideas remain what they are and influence the world, not according to their apparent and temporary meanings and natures but according to their original meaning and nature.

We have approached the definition of Islam in a different way. Keeping in mind the main point, we can say Islam means first to understand and to admit the primeval dualism of the world and then to overcome it.

The adjective "Islamic" is used in this book not only to qualify regulations which are commonly known as Islam, but also and even

---

[4]Modesty is a good excuse for a very low living standard, and respect for elders has been easily transformed into a blind respect for authority.

more so, to term the basic principle underlying them. Islam here is the name of a method rather than of a ready-made solution and means the synthesis of opposite principles. The basic principle of Islam reminds us of the pattern in which life was created. The inspiration which connected freedom of the mind and the determinism of nature in the life appearance, seems to be the same which connected ablution and prayer in a unity called Islamic *salah*. A powerful intuition would be able to reconstruct out of *salah* the complete Islam, and out of Islam the universal dualism of the world.[5]

Europe was not able to find a middle way although (England has tried in a way to be an exception in this regard). That is why it is not possible to express Islam using European terminology. The Islamic terms *salāh*, *zakāh*, *khalīfah*, *jamā'ah*, *wuḍū'*, and so forth are not prayer, tax, ruler, community, and washing. The definition that Islam is a synthesis between religion and materialism, that it exists in the middle between Christianity and socialism, is very rough and could be accepted only conditionally. It is more or less correct only in some aspects. Islam is neither a simple arithmetical mean between these two teachings, nor their average. *Salāh*, *zakāh*, *wuḍū'* are more indivisible since they express an intimate and simple feeling, a certainty which is expressed with one word and one picture only but which still represents a logically dual connotation. The parallel with man is obvious. Man is its measure and its explanation.[6]

It is known that the Qur'ān leaves an analytical reader the impression of disarrangement, and that it seems to be a compound of diverse elements. Nevertheless, the Qur'ān is life, not literature. Islam is a way of living rather than a way of thinking. The only authentic comment of the Qur'ān can be life, and as we know, it was the life of Prophet Muhammad. Islam in its written form (the Qur'ān) may *seem* disorderly, but in the life of Muhammad, it proves itself to be a natural union of love and force, the sublime and the real, the divine and the human. This explosive compound of religion and politics produced enormous force in the life of the peoples

---

[5]To define Islam as a principle is of essential importance for its future development. It has been said many times — quite correctly — that Islam and the Islamic world have become stereotyped and closed.

[6]It seems that *ayah* 30:30 from the Qur'ān speaks directly about this: "So set your face steadily and truly to the faith, God's handiwork, according to the pattern on which He has made mankind..."

who accepted it. In one moment, Islam has coincided with the very essence of life.

Islam's middle position can be recognized by the fact that Islam has always been attacked from the two opposite directions: from the side of religion that it is too natural, actual, and tuned to the world; and from the side of science that it contains religious and mystical elements. There is only one Islam, but like man, it has both soul and body. Its contrary aspects depend on a different point of view: materialists only see Islam as a religion and mysticism, as a "right wing" tendency, while Christians see it only as a sociopolitical movement, as a left-wing tendency.

The same dualistic impression repeats itself when looking from inside as well. Not one original Islamic institution belongs either to pure religion alone, or solely to science which may go along with politics and economy. The mystics have always stressed the religious aspect of Islam, the rationalists the other one. All the same, both of them have always had difficulties with Islam, simply because it cannot be put into any of their classifications. Take *wuḍū'* as an example. A mystic will define it as a religious ablution with symbolic meaning. A rationalist will look upon it as a matter of hygiene only. They are both right, but only partly. The defectiveness of the mystic explanation lies in the fact that it lets the hygienic side of *wuḍū'* become a mere form. Following the same logic in other questions, this approach will reduce Islam to pure religion, by eliminating all physical, intellectual, and social components from it. The rationalists take quite the opposite way. By neglecting the religious side, they degrade Islam to a political movement only, creating a new type of nationalism from it, a so-called Islamic nationalism, deprived of ethical-religious substance, empty and equal to all other nationalisms in this regard. To be a Muslim, in this case, does not represent an appeal or a duty, a moral or a religious obligation, or any attitude to the universal truth. It means only belonging to a group different from the other one. Islam has never been only a nation. Rather, Islam is a call to a nation, "to enjoin the right and to forbid the wrong"[7] — that is, to perform a moral mission. If we disregard the political component of Islam and accept religious mysticism, we silently admit dependence and slavery. On the contrary, if we ignore the religious component, we

[7]The Qur'ān 22:41.

cease to be any moral force. Does it matter if an imperialism is called British, German, or Islamic if it means only a naked power over people and things?

For the future and man's practical activity, Islam means the call to create a man harmonious in his soul and body and a society whose laws and socio-political institutions will maintain — and not violate — this harmony. Islam is, and should be, a permanent searching through history for a state of inward and outward balance. This is the aim of Islam today, and it is its specific historical duty in the future.

The problems discussed in this book coincide in a way with the most specific feature of the present historical situation, namely, the division of the world into two opposing camps, based on ideological conflict. The encounter between ideas is projected in reality more clearly than ever before, assuming practical, determined forms. The polarization increases, unfortunately, day by day. Today, we are faced with two worlds divided to the core, politically, ideologically, and emotionally. A gigantic historical experiment about the duality of man's world takes place before our eyes.

Still, a part of the world is not affected by this polarization, and the majority of it is made up of Muslim countries. This phenomenon is not accidental. Islam is ideologically independent — nonaligned. Islam is such by its very definition.

This process of ideological and political independence of Muslim countries will be continued. The unengagement is not only political; it is followed by the same decisive demands to rid themselves from foreign models and influences, both Eastern and Western. That is the natural position of Islam in today's world.[8]

Islam, which occupies a central position between East and West, has to become conscious of its own mission. Now, when it is more and more obvious that the opposed ideologies with their extreme forms cannot be imposed on mankind, and that they must go toward a synthesis and a new middle position, we want to prove that Islam corresponds to this natural way of thinking and that it is its most

---

[8]When this book was under preparation, two Islamic countries, Pakistan and Iran, cancelled their membership in a pro-Western treaty organization (CENTO). Some time ago, Indonesia, Sudan, Egypt, and Somalia rejected the attempts to be drawn into the orbit of the Eastern camp.

consistent expression. As Islam in the past was the intermediary between the ancient cultures and the West, it must again today, in a time of dramatic dilemmas and alternatives, shoulder its role of intermediary nation in the divided world. This is the meaning of the third way, the Islamic way.

Last, a few words about the work itself. The book is divided into two parts. The first part, PREMISES, discusses the question of religion in general. The second part deals with Islam, or more precisely, with one of its aspects: bipolarity.

In any event, this book is neither theology, nor is its author a theologian. In this regard, the book is rather an attempt at the translation of Islam into the language which the new generation speaks and understands. This fact might explain some of its faults and inaccuracies — perfect translations do not exist.

PART I

PREMISES: CONSIDERATION ABOUT RELIGION

Chapter 1

CREATION AND EVOLUTION

Man is not tailored according to Darwin, nor is the universe tailored according to Newton.

CREATION AND EVOLUTION

Darwin and Michelangelo

The origin of man is the cornerstone of every view of the world. Any discussion about how man should live takes us back to the question of man's origin. The answers given by science and religion contradict each other, as is the case with many other issues.

Science looks upon man's origin as the result of a long process of evolution from the lower forms of life where there is no clear distinction between animal and human. The point at which science considers man a human being is determined by external material facts: walking upright, making tools, or communicating through articulate speech. Here, man is a child of nature and remains a part of it.

On the other hand, religion and art talk about the creation of man. It is not a process but an act of God — not something continuous but an abrupt, painful, and catastrophic act. All religions and all art have created the visions of man thrown into matter, of his fall to earth, and of the antagonism between man and nature, of man's clash with a strange and unfriendly world.

Whether man is a product of evolution or is "created" becomes the question: who is man? Is he part of the world or something different from it?

The materialists maintain that man is the "perfect animal," "*l'homme machine.*" The difference between man and animal is one of stage, not of quality. There is no specific human essence.[1] There is only a "concrete historical and social concept of man" and "economic and social history is the only true history that really exists."[2] "Man is a system as any other in nature, subordinated to nature's inevitable, general laws."[3] The evolution of man is influenced by an external objective fact — work. As Friedrich Engels put it: "Man is the product of his environment and his work." The creation of man is represented as the result of an external biological process, determined by external, spiritual facts. The hand causes and promotes the development of psychological life. ... Its 'discovery' and the 'discovery' of language marks the end of the zoological and the beginning of the human history."[4]

These ideas *seem* quite convincing, but it is less obvious that they are at the same time a radical negation of man.

In materialistic philosophy, man is dissected into his constituent parts, and in the end he disappears. Engels demonstrated that man is the product of social relations, or more precisely, the result of the existing means of production. Man is nothing and creates nothing; on the contrary, he is only the result of given facts.

Darwin takes this impersonalized man in his hands and describes his ascent through natural selection to a human being who can speak, make tools, and walk erect. Biology completes this picture by showing that everything goes back to the primeval form of life which in turn is a physical-chemical process, a play of molecules. Life, conscience, and soul do not exist, and consequently, there is no human essence.

If we now leave this sharp and understandable but dull scientific model and turn to the interior of the Sistine Chapel and contemplate Michelangelo's famous frescoes representing man's history from his Fall to Doomsday, we are obliged to wonder about the meaning of these pictures. Do they contain any truth about the great themes they are depicting? If so, what is this truth? More precisely, in

---

[1]John Watson: "No Dividing line between Man and Brute," *Psychology Review* 20 (1913):158.

[2]Györge Lukacs: "Existentialism or Marxism," *Studies in European Realism,* trans. Edith Bone (London: Hillway Publishing Co., 1950).

[3]Ivan P. Pavlov: "Experimental Psychology," *Essays in Psychology and Psychiatry* (New York: Citadel Press, 1962).

[4]H. Berr in his introduction to Lewis H. Morgan: *Ancient Society* (Chicago: C.H. Kerr, 1907).

which way are these pictures truthful at all?

Greek drama, Dante's vision of heavens and hell, African spirituals, Faust's prologue in heaven, Melanesian masks, ancient Japanese frescoes, and modern paintings — all of these examples taken without any special order bear the same testimony. It is evident that they have nothing to do with Darwin's man, and it is not possible to imagine them as products of the surrounding nature. What kind of feelings stand behind the idea of a religion of salvation? What does this dramatic expression mean? How could there be anything dramatic in life which consists of an exchange between being and nature? What did Ernest Neizvestni see with his mind's eye when he drew Dante's Hell? Why is there fear among everything living, if man and life are the fruit of mother nature?

These questions make us wonder if the picture sketched by science is even complete. Science does give us an exact photograph of the world, but it lacks an essential dimension of reality. Science is characterized by a natural misunderstanding of the living and the human. In its strict logical analysis, it makes life devoid of life and man devoid of humanity.

Science about man is possible only if he is a part of the world or a product of it — that is, if he is a thing. Conversely, art is possible only if man is different from nature, if man is a stranger in it — that is, if he is a personality. All art is a continuous story of man's foreignness in nature.

So, in the question about man's origin, science and art are on a complete and irrevocable path of collision. Science enumerates facts leading inexorably to the conclusion of man's gradual evolution from animal to human. Art shows in exciting pictures man coming from the unknown. Science refers to Darwin and his gigantic synthesis; art refers to Michelangelo and his grandiose charter on the ceiling of the Sistine Chapel.[5]

Darwin and Michelangelo represent two different conceptions of man and two opposite truths about his origin. Neither of them will ever prevail over the other for one is supported by *so many irrefut-*

---

[5]The idea of evolution has always been connected with atheism. The first ideas about the origin and extinction of the species were expressed by Lucretius, a Roman poet well-known for his atheistic and hedonistic ideas. See, Titus Carus Lucretius, *De rerum natura,* trans. W.H.D. Rouse, 3rd ed. (Cambridge, MA: Harvard University Press, 1937).

able facts while the other is held in the hearts of all men.

It is only around man that two contradictory truths can exist. Only together can they give us the complete and true picture about him.

The statement that man, as a biological being, has an animal nature came from religion before Darwin and de Lamarck. Religion claims that the animal is an aspect of man. The difference lies only in the scope of this claim. According to science, man is nothing more than an intelligent animal; according to religion, man is an animal endowed with personality.

Let us notice that the word "human" has a double meaning in our mind. "We are human" means that we are sinful and weak. "Let us be human" is an appeal to remind us that we are something superior, that we have higher obligations, that we have to be unselfish and humane. "You think only of the human," Jesus reproached Saint Peter, giving preference to the divine.

Humanism and humanity are both derived from the word man and have a higher moral connotation. This double meaning of ideas connected to man's name is a result of man's double nature, one of them originating from the earth and the other from heaven.

The materialists always directed our attention to the external aspects of things. "The hand is not only an organ of work," writes Engels, "but also a product of it. Only through work...the human hand attained that high degree of perfection in which it could produce Raffaello's paintings, Thorvaldsen's statues and Paganini's music."[6]

What Engels is talking about is the continuation of biological and not spiritual development. Painting, however, is a spiritual, not a technical act. Raphael created his paintings not with his hands but with his spirit. Beethoven wrote his best compositions when he was already deaf. Biological development alone, even if streched out indefinitely, could never have given us Raphael's paintings nor even the crude prehistoric cave pictures. Here we are faced with two separate aspects of man's existence.

A human being is not the sum of his different biological func-

---

[6]Friedrich Engels: "The Part Played by labour in the Transition from Ape to Man," *Dialectics of Nature*, ed. Clemens Dutt (London: Lawrence & Wishart, 1941).

tions, just like a painting cannot be reduced to the quantity of the paint used or a poem to its syntax. It is true that a mosque is built from a given number of stone blocks of definite form and in definite order, from a certain quantity of mortar, wooden beams, and so forth: however, this is not the whole truth about the mosque. After all, there is a difference between a mosque and military barracks. It is possible to write a perfect grammatical and linguistic analysis of a poem by Goethe without coming anywhere near its essence. The same goes for the difference between a dictionary and a poem in the same language. A dictionary is exact but has no plot; a poem has a meaning and an unattainable essence. Fossils, morphology, and psychology describe only man's external, mechanical, and meaningless side. Man is like a painting, a mosque, or a poem rather than the quantity or quality of the material of which he is made. Man is more than all the sciences together can say about him.

Original Idealism

According to the theory of evolution, the ancestor of the most primitive type of man was the most developed type of animal. If we compare primitive man with the most developed animal, we find that there is an essential and inseparable difference. On one side, we see a flock of animals searching for food and struggling to survive; on the other side, we see primitive man, frightened and confused by his strange taboos and beliefs, or absorbed in his abstruse mysteries and symbols. The difference between these two beings cannot be only in their different stages of development.

We say man has developed, but that is true only for his mortal, outer history. Man was also created. At once, he has become aware that not only is he not animal, but that the meaning of his life is to be found in the negation of the animal inside himself. If man is a child of nature, how is it possible that he started to oppose it? If we imagine developing man's intelligence to the highest degree, we find that his needs will only increase in number as well as in kind; none of this will disappear — only the way he satisfies them will become more intelligent and better organized. The idea to sacrifice himself for the sake of others or to reject any of his wishes or to reduce the intensity of his own physical pleasure will never come from his brain.

The principle of animal existence is utility and efficiency. This is not the case with man, at least with his specific human quality.

Animal instincts are the best examples of the principle of efficiency and usefulness. Animals have a good sense of time — better than man's. For example, starlings stop eating an hour before sunset. Bees organize their workday with a surprising degree of exactness. Most flowers give their nectar only a few hours daily and only at exact times. Bees collect the nectar at the most favorable time and from the best places. For their direction, bees use different signs on the ground and the position of the sun. When it is cloudy, they orient themselves with the help of polarized lights, and so forth. These abilities are of this world. They help and enable the species to survive.

On the contrary, moral principles — both in primitive and in civilized society — reduce man's efficiency. Given two species with the same intelligence, the one with moral principles would soon be exterminated. Man has compensated for this deficiency of power which is a result of his ethics with his superior intelligence and other parallel abilities.

Intelligence, however, has a zoological and not a human origin. "Let us open a collection of anecdotes about the animal intelligence. Besides many behaviors which could be explained as imitation or as automatic association of picture, we can see as well many which we will not hesitate to admit as intelligent. In this, we may especially take into consideration, all those in which a certain manufacturing idea is manifested, whether the animal makes a rough tool or uses an object made by man..."[7]

A chimpanzee will use a stick to reach a banana, a bear a stone to get at its prey, and so forth. Much material has been collected on how bees, geese, and apes receive and transmit different information through conversation or pantomime.[8] Dr. Bler, director of the New York Zoo, has collected many interesting observations on the intelligence of animals and their ability to use objects near them. His general conclusion was that all animals are capable of thinking.

Language also belongs to the natural and zoological rather than

---

[7]Henri Bergson: *Creative Evolution,* trans. Arthur Mitchell (New York: The Modern Library, 1944).

[8]See the investigations of professors Frosch, Zinkin, and especially, Konrad Lorenz, *King Solomon's Ring: New Light on Animal Ways,* trans. Marjorie Kerr Wilson (New York: Crowell, 1952).

the spiritual side of man. We find a rudimentary form of language with animals. Linguistics — contrary to art — can be analyzed scientifically and even by strict mathematical methods. This gives it the characteristics of a science, and the subjects of science can be something external only.[9]

There is an analogy between intelligence and nature and between intelligence and language. As intelligence and matter helped to "create each other" so, in a similar way, did intelligence and language. Language is "the hand of the brain" and, as Bergson states, "the function of the brain is in limiting our spiritual life to what is useful for us in practice."[10]

Generally speaking, there is nothing in man that does not also exist in higher stages of animals, vertebrates, and insects. There is consciousness, intelligence, one or more means of communication, the desire to satisfy needs and join in societies, and some form of economy. Looking from this side, man may appear to have something in common with the animal world.[11] However, there is nothing in the animal kingdom which resembles — even in a rudimentary form — religion, magic, drama, taboo, art, moral prohibitions, and so forth, with which the life of prehistoric as well as civilized man is surrounded. The evolution of animals may appear to be logical, gradual, and easily understood, compared to the evolution of primitive man, who is possessed by strange taboos and beliefs. When an animal goes hunting, it behaves very logically and rationally. No animal will let an opportunity pass. There is no superstition or the like here. Bees treat their useless members in a most cruel way: they are simply thrown out of the beehive. Bees are the best example of a well-organized social life which completely lacks what we usually call humanism: protection of the weak and disabled, the right to life, appreciation, recognition, and so forth.

For animals, things are what they seem to be. For man, things have also an imaginary meaning which is sometimes more important for him than the real one. It is easy to understand the logic of an

---

[9]An indication of this might be the fact that in some religions abstention from speech has the meaning of fasting, for example, the "vow of silence" known in some Christian orders.

[10]Bergson: *Creative Evolution*.

[11]In a very revealing passage (6:38), the Qur'ān talks about the animal creations in terms of communities with a plan: "All of the animals walking on the earth, and the beings flying with their wings, are communities like you."

animal struggling to survive. What about primitive man? Before they went hunting, the primitive hunters and often their families too had to submit themselves to different taboos, fastings, prayers; to perform special dances; to have certain kinds of dreams; to observe special signs. When the game was within sight, other rituals had to be performed. Even the women at home were subject to many taboos. If they broke them, the hunting expedition might not be successful and the lives of their husbands endangered..."[12] We know that primitive men depicted the animals they hoped to kill before they set out hunting. They were convinced that this would have a decisive influence on their hunting success (so-called "hunting magic"). Young men were accepted among the hunters after complicated ceremonies. Hubert and Mauss describe these ceremonies as consisting of three phases: the ritual of purification, the ritual of initiation, and the ritual of acceptance. While man painted or prayed, animals went about their task "logically"; they explored the ground, listened carefully, and followed their prey from behind.

As such, the animal was an excellent hunter. Primitive man was the same, but he was at the same time the tireless creator and "producer" of cults, myths, superstitions, dances, and idols. Man always looked for another world — authentic or imaginary. This is not a difference in developmental stages but in essence.

One of the strongest things in the development of human society is that the idea of sowing was associated with the idea of human sacrifice. H.G. Wells writes in his *Short History of the World*: "It was entanglement, we must remember, in the childish, dreaming myth-making primitive mind; no reasoned process will explain it. But in the world of 12,000 to 20,000 years ago, it would seem that whenever seed time came around to the Neolithic peoples, there was a human sacrifice. And it was not the sacrifice of any mean or outcast person; it was usually of a chosen youth or maiden, a youth more often, who was treated with profound deference and even worship..."[13] "These communities displayed a great development of human sacrifice about the process of seed-time and harvest...,"[14] or a little further in the same book: "The Mexican (Aztec) civilization in particular ran in blood; it offered thousands of human victims

---

[12]Lucien Henry: *The Origin of Religion*.

[13]H. G. Wells: *Short History of the World*, Rev. ed. (New York: Pelican Books, 1946) p. 51.

[14]Ibid. p. 55.

yearly. The cutting open of living victims, the tearing out of the still-beating heart, was an act that dominated the minds and lives of these strange priesthoods. Public life, national festivities — all turned on this horrible act."[15]

In his book, *Salammbo,* Gustave Flaubert describes how the Carthaginians, when they prayed for rain, threw their own children into the glowing mouth of their god Moloch. On the basis of these horrible examples, it would be wrong to conclude that men were beasts. We find nothing similar among animals. It may sound like a paradox, but the given examples are typically human behavior. It has to do with man's suffering and wandering, both of which are repeating themselves even today in a drama of mankind where nations and individuals act unreasonably, led not by their instincts but by authentic human prejudices and errors.

Sacrifice has existed in all religions without exception. The nature of sacrifice has remained unexplained and even absurd. Sacrifice is a fact of another order, of another world. In primitive religions, sacrifice sometimes assumes terrible forms. As such, sacrifice represents a powerful, tangible, and painfully visible border line between the alleged zoological, and the human era. It represents the appearance of a principle that is contrary to the principle of interest,benefits, and needs. Interest is zoological; sacrifice is human. Interest is one of the basic concepts in politics or political economy; sacrifice is one of the basic principles of religion and ethics.

Primitive man's irrational way of thinking sometimes took on unbelievable forms: "One of the strange things that appeared in the later paleolithic and neolithic ages was the self-mangling of the body. People began to mutilate their own bodies, cutting off noses, ears, fingers and the like, and giving to these acts different superstitious meanings. ... No animal does the like," concludes Wells.[16] Compare this with the fox which, when caught in a fox trap, bites off his leg. This is an act of reason. The irrational self-mutilation of primitive man is completely extraneous to animals.[17]

---

[15]Ibid, p. 56.

[16]Ibid. p. 64.

[17]The following differences are of a similar instance: an animal is dangerous when it is hungry or in danger. Man is dangerous when fed and powerful. Much more crime has been committed out of satiety and wantonness than out of poverty.

From this, we might wrongly conclude that this is an anomaly in evolution. It seems that evolution has regressed and that the appearance of an animal with idealistic prejudices prevents further development.

This phenomenon of vacillation at the very top of evolution which makes animals look more advanced than humans, we call "the primitive man's complex." Even if this may sound strange, this complex is the expression of that new quality which is typically human and which is the source of all religions, poetry, and art. The phenomenon is important because it points out, in its own way, the originality of man's appearance and many of the paradoxes which are connected with it.

These facts could easily lead us to conclude that animals have had more favorable changes in their ascent up the evolutionary ladder while primitive man, staring at the sky and entangled in moral obligations, had all the preconditions needed to be trampled underfoot. This almost unavoidable impression of the superiority of the zoological over the human during the dawn of the human era will be repeated later in the call to destroy idealism for the sake of progress.

During this long period of man's emancipation from the animal world, it is alleged that the external differences (walking erect and the development of speech, and intelligence) were for a long time very small and hardly noticeable. It is not clear whether a being who resembled a man as well as an ape and used a stick to prolong his arm to reach food, or uttered inarticulate sounds to communicate with his fellows, was a man or an ape. The presence of any kind of cult or taboo will, however, disperse any doubts. Animals waited to become humans until the point in time where they began to pray. Whatever the merits of such a view, the decisive difference between man and animal is neither a physical nor an intellectual one. It is above all a spiritual one, manifesting itself in the presence of some religious, ethical, and aesthetical conscience. From this standpoint, the appearance of man should not be acknowledged as the time when he started to walk upright or from the development of his hands, speech, or intelligence, as science teaches us, but from the appearance of the first taboo cult. Ironically, primitive man, who 15,000 years ago enjoyed looking at flowers and the profiles of animals and then painted them on the walls of his cave, was — from this point of view — nearer to true man than the modern epicure who lives only to satisfy his physical pleasures and daily thinks of new ones, or the average modern town dweller who lives isolated in his concrete cage deprived of all elementary aesthetical feelings and sensations.

In his book *The First Law*, Atkinson writes that different kinds of prohibitions existed among primitive people everywhere in the world. The constant need for "purification from evil" and the constant dwelling on things forbidden to the touch or even to the sight, is found everywhere and this has enabled us to acquire some knowledge about the existence of primitive being. The other universal idea which dominated the minds of primitive men was the idea of banishment.

In this way, a whole system of prohibitions was created which covered different aspects of primitive life. These were later called taboos. The taboo was originally a prohibition of ethical character among early mankind.

Man does not behave as a child of nature but rather as a stranger in it. His basic feeling is fear but not the biological fear that animals feel. It is a spiritual, cosmic, and primeval fear bound to the secrets and riddles of human existence. Markin Heidegger called it the "eternal and timeless determinant of human existence." This is a fear mingled with curiosity, astonishment, admiration, disaffection — the feelings that perhaps lie at the basis of all our culture and art.

Only this position of primitive man in the world could explain the appearance of different prohibitions and concepts of "impurity," "sublimity," "damnation," "holiness," and so forth. If we were children of this world, nothing would seem either impure or holy to us. These concepts are contradictory to the world we know. They are evidence of our other origin, of which we cannot have any memory. Our inadequate reaction to this world, as expressed by religion and art, is the negation of the scientific concept of man. Why did he always express his fear and disappointments through religion? Why and from what did he seek salvation? This side of man we are talking about (good, evil, the feeling of wretchedness, the permanent dilemma between interest and conscience, the question of our existence, and so forth) remains without a rational explanation. Obviously, man did not react to the world around him in a Darwinian way.

Not even in the most developed species of animals can we find any traces of cults or prohibitions. Wherever man has appeared, religion and art have followed. Science, on the other hand, is relatively new. Man, religion, and art were always bound together. Not enough attention has been devoted to this phenomenon which might contain the answer to some decisive questions of human existence.[18]

From the materialistic point of view, the history of mankind seems to bc a process of progressive secularization.[19] Still,no one has ever explained why primitive man's life was filled with cults, mysteries, prohibitions, and beliefs. Why did he attribute life and personality to all things surrounding him such as stones, stars, rivers, and so forth?[20] Why, on the contrary, does civilized man try to reduce everything to the inorganic and the mechanical? Already for thousands of years, we have been trying to get rid of primitive man's nightmares, without understanding their nature and origin.

This phenomenon of inner life or staring at the sky, which is typical of man and alien to all animals, remains without a logical explanation and seems to have descended literally "from the sky." As it is not a product of evolution, it stands principally above or outside evolution. After studying the paintings of Neanderthal man in France, Henri Simle concluded that the psychological life of primitive man differed very little from that of modern man. "Even the cave man of 70,000 years ago suffered from 'the metaphysical giddiness,' the illness of modern man."[21] Obviously, this is not the continuation of biological evolution, but one more act of the drama which was started by the "prologue in heaven."

During the so-called zoological era, before the appearance of human beings, there is nothing that gives us any hint of the coming period of cults and primitive ethics. Even if we imagine this period to be prolonged indefinitely, the appearance of cults and taboos does not seem possible. The evolution of animals does not go toward physical and intellectual perfection, and from there toward super-intelligence and super-animal, toward Nietzsche's superman — in fact,

---

[18]Plutarch adequately observed: "We find cities without walls, kings, civilizations, literature, or theaters, but never has man seen a city without places of worship or worshippers." See *Plutarch's Morals,* ed. William W. Goodwin (Boston: Little, Brown, & Co., 1883). "There have existed and still exist human societies without science, art, and philosophy, but no human society without a religion has ever existed," Bergson wrote almost twenty centuries later. See Henri Bergson, *Les deux sources de la morale et de la religion* (Paris: Librairie Félix Alcan, 1932), p. 105.

[19]See, for example, Salomon Reinach, *Cultes, mythes, et religions* (Paris: n.p., 1905).

[20]"Primitiave man does not know a world without life." U. A. Frankfurth, *From Myth to Philosophy*, Serbocroatian trans. (Subotica-Beograd: Minerva, 1967), p.12.

[21]This assertion was made by Simle at a 1076 archeological congress in Nice.

the perfect animal.[22] Nietzsche's vision of the superman was inspired by Darwin. Evolution — zoological and external in its essence — is stretched out beyond man, but this zoological evolution remains simple and logical because it stays within the limits of nature. Super-animal is the result of evolution and as such it is a creature without inner life, without humanity, drama, character, heart, and so forth. It is the Homunculus, the creation out of the test tube, which Dr. Faust produced in his laboratory, as did nature, although through a slower process.[23]

Doubtless, the Soviet poet Voznesenski had a similar picture in mind when he wrote: "The future computers will theoretically be able to do everything that man is doing, except two things: to be religious and to write poetry."[24]

As animals have no idea of the holy or the devil, they have no idea of the beautiful. The opinion held by some scientists that apes could paint, based on the "paintings" apes had done, proved to be quite wrong. It has been confirmed that apes only imitate man. So-called "ape art" surely does not exist.[25] On the contrary, the cave men from Cromagnon onward knew how to paint and carve. Their drawings have been found in caves of the Sahara, in Spain at Altamira, in France at Lascaux, and recently in Poland at Mashicka. Many of these pictures are thought to be more than 30,000 years old. Some time ago, a group of Soviet archeologists discovered a set of musical instruments, made 20,000 years ago, near the town of Chernigov in the Ukraine.

Man's desire to adorn himself is older and stranger than his need to cover and protect his body. This fact can be traced from prehistoric times up to today. Our clothes are not only a protection; they also reflect the times in which we live and the group to which we belong. Our costume becomes a picture and poetry. The furs and feathers of animals may be very beautiful, but behind this beauty

---

[22]Nietzsche's superman is free from "ethical prejudice": "Fight against compassion, conscience, and forgiving — those human inner tyrants: suppress the weak, climb upward over their bodies. You are the children of a higher species, your ideal is superman." Nietzsche, *Thus Spoke Zarathustra*, Serbocroatian translation (Zagreb: Mladost, 1976), p.

[23]Literature has created many similar "monsters." The common characteristic of all of them is super intelligence with the complete absence of "moral sense."

[24]Andrei Voznesensky, n.p.d.

[25]There is, in this regard, the very prominent research of the Soviet scientist Bukin.

is always a function. In primitive man's songs and drama, it is not possible to distinguish between art and cult. The first stone sculpture was an idol. Religious inspiration, wrongly oriented, created those fantastic sculptures of gods and masks found in Oceania, Mexico, and on the Ivory Coast and which today are good examples of impressionistic art. All so-called plastic art is idolatrous in origin, and this is how Islam's intolerance — and that of some less personalistic religions — of this form of art should be explained. It seems that we have to go back to prehistory to understand the roots of art in religion, and how they, together with primitive ethics, have a common source: man's longing for a lost world.

This dissimilarity from animals can also be seen in man's revolt. An animal does not revolt against his animal fate. Only man revolts, the only animal who refused to be so.[26] This type of revolt is essentially human, and we also find it in well-developed societies, where civilization — zoological in its origin — tries to implement some inhumane standards of existence (order, depersonalization, general leveling and uniformity, dress of the masses, the rule of society over the individual, and so forth).[27]

Johan Huizinga discovered yet another phenomenon: playing. Animals play, but they always have some biological need for it such as sexual play, teaching their young ones, and so on. Their play is instinctive and functional; man's play is free and unconcerned. It always includes a consciousness of play that gives it a spiritual meaning: seriousness, solemnity, "aimless purposefulness."

A special kind of play is *potlatch*, a universal phenomenon of all primitive cultures. By its nature, it is typically an irrational and uneconomical (anti-utilitarian) phenomenon in the same sense as primitive art is of primitive ethics with its prohibitions, taboos, and ideas of good and evil. In the aforementioned book, Huizinga writes extensively on this subject. He finds a typical form of *potlatch* with the Kwakiut Indian tribe and describes it as a great festivity in which one of two groups prodigiously donates to the other. The single and therefore the necessary reciprocal favor is that the other group within a certain period of time repeats the festivity

---

[26]Albert Camus, *L'Homme révolté* (Paris: Gallimard, 1951).

[27]Johan Huizinga, *Homo Ludens: A Study of the Play Element in Culture* (Boston: Beacon Press, 1955).

and repays the donation. This spirit of donation permeates the whole life of the tribe: their cult, their common law, their art. In a *potlatch*, the superiority is not manifested by the simple donation of the goods, but more strikingly by destroying them to prove that it is possible to live without them. The action always promotes a form of competition: if the chieftain breaks a little copper kettle or sets fire to a heap of blankets or breaks his cane, the rival is due to destroy some object of at least equal value, if not a higher one. Such competition, whose pinnacle of excess is in calmly destroying one's own goods, is to be found throughout the world. Marcel Mauss described the same custom among the Malay people. In his book, *Essai sur le Don,*he proved that similar customs existed in the ancient Greek, Roman, and old Germanic cultures. Granet identified competitive donation and destruction of goods in Chinese traditions as well.

We find the practice of *potlatch* in pre-Islamic Arabia under the name of *muaqara*, and Mauss maintains that the Indian epic *Mahabharata* is nothing but the history of a giant *potlatch*. ... It is not a world concerned with everyday life, benefits, or the acquisition of useful goods. As far as I know, ethnology looks for an explanation of *potlatch* mostly in magic and mythical images. ... Material benefit is also not in question.[28] To destroy goods, to show indifference to useful material things, to prefer principle to things — be it only feigned — is typical for human beings. Nothing similar — not even a trace of it — can be found among animals.

For some time, Darwin's theory was considered to be the final explanation of man's origin, just as Newton's cosmos theory was once thought to be final as regards the universe. But in the same way that Newton's mechanical conception had to be disputed because it could not explain some phenomena in the universe, Darwin's theory also has to be revitalized. The theory of evolution can neither explain in a satisfactory way the first religious phase of mankind nor the same phenomena in modern times. Why are men psychologically less satisfied when they are better off materially? Why do the number of suicides and mental diseases increase with increased standards of living and education? Why does progress not mean humanization as well? The human mind, having once accepted the clear-cut visions of Darwin and Newton, finds it difficult

---

[28]Maracel Granet, *Chinese Civilization* (London: K. Paul, Trench, Trubner, & Co., Ltd., 1930).

to reject them. Newton's world is stable, logical, and continuous, as Darwin's man is simple and one dimensional: he struggles for survival, he satisfies his needs and aims for a functional world. Nonetheless, Einstein destroyed Newton's illusion and pessimistic philosophy, and the failure of civilization does so with Darwin's image of man. Man is inexplicable, unsatisfied, tormented by fear and doubts — Einstein would say "curved." The philosophy of man, which for a long time has been under the influence of Darwin's straight-lined vision, now is waiting for its Einsteinian overthrow. The new conception of man, as compared with that of Darwin, will be the same as the relation between Einstein's and Newton's universe. If it is true that we rise through suffering and sink through enjoyment, it is because we are different from animals. Man is not tailored according to Darwin, nor is the universe tailored according to Newton.

The Dualism of the Living World

Are we able to and will we forever be able to produce life? The answer is: yes, if we can understand it. Can we understand life?

Biology is not a science about the essence of life, but a science about the phenomenon of life — about life as an object, as a product.

The same incongruence that we established earlier between animal and man is met again, but one degree lower, on the level of "matter" versus life. On one side, we see homogeneity, quantity, repetition, causality, mechanism; on the other side, we find originality, quality, growth, spontaneity, organism. Life does not manifest itself as a continuance of matter — neither mechanically nor dialectically, nor as its most organized and most complex form. Looking at some of its qualities, life is contradictory to our conceptions and understanding of matter in its very definition. The nature of life is the opposite of matter.

According to biologists, entropy is the crucial point in the definition of life. All laws of nature go back to entropy, which means universal disorganization, the ultimate state of inert uniformity. On the contrary, the basic characteristic of a living organism is the state of "anti-entropy," its ability to create the complex out of the simple, order out of chaos, and to maintain a system — even temporary — on a higher level of energy. Every material system moves toward a higher degree of entropy, and every living system follows the opposite direction because "life is a movement against the wind of mechanical laws," as Kuznjetzov, a Russian scientist in the field of cybernetics puts it.[29]

Not being a biologist, I will confine myself to quoting some authorities in this field. The failure of biology to explain life is a fact which cannot be passed over in silence. I would like to point out that this comes as no surprise.

In 1950, André George put only one question to biologists, doctors, and physicists: What is life? All the answers he received were indefinite and cautious. We may take the answers by Pierre Lapin and Jean Rostand as typical examples. "The mystery remains complete. Our lack of knowledge makes every explanation of life less clear than our instinctive knowledge of it."[30] "So far, we do not know what life is. We are not even able to give a complete and exact definition of the phenomenon of life."[31]

Due to its ability to evade quick decomposition to an inert state of uniformity, the organism shows itself so mysterious that people from the most ancient times believed that a special nonphysical and supernatural force (vis à vis, entelecheia) acted in the organism. In what way does a living organism fight against its decline?... Each process, or event, or development in the world, all that happens in nature means at the same time an addition of entropy... The organism can retain that process — that is, survive — only by the constant taking of negative entropy from the outside... Therefore, the organism feeds on the negative entropy."[32]

French paleontologist Teilhard de Chardin writes very similarly: "Indeed, in spite of many obstacles, the curve running from the big molecules toward polycell organisms continues incessantly: this is just the one along which the indeterminations, self-arrangements, and consciousness emerge... Hence the question: is there a connection between this mysterious movement of the world toward states more and more complex and internal and the other movement (better

---

[29]Boris G. Kuznjetzov, *Einstein*, trans. Vladimir Talmy (New York: Phaedra, 1970).
[30]Pierre Lapin, n.p.d.
[31]Jean Rostand, *Life, The Great Adventure* (New York: Scribner, 1956).
[32]Erwin Schrödinger, *What is life? — The Physical Aspect of the living Cell* (New York: The Macmillan Company, 1945).

studied and better known) which pulls the same world toward the more and more simple and external states? ... The essential secret of the universe might be formulated in this question."[33]

"The spontaneous ability of cells to create the organs and social behavior of some insects are among the basic facts which we learned by means of observation. We cannot find an explanation of them in the light of our present understanding."[34]

Karl Jaspers, in his *General Psychopathology* writes about the aforementioned inverse character of the living as follows: "Psychic facts appear as quite new and in a fashion that cannot be understood. They are coming one after another and not one from another. The phases of phychic evolution of a normal life, as well as of an abnormal life, give such unintelligible successions in time. So, a longitudinal cross section of the psychic cannot be understood, even approximately in its emergence. The psychic facts cannot be studied from outside as the natural facts cannot be from inside."[35]

In the same book, Jaspers also points out the difference between "to comprehend" *(verstehen)*, which can be achieved by psychological penetration, and to explain *(erklaren)*, which means to uncover the objective connection between cause and effect by natural science. Jaspers concludes: "Here we are talking about the ultimate souces of our knowledge which deeply differ one from another."[36]

Louis de Broglie, the French physicist and Nobel Laureate, said in 1929: "We cannot explain life with our present knowledge of chemistry and physics."[37]

The Swiss biologist Guyenot maintains that there is an essential difference between physio-chemical relations and life:

---

[33]Pierre Teilhard de Chardin, *Activation of Energy*, trans. René Hague (New York: Harcourt Brace Jovanovich, 1971).

[34]Alexis Carrel, *Man: The Unknown* (New York: Harper & Brothers, 1939).

[35]Let us remember Hegel's sentences: "Material is outside itself," "The soul has its center in itself," "The soul is the existence inside itself," and so forth. See, Georg W.F. Hegel, *Sämtliche Werke*, ed. Herman Glockner (Stuttgart: F. Frommann, 1961).

[36]Karl Jaspers, *General Psychopathology*, trans. J. Hoenig and Marian W. Hamilton (Chicago: University of Chicago Press, 1963).

[37]Louis de Broglie, "Address Delivered at Stockholm on Receiving the Nobel Prize, December 12, 1929," *Matter and Light: The New Physics*, trans. W. H. Johnston (New York: Dover Publications, 1946), p. 165-179.

> Physicists must realize that although we biologists have worked hard to explain life in physical and chemical formulas, we have come across something that we could not explain. That is life. Life has found an organized form. And not only once, but a million times during billions of years. Here we are faced with a constructive ability which can be explained neither physically nor chemically.[38]

André Lwoff, the French biologist and Nobel Prize winner in 1965, well-known for his work on the genetical mechanism of viruses and bacteria, said:

> Life can be defined as a quality, or a manifestation, or a state of an organism. An organism is an independent system of mutually dependent structures and functions which is able to reproduce itself... It has often been said that a virus is the connection between organic substances and living matter. In reality, living matter does not exist. One element of a cell, such as albumen, an enzyme or nucleic acid, is not a living substance. Only an organism is alive, and this organism is much more than the sum of its parts. We have succeeded in creating a synthesis of viral nucleic acids. On the basis of this, we cannot talk about a synthesis of life, because in all these experiments one substance lent to the virus, which is genetical matter specific to the nucleotide, takes part... Sometimes life is born spontaneously. It is easy to synthetically produce some parts of albumen or nucleic acid, but up to now it has not been possible to create an organism... To reproduce one single bacteria — that is still beyond our reach...[39]

The famous Russian psychologist and experimenter Ivan Pavlov expresses similar skepticism:

> Already for thousands of years, mankind has been investigating psychological events, phenomena of spiritual life,

---

[38]Guyenot, n.p.d.

[39]André Lwoff, *Of Microbes and Life,* ed. Jacques Monod and Ernest Borck (New York: Columbia University Press, 1971).

> the human soul, and not only are psychologists and specialists working on this question, but also all forms of art and literature — these mechanical expressions of mankind's psychological life — deal with this problem. Thousands of pages have been filled with descriptions of man's inner world, but so far we have not been successful in this effort. We have not been able to find any law that regulates man's psychological life.[40]

Alexis Carrel doubts man's ability to understand fully the life within the cell:

> The methods which are used by the organs in their own construction are strange to the human mind... All this material emerges from one single cell, which would be like a whole house being produced from a magic brick, which would be like a whole house being produced from a magic brick, which would then spontaneously produce the other bricks... The organs develop in a way which has been used by fairies in children's fables... Our reason can by no means find itself in that world of inner organs.[41]

Also, somewhat further:

> So far, we have not been able to reach the secret of the organization of our body, its food, or its nervous and spiritual energy. The laws of physics and chemistry can be fully applied only to dead matter and only partly to man. We should free ourselves completely from the illusions of the nineteenth century and Jacques Loeb's dogmas — those childish physio-chemical theories about human beings which, unfortunately, many physiologists and doctors still believe in."[42]

Life is a miracle rather than a phenomenon. Look, for instance, at the human eye. The human eye is lying in a cavity filled

---

[40]Pavlov, "Experimental Psychology."
[41]Carrel, pp. 127-128.
[42]Ibid.

with fat. It is protected by an upper and a lower lid, eyelashes, eyebrows, mucous membranes, and the conjunctiva. The movement of the eye in all directions is made possible by motor muscles, two straight ones and two oblique ones, and it is aided by the tear apparatus which consists of the lachrymal gland, the lachrymal sac, and the tear canal which keeps the eye humid and protects it from infections. The eyeball consists of three coats. The outer one is the compact and nontransparent white of the eye, which is transformed into the transparent cornea on the front side. The vascular net lies under the white of the eye and through it flow the blood vessels which nourish the eye. For the function of the eye, the most important part is the third layer, the retina. This is where the sensory cells are situated — the rods and cones, connected with bipolar cells and fibers that collectively form the optic nerve. The interior of the eyeball is filled with an elastic, transparent, and watery fluid. The crystalline lens attached to the iris and connected with the ciliar body lies in the front part. When rays of light pass through the cornea, they change their shape to enable focusing at the back of the eye and an upside down picture is transmitted to the optical center of the brain. Each eye receives the image from a different angle. These nerve impulses from both eyes travel over the optic nerve. Collective impulses arrive at midbrain junctions on either side of the brain and travel over fibers which ramify to the occipital lobe where the impulses are "seen." For the functioning of the eye, tears are very important. They are produced by the lachrymal gland, and they keep the cornea wet. Among other substances, tears contain lysozyme, an antibacterial substance which protects the eye from infections. The flow of the tears is controlled by the seventh cranial nerve, the nervus facialis. As a bactericide, the human tear is more effective than any pharmaceutical product and is supposed to destroy more than 100 different kinds of bacteria. This ability is retained even when diluted up to 600 times.

Likewise, the liver has several different functions. As a gland, it produces bile which helps in food digestion. The liver is an incomparable chemical plant. It can modify almost any chemical substance. It is a powerful detoxifying organ, breaking down many kinds of toxic molecules and making them harmless. It is a blood reservoir and a storage organ for some vitamins and for digested carbohydrates (in the form of glycogen) which is released to sustain the blood sugar level. It is a manufacturing site for enzymes, cholesterol, proteins, vitamin A, blood coagulation factors, and other elements. Under some circumstances, it can even resume its embryonic function of red blood cell production.

Our blood transports nutriments to the different parts of the body, carries oxygen from the lungs to the cells, and carbon dioxide away from the thirty trillion cells of the human body. Moreover, it transports the hormones and antibodies which form our internal defense. Blood also influences the regulation of body temperature. The white blood cells destroy, digest, and ingest invading bacteria as well as nonbacterial foreign particles.

The brain consists of the cerebrum which is divided into two hemispheres: the thalamus, including the medulla oblongata and the pons; and the midbrain, including the cerebellum and the spinal cord. The brain is protected by three coats: the hard, the soft, and the connective tissue. The mass of the brain consists of grayish-white substances. The gray tissue contains nerve cells, and the white is the end station of the motor and sensory fibers. The medulla oblongata forms the relay and reflex center and connects with higher brain centers via the pons. The cerebellum is concerned with equilibrium, muscular coordination and the automatic execution of fine movements. The "seeing center," known as the occipital lobe, is located in the back part of the brain. Areas for hearing and smelling are located in the temporal lobe at the side of the head. The most conspicuous part of the brain is the massive cerebrum. Its outer rind, the cerebral cortex, is a grayish layer of nerve cells. Beneath is white tissue, at the base of which is an extra small center of gray substance called the basal ganglion. "Gray matter" is not necessarily superior to white, or vice versa; it is concerned with the distribution of impulses across selcted synapses while white matter sees to impulse conduction along fibers. Together they enable the creation of main psychological functions and conditional reflexes. The average weight of a human brain is about 1,300 to 1,450 grams, and it contains about 14 to 15 billion cells.

Animals possess apparatus which are often stronger and more perfect than tools manufactured by man. There are many examples: the lights of some birds, the violin of grasshoppers, the cymbal of crickets, and whole sets of traps, nets, snares, glues, and so on. André Tetry has written a whole book on this subject, *Les Qutils chez les êtres vivants.*[43] It is evident that evolution did not progress blindly or mechanically as Darwin thought. Evolution seems to have followed the principle of usefulness, the direction which was

[43]André Tetry, Res putils chez les êtres vivants [Tools among Living Beings.] (n.p., n.d.).

helpful for the individual. This points to a certain idea which cannot be found in materia.[44]

The rattlesnake has an extraordinary ability to feel infrared rays. Scientists at Colorado University in the US have proved that this infrared detector is placed on the head of the snake, and that it consists of very thin nerves with specific cells which change while the light shines on them. Experiments have shown that within 35 milliseconds after the rays are sent, the snake reacts. This is a record reaction time for any biological system known so far.

In a similar way, sharks have a very sensitive electric antenna on their nose which enables them to find food hidden in the sand on the sea bottom. All organisms in the sea transmit weak electric waves which sharks intercept with the help of their sensitive antennas.

Dr. Alexander Gorbovsky, a member of the Soviet Academy of Science, readopts the old idea which, Einstein among others, supported that there are some enigmatic traits in the structure of the cosmos and matter. I will quote here some interesting instances from his work:

> Many thousands of termites cooperate to build a termite hill. When completed, it is a very complicated construction with an area of more than a hundred square miles of channels, storage for wood, rooms for eggs, and so on.
>
> The following test was performed: a termite hill, the construction of which had just been started, was partitioned into two parts so that the termites would be completely separated from each other. In spite of this, the construction continued successfully and all passages, channels, rooms, and stores were built identically in both parts, and they even had common connections...
>
> We might think that every termite was very well informed of his neighbor's work in the other part, as they had worked in exactly the same way. However, he had no knowledge of his neighbor's work, for he could not communicate with him. Let us try to explain this

---

[44]For more information on this subject, see Lucian Cuenot's *Invention et Finalite en Biologie* (Paris: Masson et Cie. Editeurs, 1951.)

> phenomenon...
> It is obvious that the individual termite does not possess all the information on the construction of a termite hill. Each individual 'knows' only a part of the complete process in which he is involved. Accordingly, we may conclude that only the population as a whole has the complete knowledge. In other words, only individuals as members of the group have the 'great knowledge.' Individually, they do not possess it...
> For a long time it was thought that flocks of migratory birds on their way to warmer regions were guided by older and more experienced birds, but this has not been confirmed by facts. Professor Jamoto Hirosuke, a Japanese ornithologist, has found that a flock of birds has no guiding bird. If there happens to be a bird in front, it is not necessarily guiding the flock. Sometimes, a very young and even featherless bird is in front. It is evident that such a bird 'does not know' the traditional route and cannot direct the others who know their way very well.[45]

Gorbovsky continues:

> It is a known fact that, from the biological point of view, the relation between newborn males and females is equal. If this normal relation is upset, a spontaneous process of adjustment occurs. If there are less females in a society, there will be more females born, but if we have less males, their number will increase successively. This process will continue until the balance is reestablished...
> It is obvious that the individual independent organism cannot influence the sex of its offspring. In other words, again we have a phenomenon with laws of its own. We are again confronted with an influence coming from outside of each individual organism...
> This is a phenomenon well-known to mankind. Demographers call it 'the phenomenon of war years'. During and after wars many men are killed, but very soon after

---

[45]Alexander Gorbovsky, n.p.d.

a war the number of men born always increases until the balance is reestablished.[46]

The preceding examples are taken from the first biology textbook that was at hand. These true miracles in nature are explained by religion as acts by the Highest Reason — God. All scientific explanations can be summarized as miracles created by themselves. Is it not the greatest superstition intruded on the human mind? To ask one to accept that something as perfect and complex as man's eye and brain were created by chance, by themselves, is to ask one to accept Greek mythology as truth. Let us conclude, therefore, with the words of the great Islamic philosopher Muhammad Al-Ghazāli that all miracles are natural and all nature is miraculous.

What then about 'self-organizing matter' and 'the self-creation' of all these very complex systems of which the living world is full?

Let us look at the self-organizing (creation by accident) of one molecule of albumen which is the basic material of all living organisms known to us.

The Swiss physicist Charles Eugene Guye has tried to make a probability count of the accidental creation of one molecule of protein. It is known that a molecule of protein consists of at least four different elements. To simplify the count, Guye assumed that a molecule of albumen consists only of two elements of 2,000 atoms with the atomic weight of 10 and with the molecule dissymmetry of 0.9. With these simplified preconditions, the probability that protein could be created accidentally amounts to 2.02 x 10 - 231 according to Guye's calculations. If we consider this result within the age and size of our planet, the creation of such a molecule would take 10243 billion years under the condition of 5.1014 vibrations per second. Consequently, there is no possibility that life could have been created accidentally during the 4.5 billion years the earth is supposed to have existed.

The count was repeated by Manfred Eigen of the Max Plank Institute for Biophysical Chemistry in Göttingen, Germany, a Nobel Prize winner for chemistry in 1968. He has proven that all the water of our planet is not sufficient to accidentally produce one

---

[46]Ibid.

molecule of protein. Even if the whole universe were full of chemical substances which were permanently combining with each other, the ten billion years since the creation of the universe would not have been enough to produce any type of protein. Faced with this fact, Eigen formulated the hypothesis of evolution before life — that is life before life as this theory is called — because he admitted that nucleic acid has a kind of life capability. A principle of order, selection, and adaption is all at once attributed to matter — a principle which by no means enters the definition of matter.

When two British scientists, Frederic Hoyle, the former President of the Royal Society of Astronomy, and Chandra Vikrama of the University of Cardiff, studied the same problem, they defined the hypothesis that life was not created on earth but was imported with the help of cosmic dust clouds from the depths of the cosmos. According to them, the biological activity in the cosmos must have started before the creation of the earth.

The Russian scientist Balandin writes: "If a million laboratories on earth worked for a few million years combining chemical substances, the probability of creating life in a test tube would be minimal. According to Holden's calculations, the chance is one to 1,310."[47]

This is how things stand with the self-organizing of one molecule of protein which, compared to a living organism, is as one brick compared to the completed building.

Science, especially molecular biology, has managed to reduce the huge gap between living and dead material to a very small space, but this small space has remained unbridgeable. To underestimate it would be scientifically unsound, but this is a tendency of the official materialism.

How can the following paradox be explained? If, in an archeological excavation, we find two stones put in a certain order or cut for some purpose, all of us would surely conclude that it is the work of a man of older times. If, near the same stones, we find a human skull incomparably more perfect and complex than the stone tools, some of us would not think that it is the work of a conscious being. They look upon this perfect skull or skeleton as being created by itself or by accident — that is, without the intervention

---

[47]Balandin, n.p.d.

of a brain or consciousness. Is not man's negation of God sometimes capricious?

Modern man's narrow-mindedness is best shown in his belief that there is no riddle before him. His wisdom is the sum of his knowledge and his ignorance, of which he is not aware, he accepts it as knowledge. Even in the face of the greatest mystery, he behaves self-consciously and conceitedly. He does not even see the problem. It is in this that the true measure of his ignorance and prejudice is manifested. In autumn, the swallows fly from Europe to Africa. In springtime, they return to the same roof where they set their nest. How do they know that they have to go and when they must leave? Coming back, how are they able to find the same roof among thousands of roofs in a big town? To this question, our conceited man answers that it is instinct which leads them, or that it is a question of natural selection — only the birds which "understood" that they had to move to warmer regions survived. The others who did not "understand" this died out. Their instinct to migrate is the result of the accumulated knowledge of thousands of generations.

The problem does not lie in this empty answer. It lies in the fact that our disputant thinks that he gave an answer at all: he eliminates questioning which is the first condition for exploring the truth. The appearance of the general theory of relativity is due to the fact that Einstein saw a problem where everything seemed clear and defined.

The meaning of art, philosophy, and religion is to direct man's attention to riddles, secrets, and questions. It sometimes leads to a certain knowledge but more often to an awareness of ignorance or to transforming our ignorance of which we are not aware into ignorance of which we are aware. This is the dividing line between the ignorant and the wise. Sometimes both of them know very little about some question, but the ignorant, contrary to the wise, takes his ignorance as knowledge and behaves accordingly.

He is simply blind to the problem and, in our case, blind to the miracle. This situation sometimes has tragic consequences in practical life: ignorant persons are very sure of themselves, while the wise behave in a Hamletian way, which gives the first group obvious advantages. This state of affairs is the exact opposite of the state of meditation. No meditation is needed if "everything is clear," as is the case with the state of mind of the so-called "mass-man." This type of man does not litter his mind with any riddles or secrets. He does not wonder nor admire when confronted with the unknown. If a problem arises, he terms it and goes on living, believing that the problem has been solved in this way. Such terms are "instinct," "self-organizing matter," "complex form or highly organized matter," and so forth.

We cannot explain life by scientific means only because life is both a miracle and a phenomenon. Wonder and admiration are the highest forms of our understanding of life.

The Meaning of Humanism

To strive for enjoyment and to flee from pain — with this lapidary sentence, two great materialistic thinkers, Epicurus in antiquity and Holbach in modern times, defined the basic principles of life, not only of human life but also that of animals. Materialism always stresses what is common to animals and humans, while religion stresses what makes them different. The meaning of some cults and religious prohibitions is only to underline these differences.

In its effort to emphasize the animal nature of human beings, materialism sometimes shows more than a common concern for truth.[48]

Darwin did not make man an animal, but he made him aware of his animal origin. Out of this "awareness," the others continued to draw the "appropriate conclusions," both moral and political: a human society is a flock in civilized form, and civilization is the human awakening which goes accompanied with the rejection of prohibitions, power over nature, living with the senses instead of the spirit, and so forth.

By establishing the unity (or continuation) between animal and man, evolution abolished the difference between nature and culture. Starting from a quite different point, religion reestablished this difference. Therefore, from the act of creation, man — and all cul-

---

[48]A good example of this is the stubborn insistence that sexual relations were completely free during a great part of prehistory. Every woman belonged to every man and every man to every woman. Engels openly admitted that there is no direct proof that it was really so, but still he continued to insist upon it in his *The Origin of the Family, Private Property, and the State*. Serbocroation trans. (Zagreb: Naprijed, 1945), p. 28. Not scientific truth but ideological decision is the decisive factor here.

ture with him — inexorably has opposed the whole development of human history. The divergence between culture and civilization began here. While Camus indicated that "Man is an animal which refuses to be so,"[49] Whitehead saw in this negation the essence of the religious attitude, "this great rejection."[50] Religion seems to say: look what the animals do, and do the opposite; they devour — you should fast; they mate — you should abstain; they live in flocks — you should try to live alone; they strive for enjoyment and flee from pain — you should expose yourself to difficulties. In a word, they live with their bodies, but you should live with your spirit.

Rejection of this zoological position, this "negative desire" which cannot be explained by Darwinian and rational theories, is the crucial fact of human life on this planet. This fact may be the human damnation or privilege, but it is the only specific quality which makes one a human being.

In reality, there exist both a complete parallelism and an absolute incongruity between man and animal. We find conformity in the biological, constitutional — that is, the mechanical aspect, but on the other hand, there is actually no parallel since an animal is innocent, sinless, and morally neutral like a thing. Man is never so and from the moment "animal became humanized," from the dramatic "prologue in heaven," or from the famous "fall to earth," man cannot choose to be an innocent animal. Man was set "free without the option to return," and so every Freudian solution is excluded. From that moment on, he could no longer be an animal or a man; he could only be man or non-man.

If man was simply the most perfect animal, his life would be simple and without mysteries. Still, since he is not so because he is a "worm of the earth and a child of heaven" and because he was created, he is a disharmonious being, and Euclid's harmony is not possible. Not only our fundamental truth but also our sins and vices are based on the fact of the creation.

There we find our human dignity, moral striving, and tragedies as well as our dilemmas, dissatisfaction, damnation, cruelty, and malice.[51] An animal knows none of them and in this lies the meaning of this epoch-making moment.

---

[49]Camus: *l'Homme révolté*.

[50]Alfred Whitehead: *Science and the Modern World* (New York: Macmillan, 1926).

[51]Compare the Qur'ān, 91:7-8.

The question of creation is really the question of human freedom. If one accepts that man has no freedom, that all his actions are predetermined — either by what is inside or what is outside him — one may consider that God is not necessary for an explanation and understanding of the world. However, if one gives man freedom, if one considers him responsible, one recognizes the existence of God, tacitly or openly. Only God was able to create a free creature, and freedom could only arise by the act of creation.[52] Freedom is not the result or product of evolution. Freedom and product are disparate ideas. God does not produce or construct. He creates. We used to say the same for artists, for the artist who constructs does not create a personality but rather a poster of man. A personality cannot be constructed. I do not know what a portrait could mean without God. Maybe, sooner or later, during this century or after a million years of continued civilization, man will succeed in constructing an imitation of himself, a kind of robot or monster, something very similar to its constructor. This human-looking monster may look very much like a man, but one thing is certain: it will not have freedom, it will be able to do only what it has been programmed to do. In this lies the greatness of God's creation which cannot be repeated or compared with anything that has happened before or after in the cosmos. In one eon of eternity, a free being started to exist. Without a divine touch, the result of evolution would not have been man, but rather a more developed animal, a super-animal, a creature with a human body and intelligence but without a heart and personality. Its intelligence without moral scruples might even be more efficient but, at the same time, more cruel. Some people imagine this type of creature as coming from a far planet in the universe; others see it as a product of our civilization on some high level of development. There is such a creature in Goethe's *Faust*, but it is a quasi-man — a homunculus. It should be noted that there is no analogy between this cruelly indifferent creature, homunculus, and the worst criminal. Man can choose to go against the moral laws, but he cannot, as a monster, stay out of the moral sphere, beyond good and evil. He cannot "switch off" him-

---

[52]Compare Karl Jaspers: "When a man really is conscious of his freedom, he at the same time becomes convinced of the existence of God. Freedom and God are inseparable," and further: "If the consciousness of freedom contains the consciousness of God, then there exists a connection between the denial of freedom and the denial of God" *Karl Jaspers, Intruduction to Philosophy*, Serbocroatian translation (Beograd: Prosveta, 1967) p. 158.

self.

Practical moral experience shows man's greater inclination to sin than his striving to do good. His ability to fall deep into sin seems to be greater than to soar up into the heights of virtue.[53] Negative personalities always seem truer than positive ones, and the poet who describes negative characters has an advantage over the one who describes heroes.[54]

Anyhow, men are always good or bad but never innocent, and this could be the ultimate meaning of the biblical story about the fall, the original sin. From the moment of the expulsion from paradise, Adam (man) could not rid himself of his freedom, nor escape from the drama, to be as innocent as an animal or an angel. He has to choose, to use his freedom, to be good or evil; in one word, to be man. This ability to choose, regardless of result, is the highest form of existence possible in the universe.

Man has a soul, but psychology is not the science about it. There cannot exist a science about the soul. Psychology deals with some forms of apparent inner life. This is why it is possible to talk about psycho-physiology, psychometry, psycho-hygiene, and the physics of the psyche. The possibility of quantitative psychology confirms the thesis of the outer, mechanical, and quantitative, that is, the soulless nature of thought and feeling. Animal and human psychology may complement each other, for psychology has nothing to do with the soul, only with the psychological manifestations. John Watson writes: "Human psychology, as understood by behaviorism, must be built upon the example of the objective and experimental psychology of animals, borrowing from its way of examining, its method, and its aim. As such, there do not exist two

---

[53]The Qur'ān 12:53.

[54]It is interesting to note the polemic that took place in China in 1974 about a Chinese novel from the fifteenth century, *The Water Boundary*, better known in the West in Pearl Buck's English translation *All Men are Brothers*. The novel, one of the best in Chinese classical literature, describes the revolt of the peasants against the imperial administration during the twelfth century. Because of its message that all men are brothers, the novel was cited as "a negative instructive example" of an "unclass approach" because "all men are not brothers," as stated during this polemic in 1974.

In Hungary, the Ministry of Education ordered the classification of all children according to the class they belonged to, six categories "a" to "f." The reaction of the public, although very careful, showed that this classification was looked upon as a discriminatory measure. New forms or reasons for making differences among people are, no doubt, connected with official atheistic philosophy.

types of psychology (human and animal), separated from each other; by an iron curtain, not knowing each other; having basically different objects, methods, and aims; but only one psychology which takes its place among the natural sciences."[55] This quotation needs no comment. If we use Islamic terms, we may say that psychology is the science of the *nafs* and not of the *rūh*, that is, a science on the biological and not on the personal level. There are three circles (the mechanical, the biological, and the personal) which correspond to the three degrees of reality (matter, life, and personality). This way of thinking leads to the application of the scientific method, which always implies an absolute causality, and this by itself means the negation of freedom which is the essence of the soul. Our attempt to "study" the soul in psychology brings us necessarily to the negation of the "subject of this study." There is no way out of this bewitched circle.

The equality and brotherhood of people is possible only if man is created by God. The equality of men is a spiritual and not a natural, physical, or intellectual fact. It exists as a moral quality of man, as the human dignity, or as the equal value of the human personality. On the contrary, as physical, thinking, and social beings; as members of groups, classes, political groupings, and nations; people are always very unequal. If man's spiritual value is not recognized — this fact of religious character — the only real base of human equality is lost. Equality, then, becomes a mere phrase without a base and content and, as such, it will soon retreat, faced with the evident facts of human inequality or with the natural human desire to rule and to obey and thus to be unequal. As soon as the religious approach is removed, the empty room is filled by different forms of inequality — racial, national, social, or political.

Man's dignity could not be dicovered by biology, psychology, or by any other science, Man's dignity is a spiritual question. After "objective observations," it is easier for science to confirm the inequality of man, and so, "scientific racism" is quite possible and even logical [56]

The ethics of Socrates, Pythagoras, and of Seneca were not in-

---

[55]Watson, p. 158

[56]Evolutionism, can, neither be reconciled with the idea of equality nor with the concept of natural human rights. The "égalité" of the French revolution is also religious in its origin (see Chapter XI of this book).

ferior to the ethics of the three revealed religions (Judaism, Christianity, and Islam) even though there remains one clear distinction: only the ethics of the revealed religions postulated clearly and without ambiguity the equality of all men as God's creatures. Even Plato accepted it as necessary that men were unequal. On the contrary, the cornerstone of the revealed religions is the common origin, and therefore the absolute equality, of all men. This idea has had a fundamental impact on all later spiritual, ethical, and social development of mankind. Moreover, the history of ethics seems to prove the connection between the idea of the equality of men and the idea of immortality — a topic which has not yet been studied enough. Religious and moral systems which do not recognize or otherwise have a confused idea about immortality, do not recognize this equality either. If there is no God, men are obviously and hopelessly unequal.

Nietzsche claimed that religions were invented by the weak to delude the strong. Marx maintained the opposite. If we accept that religions were imagined, Nietzsche's interpretation seems more convincing because only on religion could the weak base their demand for equality. Science and everything else except religion have confirmed their inequality.

Why are there so many handicapped people around the mosques, churches, and temples which we enter? Only the houses of God have opened their doors to the ones who have nothing to show and to prove, who are poor in health and wealth, who are shut out from all the feasts of this world where one is asked for name, family, talents, and knowledge. The sick and the uneducated remain in front of the factory door too, while the healthy and educated enter. In the house of God, a poor and blind man can stand by the side of a king or a noble and he may even be better than they are.[57] The most important cultural and human meaning of the temples lies in this recurring proof of equality.

The utmost meaning of art is to discover the human quality in men who have been degraded by life and to find human greatness in the small, forgotten people — in a word, to reveal the human soul of the same value in every human being. The lower the social status of a man, the more striking is the discovery of his dignity. In

---

[57]The Qur'ān 80:1-9.

this lies the true value of classical Russian literature.[58] French literature equally featured this in such personages as Quasimodo, Fantine, and Jean Valjean.

Humanism is not charity, forgiveness, and tolerance, although that is the necessary result of it. Humanism is primarily the affirmation of man and his freedom, namely, of his value as a man.

Everything that debases man's personality, that brings him down to a thing, is inhuman. For instance, it is human to state that man is responsible for his deeds and to punish him. It is not human to ask him to regret, to change his mind, to "improve," and to be pardoned. It is more human to prosecute a man for his beliefs than to force him to renounce them, giving him the well-known chance called "taking into consideration his sincere attitude." So, there are punishments which are human, and pardonings which are most inhuman. The inquisitors claimed that they burned the body to save the soul. Modern inquisitors do the opposite: they "burn" the soul as the compensation for the body.

To reduce a man to the function of a producer and a consumer, even if every man is given his place in production and consumption, does not signal humanism but dehumanization.

To drill people to produce correct and disciplined citizens is likewise inhuman.

Education, too, can be inhuman: if it is one-sided, directed, and indoctrinated; if it does not teach one to think independently, if it only gives ready-made answers; if it prepares people only for different functions instead of broadening their horizons and thereby their freedom.

Every manipulation of people, even if it is done in their own interest, is inhuman. To think for them and to free them from their responsibilities and obligations is also inhuman. Our quality of man obliges us. When God gave man the ability to choose and

---

[58]In the essay "The Russian Point of View" Virginia Woolf describes this lively quality of classical Russian prose: "The soul is the leading character in Russian artistic prose. Delicate and subtle with Checkhov, deeper and greater with Dostoevski, inclined to violent and furious convulsion but always dominating...Dostoevski's novels sow gales, whirlwinds of sand, gushes of water bubbling and gurgling, absorbing us. They consist of soul only. See Virginia Woolf, *The common Reader* (New york: Harcourt, Brace & Co., 1925).

threatened him with severe punishments, He confirmed in the highest way the value of man as a man.[59] We have to follow the example set by God: let us leave man to struggle for himself, instead of doing it for him.

Without religion and the concept of man's ever-striving spirit, as stated in the "prologue in heaven," there is no authentic belief of man as the highest value. Without it, there is no belief that man as man is at all possible and that he really exists. Atheistic humanism is a contradiction because if there is no God, then there is no man either.[60] Also, if there is no man, humanism is a phrase without essence. The one who does not acknowledge the creation of man does not understand the real meaning of humanism. Since he has lost his basic standard, he will always reduce humanism to the production of goods and their distribution according to need. To make sure that all people are fed is of course a matter of great concern, but knowing affluent societies of today, we cannot be sure that in this way we would get a better and more humane world. It would be even less humane if the ideas of some people about general leveling, uniformity, and depersonification were put into practice. In such a world, as described by Aldous Huxley in *Brave New World*, there would be no social problems, and evenness, uniformity, and stability would reign everywhere. Nonetheless, all of us consciously or instinctively reject this vision as an example of general dehumanization.

"Man is a product of his environment" — this basic postulate of materialism served as the starting point of all subsequent inhuman theories in law and sociology, and of the practice of manipulating human beings, which in our time reached monstrous proportions during the time of Nazism and Stalinism. All other similar seductive theories of society's priority over individuals, of man's obligation to serve society, and so forth, belong here as well. Man must not

---

[59]Verily, We have created man into toil and struggle... Have we not made for him a pair of eyes? And a tongue and a pair of lips? And shown him the two highways? But he has made no haste on the path that is steep. And what will explain to you the path that is steep? It is freeing the bondman; or the giving of food in a day of privation to the orphan with claims of relationship; or to the indigent down in the dust. Then will he be of those who believe and enjoin patience and constancy and self-restraint and enjoin deeds of kindness and compassion (The Qur'ān 90:8-17).

[60]Nikolai Berdyaev, *The Beginning and the End*, trans. R. M. French (New York: Harper, 1857).

serve anybody; he must not be a means. Everything must serve man, and man must serve God only. This is the ultimate meaning of humanism.

Chapter 2

CULTURE AND CIVILIZATION

Civilization cannot be rejected even if we like that. The only thing that is necessary and possible is to destroy the myth of it.

CULTURE AND CIVILIZATION

Tool and Cult

Two antagonistic facts are connected to man's emergence: the first tool and the first cult. The first tool was a piece of wood or a roughly shaped stone — a fragment of nature. The making of tools and their usage represents a continuation of biological evolution, which is exterior and quantitative, and which can be followed from primitive forms of life to the appearance of man as a perfect animal. Upright bearing, perfection of hand, language, and intelligence are various states and moments in evolution which remain zoological in nature. By using for the first time a stone to smash a hard fruit or to hit an animal, man did something very important though not anything entirely new since his alleged animal ancestors had already tried to do it. However, when he set the stone in front of his eyes and looked at it as a symbol of a spirit, he did something that became the universal and unavoidable trait of man all over the world, something completely new in his development. Similarly, when man for "the first time drew the line around his shadow on sand and so made the first picture,"[1] he began an impossible activity belonging to him alone, any animal being a priori incapable of it — regardless of its degree of evolution, present and future.

---

[1]Leonardo da Vinci: *The Notebooks of Leonardo da Vinci*, ed. Jean Paul Richter (New York: Dover Publications, 1970).

The biological aspect of man's emergence may be explained by the preceding history. The spiritual aspect of his emergence cannot be deduced or explained by anything that had existed before him. Man came from another world, from the sky, as religion has picturesquely said.

The cult and tool represent two natures and two histories of man. One history is human drama, beginning with the "prologue in heaven," developing through the triumph of the idea of freedom and ending with the last judgment, which is the moral sanction of history. The other is the history of tools, which is the history of things, and it will end by entering the classless society, the entropy, as the rest of the material world.[2] The two histories have the same relation as the cult and the tool, which is the same as culture and civilization.[3]

Reflex of the Life Dualism

A singular confusion exists about the notions of "culture" and "civilization."

Culture began with the "prologue in heaven." With its religion, art, ethics, and philosophy, it will always be dealing with man's relation to that heaven from whence he came. Everything within culture means a confirmation or a rejection, a doubt or a reminiscence of the heavenly origin of man. Culture is characterized by this enigma and goes on through all time with the steady striving to solve it.

On the other hand, civilization is a continuation of the zoological, one-dimensional life, the material exchange between man and nature. This aspect of life differs from other animals' lives, but only in its degree, level, and organization. Here, one does not find man embarrassed by evangelical, Hamletian, or Karamasovian problems. The anonymous member of society functions here only by adopting

---

[2]Compare: "The changes of mankind follow the changes of tools." Georg Hegel, *Philosophy of History*, Serbocroatian trans. (Zegreb: Naprijed, 1966). Contrarily: "All history flows toward Christ and emanates from him." Pierre Lacomb, *History Considered as Knowledge* (n.p., n.d.).

[3]Culture is etymologically connected to the word "cult" (Latin: cultus) and culture. Both words have a common origin in the Hindu-European word "kwel." On the other hand, civilization is linked to the word cives = citizen.

the goods of nature and changing the world by his work according to his needs.

Culture is the influence of religion on man or man's influence on himself, while civilization is the effect of intelligence on nature, on the external world. Culture means the "art of being man"; civilization means the art of functioning, ruling, and making things perfect. Culture is a "continual creating of self"; civilization is the continual changing of the world. This is the opposite man-thing, humanism against chosism.[4]

Religions, creeds, drama, poetry, games, folklore, folk tales, mythology, moral and aesthetic codes; elements of the political and juridical life affirming a personality's value, freedom and tolerance; philosophy, theater, galleries, museums, libraries — this is the unbroken line of human culture, the first act of which has been played in heaven between God and man. That is "climbing the holy mountain, the top of which remains unreachable; marching through darkness by means of the blazing candle carried by man."[5]

Civilization is the continuation of technical rather than spiritual progress, in the same way that Darwinian evolution is the continuation of biological rather than human progress. Civilization represents the development of the potential forces that existed in our less developed ancestors. It is a continuation of the natural, mechanical elements — that is, of the unconscious, senseless elements of our existence. Therefore, civilization is neither good nor bad in itself. Man must create civilization, just as he must breathe or eat. It is an expression of necessity and of our lack of freedom. Culture, on the contrary, is the ever-present feeling of choice and expression of human freedom.

Man's dependency on matter in civilization is constantly growing. Somebody found that every American — man, woman, and child — uses 18 tons of different materials yearly. Forever creating new necessities and developing the need for the needless, civilization tends to intensify the material exchange between man and nature, to induce the external life at the expense of the internal one. "Produce to gain, gain to squander" — that is innate in civilization. On the other hand, every culture (owing to its religious nature) tends to re-

---

[4]From the French word "chose" = thing, used first by Durkheim. It is the method of examining a phenomenon objectively, from the outside and only as a thing.

[5]André Malraux: *Antimemoirs*, Serbocroatian trans. (Zagreb: Naprijed, 1969), p. 276.

duce the number of human needs or the degree of their supply, enlarging in this way man's internal freedom. This is the true sense of the various kinds of asceticism and self-denials known in all cultures, which assume an absurd form in the "dirtiness vow" — that of thc monks or of the hippies — all the same. Contrary to the maxim of Islam: "Restrain desires," civilization, ruled by an inverse logic, had to hoist an opposing motto: "Make new desires ever and ever again."[6] The true meaning of these contradictory demands can be understood only by one who realizes that they are not accidental in either of the two examples. They show that man is a being of discord, simultaneously reflecting the ambiguity of human nature and the antagonism between culture and civilization.

The bearer of culture is man; the bearer of civilization is society. The meaning of culture is self-power attained through upbringing; the meaning of civilization is power over nature by means of science. Science, technology, cities, and states belong to civilization. The means of civilization are thought, language, and writing.[7] Culture and civilization relate to each other as the celestial empire to this world, as *civitas dei* to *civitas solis*. One is a drama, the other is utopia.

Tacitus says that barbarians treated their slaves much better than the Romans did.[8] Generally, ancient Rome is very convenient for drawing the line between culture and civilizations. Robbery wars, *panem et circenses*, inhuman ruling classes and faceless masses, lumpen-proletariat, false democracy, political machinations, persecution of Christians, gladiatorial games, Nero and Caligula — all that cannot call into question the Roman civilization, but we must wonder how much culture was left there. "Hellenic soul and Roman intellect — that is the difference between culture and civilization."[9] Romans give the impression of civilized barbarians. Rome is an example of

---

[6]*The New York Times*, in a recent article, calls this motto "the first commandment of the new era."

[7]Marshal McLuhan proved that writing causes changes in the way of thinking. "The use of an alphabet produces and supports the habit of expressing in visual and space terms, especially in terms of uniform space and uniform time, continually and constantly." McLuhan, *The Gutenberg Galaxy*, Serbocroatian trans. (Beograd: Nolit, 1973), p. 32.

[8]Tacirus: *Agricola and Germania*, trans. Maurice Hutton (Cambridge, MA: Harvard University Press, n.d.).

[9]Oswald Spengler: *The Decline of the West* (London: George Allen and Unwin, Ltd., 1971), p. 32.

a high civilization deprived of culture. The Mayan culture might be an opposite example. According to our knowledge concerning the life of the ancient Germans and Slavs, they seem to have been on a higher level of culture than the Romans in the same way as the Indian indigenes were "more cultured" than the white colonizers.

The European Renaissance represents an expressive example of this phenomenon. This cultural period, one of the most stirring in human history, turned out to be a decline from the point of view of civilization. During the century preceding the Renaissance, a true economic revolution took place in Europe, one which resulted in increased production and consumption as well as in a notable increase in population. During the two following centuries known as the Age of Renaissance (1350-1550), the achievements of that revolution were mostly lost. Completely focused on man instead of the world and obsessed by the human face, the Renaissance seemed to be indifferent to what was happening in reality. While the greatest art works of Western culture were created, a general stagnation and an evident decay were present, followed by population decreases in most European countries. By the middle of the fourteenth century, England had about 4 million inhabitants; one hundred years later it had only 2.1 million. During the fourteenth century, the number of inhabitants of Florence fell from 100,000 to 70,000. There are evidently two "progresses" having basically no interconnection.[10]

Education and Meditation

Civilization educates; culture enlightens. One needs learning, the other meditation.

Meditation, an internal effort to know one's self and one's place in the world, is quite a different activity than learning, education, and the gathering of knowledge of facts and their relations. Meditation leads to wisdom, gentleness, internal calm, to a kind of Greek catharsis. It is devotion to secrets and immersion into the self to

---

[10]This "unscientific" state of mind during the Renaissance can be illustrated by an interesting fact on the superstitions spread not only among common people but even among artists and humanists. "Astrology was especially prized by freethinkers; it acquired a vogue which it had not had since ancient times." Bertrand Russell, *History of Western Philosophy* (London: n.p., 1948), p. 523. Also see Serbocroation translation (Beograd: Kosmos, 1962), p. 485.

reach some religious, moral, or artistic truths. Learning, on the other hand, is facing nature in order to know it and to change the conditions of existence. Science applies observation, analysis, division, experiment, and examination, while contemplation means pure understanding and in neo-Platonism even a super-rational way of understanding. Contemplative observing is "free from will and wish";[11] it is observing without any function or interest. Contemplation is not the attitude of a scientist but of a thinker, a poet, an artist, or a recluse. A scientist also has some contemplative moments, but not in the capacity of a scientist, rather in his capacity as a man or artist (all men being artists in a way). Meditation provides power over self; science provides power over nature. Our schooling promotes only our civilization and does not contribute to our culture.

In our time, people learn; in the past, they used to meditate. "Sages from Laputa, absorbed in meditation, could not notice or hear those who disturbed them by asking questions."[12] A legend says that Buddha, before being inspired, was standing by the riverside for three days and nights, fixed in thought, unconscious of time. Xenophon left a similar story about Socrates: One morning he was thinking about something that he could not resolve. He would not give up and continued thinking from early dawn until noon — there he stood fixed in thought; and at noon, attention was drawn to him, and the rumor ran through the curious crowd that Socrates had been standing and thinking about something since the break of day. At last, in the evening after supper, some Ionians, out of curiosity, brought out their mats and slept in the open air that they might watch him and see whether he would stand all night. There he stood until the following morning, and with the return of the light, he offered up a prayer to the sun and went on his way."[13]

Tolstoy spent his life thinking about man and his destiny, while Galileo, the prophet of European civilization, was obsessed all his life by the problem of a falling body. To meditate and to learn (or to study) are two different activities or two kinds of energies aimed in opposite directions. The first led Beethoven to the creation of *The Ninth Symphony*. The second led Newton to the discovery of the

---

[11]Arthur Schopenhauer: *The Works of Schopenhauer*, ed. Will Durant (Garden City, NY: Garden City Publishing Company, Inc., 1928).

[12]Payot: *The Art of Being Man*, Serbocroatian trans. (Beograd: Rad, 1960), p. 21.

[13]See, Xenophon: *Hellenica, Anabasis, Apology, and Sympocium*, ed. C.L. Brownson and O.J. Todd (Cambridge, MA: Harvard University Press, n.d.).

laws of gravitation and motion. The antagonism between meditation and learning repeats once more the antagonism between man and world, soul and intellect, or culture and civilization.

What is the subject of meditation?

In nature, one can find both the world and man; in fact, everything can be found except one's "self," one's personality. It is just through that self that one is connected to eternity. Through one's self — and only through it — one feels freedom and has a sight of the other world of which one is the simultaneous inhabitant. Only alone can one attest that the world of spirit and freedom exists. Without that self, one does not witness a world beyond the world of nature because everything else besides one's self is exterior and phenomenal. Meditation is the immersion into the self — an attempt to reach and find, through one's entity, the truth of one's life and existence. That is why meditation does not try to answer the questions of society or mankind. It is a matter of the questions that man is putting to himself.

Strictly taken, meditation is not a function of intelligence. A scientist designing a new type of plane does not meditate. He thinks, studies, investigates, examines, and compares, but all these activities, separately or together, are not meditation. A monk, a poet, a thinker, an artist meditate. They are trying to reach a great truth, the only great mystery. This truth means everything and nothing: everything for a soul, nothing for the rest of the world.

Therefore, meditation is a religious activity. For Aristotle, the difference between reason and contemplation is the difference between the human and the divine.

In Buddhism, prayer consists only of meditation. In Christianity, we find the monastic contemplative order, a quite logical phenomenon. Spinoza held contemplation to be the supreme form and aim of morality.

Education by itself does not bring men up, nor does it make them better, more free, or more human; it makes them more capable, more efficient, more useful to society. History has proven that educated men and peoples can be manipulated and can also serve evil, even more effectively than backward people. The history of imperialism is a series of true stories about civilized peoples who waged unjust, extirpative, and subjugating wars against less-educated and underdeveloped peoples who defended their liberty. The high educational level of the invaders had no effect on their aims or methods; it helped only their efficiency and forced the defeat of their victims.

Technological and Classical Education

Nevertheless, education is not a one-sided phenomenon. If we look at it closely, we shall notice two different, equal but independent tendencies.

School education in the civilized world is too intellectual and insufficiently humane. If we use the usual terms, we can say it is too technological and insufficiently classical.[14] Today, it is quite possible to imagine a young man who has passed through all educational degrees, from primary school to college, without ever having been told to be a good and honest man. First he learned to write and reckon, then he studied physics, chemistry, ethnology, geography, political theories, sociology, and many other sciences. He gathered a mass of facts and, at best, learned how to think, but he was not enlightened. We hear increasingly less about history, the arts, literature, ethics, and law.

In relation to civilization, technological education appears to be both its cause and its consequence. This type of education prepares a member for society, and all its aspects are shaped by that measure. This education is directed at a precise end and is interested in dominating nature, the external world. Classical education, on the contrary, begins and ends in man, being "aimlessly purposeful."

The dilemma of technological education versus classical education is not a technical but rather an ideological question. A certain specific philosophy lies behind it. In these two systems of education, the opposition between culture and civilization is projected with all its consequences. A non-industrial society will always be inclined toward classical education, while an industrial society, especially a socialist one, will tend toward the technological education. It is, of course, just a principle, suffering many deviations in practice. Still, the main tendency remains, being realized through the unavoidable corrections. A comparison between the school programs in the USSR, France, China, or Japan, especially in the topics of history, law, ethics, literature, Latin and Greek, would be very instructive.

---

[14]In some countries, the terms "exact" and "grammar" education are used.

The logical sequence of a technological education is specialization. First of all, we can see that intelligence, science, and industry form one line and relate to each other as cause and consequence. Science is a result of intelligence, just as industry is only an applied science. They all are conditions and forms of man's bearing in nature, in the external world. Specialization affords better and deeper setting of the individual in the social scheme, in the social mechanism. It degrades personality, but it promotes society and makes it more efficient. Society gets the capacity of the whole, while man becomes an ever-decreasing part of the social mechanism. The atomization of work and depersonalization of man as the working subject tend, in their progressive march, to the ideal state of utopia.

The expansion of education is vertiginous. For example, in 1900, all colleges and universities in the US employed 24,000 professors; in 1920, about 49,000; while by the end of the century, a number somewhere around 480,000 is expected. All the colleges and universities of the country had 238,000 students in 1900; 3,777,000 in 1959; and ten years later, they numbered 14,600,000. The total expenses for education rose from the symbolic sum of 270 million dollars in 1900 to the sum of 42.5 billion dollars in 1970.[15] The increase is similar in the socialist countries, but, of course, their educational budgets started from lower points.

The two greatest scientific forces in the world, the US and the USSR, are the two strongest military forces, but they are not the world's most cultured countries. These two countries allocate the biggest funds for research and education (USSR 4.2 percent and US 2.8 percent of the national income). The average American over 25 years of age has 10.5 years of schooling, followed by a British man with 9.5 years of school, and then a Russian with 5 years.[16]

What kind of education is this? As a rule, this is the typical education according to the civilization recipe.

In communist countries, education consists of indoctrination in the ideological and political system of the state and is subordinated to its interests. In capitalist countries, education generally conforms to the economic requirements and serves the industrial system. In both cases, the education is functional, in the service of the system.

---

[15]Data from the Education Office of the US Department of Health, Education, and Welfare.

[16]Data from 1960.

This tendency prevails, despite flowery proclamations on the many-sided advances of man's personality, on the humane character of education, and so on. We shall support this assertion by two competent sources.

Lenin repeatedly stressed that education must not be "neutral," objective, or apolitical. At the first Congress of Soviet Education, held in 1918, he put forth the following principle: "Our work in the field of education has the purpose of destroying the bourgeois class, and we declare that there is no school outside of politics. That is a lie and hypocrisy."[17] Indoctrinated education remains the principle of the educational system in the USSR up to the present day.

The well-known economic theorist and one of the best connoisseurs of the industrial system in today's world, John K. Galbraith, says: "... Certainly, the modern high school is thoroughly adjusted to the needs of the industrial system. ... The great esteem enjoyed by pure and applied science and mathematics is but a reflex of the techno-structure requirements, ... while the less esteem and support given to the arts and human sciences reflect their inferior importance. ... Business and technical schools are very esteemed because of their utility character. ... The industrial system has animated a large development in education. We can bid welcome to it. But, if the tendencies would not be clearly noticed and resisted, the system will stimulate only the emotional aspect which would best serve its needs and call the least in question its objectives."[18]

Anyway, what are the common characteristics of educational systems on all sides? First of all, it is a strict selectivity causing a destructive competition, an artificial "specialistic" language developed in most of the disciplines, and an austerely functional architecture of the school buildings adjusted solely to the standards of utility and hygiene. That is so because the school serves the ruling bureaucracy or the highly concurrent industrial system, preparing the experts who will serve and further promote these two mechanisms. Appeals for humane schools, heard here and there, have remained just nice speeches so far.

If we would estimate the cultural content of the education

---

[17]Vladimir I. Lenin: *The Lenin Anthology*, ed. Robert C. Tucker (New York: Norton, 1975).

[18]John Galbraith and M. S. Randhawa: *The New Industrial State* (Boston: Houghton-Mifflin, 1967), pp. 339-341.

supplied by the schools, we could say: the school is a component of civilization; it contributes to culture to the degree that it is not a "dressage," for it develops critical thinking and leaves room for man's spiritual freedom. The school which introduces ready-made ethical and political solutions, from the point of view of culture, is barbarian. It does not create free persons but dependents. It promotes civilization, perhaps, but it degrades culture.

Mass Culture

In the light of these considerations, the reader will on his own find the place for so-called mass culture. Is it culture or just an aspect of civilization?

The subject of any culture is man as an individual, as a personality, as the "unrepeatable individuality." The subject or object of mass culture is a mass or a "man-mass."[19] A man has a soul; a mass has nothing but needs. Therefore, every culture is a bringing up of man, while mass culture is just a supply of needs.

Culture tends toward individualization; mass culture leads in the opposite direction, to spiritual uniformity. At this point, mass culture diverges both from ethics and from culture. The mass production of "spiritual goods," the copies, the tawdry and worthless literature, leads to impersonalization. Mass culture, as distinguished from authentic culture, limits human freedom by just this "uniforming" tendency since "freedom is resistance to uniformity."[20]

One widespread mistake is the identification of mass culture with popular culture. This is injurious to the latter, for popular culture, distinguished from mass culture, is authentic, active, and immediate. It is innocent of tawdriness and kitsch,[21] which are entirely the products of the big city.

---

[19]The term "man-mass" was introduced into literature by José Ortega Y. Gasset in his *The Revolt of the Masses* (New York: W. W. Norton & Company, 1932). A mass is a group of anonymous, faceless units. A group of people, having lost their personalities, becomes degraded to a mass. Man-mass is the final product of civilization without culture. He is free of the doubts and the "prejudices" of culture.

[20]Max Horkheimer: *Dialectic of Englightenment*, trans. John Cumming (New York: Herder & Herder, 1972).

[21]The latter term stands for artistic or literary material of low quality, designed to appeal to current popular taste.

Popular culture is based on consensus and participation, while the predominating principle of mass culture is manipulation. Rites, dances, and songs are common possessions of a village or a tribe. The performers are the spectators and vice versa. When the feast begins, everybody takes part in it, everybody becomes a performer. Mass culture offers quite a different example. People are strictly separated into "producers" and "consumers" of "cultural goods." Is there anybody who really believes that he can influence the television programs, of course unless he belongs to the small group of those who make them? The so-called "mass media" (press, Radio, and television) are in fact the means of mass manipulation. On one side are the editorial offices of a small number of people who created the program, on the other side is a passive audience of millions.

An inquiry carried out in 1971 showed that the average Englishman spends 16 to 18 hours a week watching TV.[22] Television has been steadily replacing literature, its equivalent in the cultural field. Every third French person never reads a book, and the French nation spends its free time watching TV.[23] The inquiry also indicated that, for more than 87 percent of the population, the main "cultural" pastime is watching a TV program, while ballet and opera hold the last place on the list. An inquiry taken on the occasion of the "Book Week" in 1976 showed that the situation in Japan is the same. About 30 percent of the Japanese do not read books, while each of them spends 2.5 hours daily watching TV. Professor Horikava from San Francisco University claims that the aptitude of the rising generation is below university criteria. Horikava explains that, in a simple way, television has replaced literature and thinking and has therefore reduced intellectual activity. It offers ready-made solutions for all problems in life.[24] Our time offers examples of how mass culture media (radio, film, and television, being a government monopoly) can be used for a mass delusion of the worst kind. There is no need for brutal force to rule people against their will. That can be now attained in a "legal way" by paralyzing the people's will, by offering them cut-and-dried truths, and by preventing them from thinking and arriving at their own opinions of men and events.

---

[22]Data from the publication *Society Trends*, a statistical annual of the British government.

[23]These are the conclusions of the inquiry made by the magazine *Le Point* in 1975.

[24]Naoyoshi Horikawa: *Gendai masu komyunikeshon ron* (n.p., 1974).

"Mass" psychology proved, and practice confirmed, that it is possible by persistent repetition to convince people of myths which have nothing in common with reality.[25] The psychology of mass media, especially of television, has been conceived in such a way as to subordinate not only the conscious but even the instinctive and emotional side of man and to create in him the feeling that the imposed opinions are his own.[26]

All totalitarian societies saw their opportunity in television and rushed to use it. Television, therefore, became a threat to freedom, more dangerous than the police, the gendarmes, the prisons, and the concentration camps. I think that the following generations, if their ability to think freely will not be fully destroyed, will be shocked by the martyrdom of the present generation which is exposed without interruption to the impact of that uncontrolled power. If past constitutions were made with the aim of restraining rulers' power, a new constitution would be needed to restrain the power of this new danger threatening to establish a spiritual slavery of the worst kind.

Mass culture is characterized by a state of mind, the one Johan Huizinga referred to as "puerility." Huizinga notices that contemporary man behaves childishly, in the negative sense of the word — that is, in a way which is equal to the mental level of puberty: banal amusements; the absence of authentic humor; the need for strong sensations; the inclination to mass parades and slogans; and the expression of an exaggerated hate or love, blame or praise, which have a mass and brutal aspect.

Finally, we meet up with different attitudes to the machine and technology. Culture has a "fear of machines," an instinctive aver-

---

[25]Until 1945, the Japanese were taught that Micado had been the child of the goddess of the Sun and that Japan had been created before the rest of the world. Students were taught that myth even by university professors. That case belongs now to the past. Today, we are meeting some new myths in the forms of the "leader cults" in Russia, China, and North Korea (the cults of Stalin, Mao Tse Tung, and Kim Il Sung). All these myths have the same pattern. For example: "Every word of the esteemed and beloved leader comrade Kim Il Sung has entered deeply into our hearts like water penetrating the thirsty earth. ... We shall resolutely continue the performance of the great plan of the communist development designed by our esteemed and beloved leader comrade Kim Il Sung," from the article *All That People Love Is Good* by Kim John Hui. A stone on which the "esteemed and beloved comrade" sat during a speech is exhibited in a glass sarcophagus in a factory yard.

[26]In this matter, we can recommend Djura Susnjic's excellent book *Fishermen For Human Souls* (Belgrad: Zadruga, 1977).

sion to technology: "The machine is the first sin of culture."[27] This attitude comes from the feeling that the machine, from the beginning being a means for manipulating things, now becomes a means for manipulating man — let's remember the warnings expressed by Tagore, Tolstoy, Heidegger, Neizvestni, Faulkner, and others. On the other hand, the Marxist Henry Lefèbvre holds a quite different opinion: "The highest level of freedom will be reached only in a society in which technology develops all its potential — in a communist society."[28] In fact, a society which has utopia as its direct or indirect paragon finds its natural ally in machines and technology. Machines help — they do not prevent — the manipulation of men and things. They help create uniformity by means of education and mass media; they require the collaboration or the group work of a great number of people organized in a similar mechanism (a "collective") and centrally managed; and finally, they offer the prospect of complete control by society (read: authority) over the individual by means of direct or indirect inspection into what he is doing, saying, and thinking.

The Countryside and the City

The poets speak about the "hell" of a large city, while the Marxists speak about "idiotic country living."[29] The aversion felt for the city, as nonfunctional as it can be, is a purely human reaction since every man is a poet in a way. Today, as well as before, the protest against the city and urban civilization is coming from religion, culture, and art. For the first Christians, Rome was the devil's kingdom, which was to be followed by the end of the world — doomsday.

Religiousness decreases in proportion to the city's size, in fact, to the concentration of the urban elements alienating man. The larger

---

[27]Nikolai Berdyaev: *The Modern Crisis of Culture*, Serbocroatian trans. (Beograd: Hriscanska Biblioteka, 1932), and: "The only people who saw through industrialism in those early days were the poets. Blake, as everybody knows, thought that mills were the work of Satan. ... It took a longish time — over twenty years — before ordinary men began to see what a monster had been created," in Kenneth Clark: *Civilization* (London: British Broadcasting Corporation, 1962), p. 321.

[28]Henri Lefèbvre: *Everyday Life in the Modern World*, trans. Sacha Rabinovitch (New York: Harper & Row, 1971).

[29]Karl Marx and Friedrich Engels: *The Communist Manifesto: principles of Communism*, trans. Paul M. Sweezy (New York: Monthly Review Press, 1964).

the city, the less nature and sky over it: there is more smoke, concrete, technology, and crime. Religiousness is inversely and crime is directly proportional to the largeness of a city.[30] These two phenomena have common causes. They are connected to the so-called "experienced aesthetics."

A country man has the opportunity to watch the starry skies, fields, flowers, rivers, plants, and animals. He is living in touch with nature and its elements. The rich folklore, the wedding customs, the folk songs, and dances offer a kind of cultural and aesthetic experience almost entirely unknown to a man of the city. In most cases, the urban man is living in the barracks of a big town, crammed with passive knowledge of the mass media and surrounded by ugly objects of mass production. Has not the sense of rhythm, possessed by all primitive peoples, almost died out with modern man? The opinion that an urban dweller has more opportunities for the artistic or aesthetic experience is one of the most grotesque mistakes of our day. As if the concerts, museums, and exhibitions frequented by a very small percentage of the city inhabitants could be a compensation for the everyday perhaps unconscious but very strong aesthetic excitement of the countryman who witnesses the wonderful sight of the sunrise or the awakening of life after winter! Most of the urbanites experience their strongest excitement in the naturalistic setting of a football or boxing match. Overall, a country man is alive and genuine; overall, an urban industrial worker is dead and mechanical.

Only here, in the different spiritual climate and different experiences rather than in the different material living conditions and educational levels should we ask for an explanation of the country man's religiousness and the urban industrial worker's atheism.[31] Religion belongs to life, arts, and culture; atheism belongs to method, science, and civilization.

---

[30]According to an inquiry, 12 to 13 percent of the inhabitants of Paris come to the Catholic mass, in Lyon 20.9 percent, and in St. Etienne 28.5 percent. Data about crime would certainly show the inverse gradient.

[31]Neither can the phenomenon in question be explained by economic insecurity. An urban industrial worker's existence is not more secure than a countryman's. The market is as inconsistent and changeable as is the sky. Marx showed that, for the urban industrial worker, the market is a fetish-power beyond his control.

The Working Class

Being a product of the city, the working class has suffered the most from the negative influence of the so-called "sheer civilization" (civilization with the least share of culture). The factory jades and tyrannizes the personality. A sociologist wrote: "The workmen, being subjected to a strict discipline, transmit the habits they get in the production process to their own organizations. They cede their power to the bureaucracy that they spontaneously create and which plays a conservative role both in the capitalist and in the socialist countries."[32]

Herbert Marcuse discovered that workers in a developed capitalist country where the influence of technology and factories is the strongest ceased to be a revolutionary force. The working class is an example of a manipulated group which is flattered and cited but is seldom consulted and followed. The two largest working classes in the world, those of the US and the USSR, have no real influence upon the political structure of their states and the decisions made by them.[33]

One of the byproducts of this situation, besides the alienation from religion and art, is the poverty of thought — theoretical sterility within the working class movement, a fact recognized by communist writers such as Gorz, Garaudy, Basso, and Malle. In a 1965 interview with a reporter of the Italian newspaper *Il Contemporaneo*, the well-known Marxist writer György Lukacs said: "After Marx, nobody except Lenin has made any theoretical contribution to the problems of capitalistic development." Then, considering Stalin's period in the USSR, Lukacs stated: "Every free thought was suppressed and personal opinions were proclaimed to be theoretical laws. A complete generation grew up in this deterioration of theoretical sense." In fact, after Marx, who himself did not originate from the working but from the middle class, we hardly find a worthy and original idea coming from the working class, excluding the idea of self-management in Yugoslavia, which, in spite of some difficulties, represents a particular and original course. In any event, this idea means an emancipation from the models and the dogmas in which official Marxism fettered the development of working-class thought.

[32]Moreover, there are sound indications that a great influence is exerted by the underworld and the Mafia in the management of some American union organizations.
[33]Herbert Marcuse: *A Critique of Pure Tolerance* (Boston: Beacon Press, 1969).

The strikes which shake the capitalist economy are usually of an economic order and finish with compromise formulas about wage increases. Since the process of economic development was not followed by the impoverishment of the working class, as Marx predicted, it found a way to arrange class peace instead of class war with the antagonistic groups in the society.[34]

The classical form of the working class, the class of oppressed factory proletarians which would, according to Marx, exist "until that class cancels itself," was just a temporary form. Machines are taking over the manual work while the activity of man becomes more and more the control and management of large automatic systems.[35]

The development of science and technology, "the development of the productive means," did not result in the power of the working class but in its abolition as such. Development did not give power to the laborer, but rather transmitted the decisive point of production, and the social importance as well, to the technical intelligence. The last traces of idealism and revolutionary romanticism have disappeared. Technocracy, the rational and heartless power, the typical product of a consistent civilization, is arriving on the scene.

Religion and Revolution

Revolution has never been a happening only in the domain of civilization, economy, society, or politics. Every true revolution is a member of faith, exaltation, justice, longing, sacrifice, and death — the feelings which are beyond interest and existence. Everybody who took part in a revolution or followed its development from close by could affirm the presence of those ethical features. They saw it

---

[34]The economic importance of strikes is not as high as it might seem at a glance. According to 1978 data of a Swedish institution, in the biggest capitalist countries (the U.S., England, Italy, and Canada) strikes during the last 5 years (1973-1978) have been taking less than I percent of the total working time. In Sweden, it takes 6 minutes a worker per year, while in Switzerland the amount is even more insignificant.

[35]According to an analysis, a worker working at a completely automatic machine operates actively only one hour per week, while the other 39 hours he just watches the machine. The development in this direction is very fast, and automation is becoming prevalent in a great number of industrial branches. Marx, a great dialectician, either did not notice that development or did not make the appropriate conclusion from it. He considered the phenomenon of the working class in a static way, not in a dialectical one.

as an epic poem and not just a mechanical overthrow or a simple change of the ruling machinery. This might explain the inability of the workers in today's capitalist countries to revolt and, on the other hand, the enthusiasm of poets, artists, and other religious people for a revolution which can be atheistic in its declarations. Considered from the inside, not as a process but as a part of life, revolution appears as a drama which affects men as only religions do. From the outside, political, "real" point of view, it can have a quite different character and aim.[36]

A community affected by the feelings of solidarity, sacrifice, and a common destiny is in a "state of religion." This is the atmosphere of "increased temperature," which appears in emergencies and at feasts, when people feel like brothers and friends.

A society incapable of religion is also incapable of revolution. The countries in revolutionary fervor are the countries of living religious feelings as well. The feeling of brotherhood, solidarity, and justice — religious in their very essence — are in revolution turned to this world's justice, to this world's paradise.

Both religion and revolution are born in pain and suffering and die in well-being and comfort. Their true life is as long as their struggle to be realized. Their realization is their death. Both religion and revolution, in their stage of becoming real, produce institutions and structures which eventually suffocate them. The official institutions are neither revolutionary nor religious.

If a revolution had its adversaries in religion, it had them in the official religion only, in the church and hierarchy — in the institutional, false religion. Conversely, the pseudo-revolution — revolution converted into structure, bureaucracy always had its ally in the religion converted into structure, into bureaucracy. Having begun to lie and betray itself, the revolution could go along with the false religion.

---

[36]In the well-known poem "Twelve of Them" by the Russian poet Alexander Blok, the members of the Red Guard are led by Christ. That is how the poet sees the happening. The poem was written just after the revolution, and official critics denounced it as religious. We do not know how much the Minister of Culture, Lunatcharski, succeeded in protecting Blok by claiming that the poem was just "a vision based upon the tragic (London: Chatto and Windus, 1920).

Progress Against Man

According to the American scientist Julius Robert Oppenheimer, the creator of the American hydrogen bomb, the human race has realized more technical and material progress during the last 40 years than during the last 40 centuries. From 1900 to 1960, the distances available to man have increased from 10^{10} to 10^{40}, the temperature from 10^{5} to 10^{11}, the pressure from 10^{10} to 10^{16}. ... In 30 years, the old piston engines will be completely replaced by nuclear-driven boats. The day when electric cables under the roads will keep the electrical vehicles on the roads in motion is near.[37] Jean Rostand envisages the magical potential of biology. Using separated hereditary substances from extremely intelligent people, mankind will be able to transform itself. If the scientists could succeed in producing artificial DNA (the chemical base of heredity identified in chromosomes), new unlimited possibilities would arise. Everybody could have a child according to his wish. The human brain, having 10 billion cells so far, could add a few billion more taken from somewhere or produced by a special process. Transplantation of body parts and organs taken from corpses would be an ordinary event, and the discovery of how brain lag is caused would make possible ancient man's aspiration for the prolongation of life by the reduction of sleep.[38] The economic possibilities of the developed world would allow a notable shortening of the working week. It would soon be reduced to 30 hours, while the working year would be reduced to 9 months. In 1965, there were 69 million cars, 60 million TV sets, 7.7 million boats and yachts in the US. In the same year, Americans spent 30 billion dollars just for holidays. Two-fifths of all personal goods in the US are luxury items. Someone has calculated that the rich countries, which make up one-third of the world, could spend 15 billion dollars a year on cosmetics alone. In these countries, the living standard of today is five times higher than it was in 1800, and in the next 60 years, it will be five times higher than it is today, and so forth. After such an optimistic vision, we might ask ourselves: does this mean that life will be five times richer, happier, and more humane as well? The answer is a decisive no.

---

[37]Julius Robert Oppenheimer: "On Science and Culture," *Encounter* (October 1962): n.p.

[38]Jean Rostand: *Humanly Possible: A Biologist's Notes on the Future of Mankind*, trans. Lowell Bair (New York: Saturday Review Press, 1973).

In the US, the richest country in the world, 5 million crimes were committed in 1965, while the increase in dangerous crime was fourteen times faster than the increase in population (178 percent as against 13 percent). In the same country, there is a crime every 12 seconds, a murder almost every hour, a rape every 25 minutes, a robbery every 5 minutes, and a car theft every minute.[39] The tendency is especially disturbing: in the US of 1951, there were 3.1 murders per 100,000 inhabitants; in 1960, 5 murders; and in 1967, 9 murders. Also, within 16 years, the number of murders tripled. In West Germany, 2 million crimes were reported in 1966, and 2,413,000 in 1970. The number of premeditated murders in England increased by 35 percent during the last 10 years, while violent crimes in Scotland in the same period grew by 100 percent. From 1962 to 1970, the number of murders in Canada increased 98.2 percent. The abolition of capital punishment in 1962 might have had a certain but not decisive influence upon the phenomenon. In some recent public opinion polls, the French put the fear of violence at the top of their everyday problems. The increase in the number of crimes, especially those committed by young people, is frightening. During 10 years (1966 – 1967), the number of thefts in France increased by 177 percent. In Belgium, the number of crimes doubled from 1969 to 1978.

At the Seventh International Congress of Criminologists in Belgrade (September, 1973), it was unanimously concluded that the present moment was characterized by the prodigious increase of crime at all meridians. Explaining the causes of the situation, American criminologists resignedly said that our planet is an ocean of delinquencies, that all men are more or less delinquents, and that there is no way out in sight.

In the UN report *The Situation of the World in 1970*, it was stated that in a developed industrial country (the name is not given), the number of teenagers that the police had to deal with increased from 1 million in 1955 to 2.4 million in 1965.[40]

The General Secretary of the UN says in a report: "Some of the most developed countries have serious problems with delinquency. ... In spite of material progress, human life has never been less sec-

---

[39]Data from the yearly report of the FBI for 1965.

[40]UN Report: *The Situation of the World in 1970* (Paris: United Nations Educational, Scientific, and Cultural Organization, n.d.).

ure than it is nowadays. Different forms of crimes (personal and public), thefts, deceits, corruption, and organized robberies represent a high price for the modern way of life and progress."[41]

Research by the Russian psychiatrist Hodakov showed a frightful expansion of alcoholism, especially in civilized countries, after the Second World War. The sale of alcohol worldwide doubled from 1940 to 1960. In 1965, it was 2.8 times higher; in 1970, 4.3 times; and in 1973, 5.5 times. A specific phenomenon is the expansion of alcoholism among women and young people.[42] According to the data of the British charitable institution "Offered Help," in 1973 there were about 400,000 alcoholics in England, more than 80,000 of them women. Every other woman drinker eventually becomes a patient of a psychiatric hospital, while every third one is a potential suicide. First place on the alcohol consumption list in Europe is held by France, followed by Italy and the USSR. According to the number of deaths caused by alcohol, West Berlin takes first place with 44.3 victims of alcohol per 100,000 inhabitants, followed by France with 35 deaths per 100,000 inhabitants, and Austria with 30 deaths per 100,000 inhabitants.[43]

In our century, alcoholism has become a problem of the rich and developed countries. If alcohol or drugs are a refuge, for what refuge are the rich looking, and from what are they fleeing? We used to connect alcoholism to poverty and backwardness, and we had some hope. The dilemma is total now: "For some reasons which cannot be identified or named, the symptoms of these social ills are more openly expressed in Sweden than in any other country," says a Swedish expert on these problems. Confronted with the fact that every tenth Swede, man or woman, is a common drinker, the Swedish government applied successive and drastic increases on alcohol taxes, but the effects were minimal.

The brutal invasion of pornography certainly has the same roots. The most civilized countries — France, Denmark and West Germany — hold first place here as well. In 1975, porno films were more than half of all French cinemas' repertoires. In Paris alone, 250 cinemas show only this kind of film. The public workers

---

[41]From the UN General Secretary report *Prevention and Fighting Against Criminality* (Paris: United Nations Educational, Scientific, and Cultural Organization, 1972).
[42]Hodakov, n.p.d. Lydia Hodakova: *Sociology of Work* (Bratislava: SPN, 1968).
[43]Data for 1971.

are confused. The well-known psychiatrist, Professor Blanchard, tried to explain the phenomenon: "The ruling ideology is repressing the personality more and more; it directs man to the automatized life according to the scheme of sleep — tube — work, which offers a certain standard but deprives him of all true experience and excitement. Everything is prepared in advance, even the holidays are organized and planned, and the partaker cannot change anything. ... Because of that, most people instinctively need to get away from themselves and experience new and cheap thrills. That need is met through porno films.[44]

Even games of chance meet with their "progress" in civilization. They also follow the general trend of vices, together with alcoholism, pornography, kitsch, and other afflictions. The largest gambling cities of the world lay in the high civilization areas: Dauville, Monte Carlo, Macao, and Las Vegas. In Atlantic City, a room in a huge casino can hold up to 6,000 players. Government data indicate that the French spent 115 billion francs on chance games in 1965 and Americans 15 billion dollars. Every third Hungarian buys lottery tickets. According to money earmarked by each inhabitant, the biggest interest in chance games is found in Sweden, followed by Israel and Denmark — a curve corresponding to the civilization level curve with only small deviations.

According to official New York police data, there were more than 23,000 young people in New York registered as addicts of heroin and other strong narcotics in 1963. The real number was estimated to be more than 100,000. At New York's Hunter College, more than half of the students use marijuana, which is the first step to taking stronger narcotics.

After the Second World War, in just those countries of prosperity and abundance, a sad young generation appeared, having everything but wanting nothing. Those were "the beatniks" or the so-called "beaten generation," who preached the philosophy of the absurd; the halbstrikers, the minors prone to delinquency; and the hippies, who ignored reality, mocked all order and rules, and whose manners and ideas spread like a plague in all large cities of the world.

It is quite wrong to consider, based on words and outer man-

---

[44]Kenneth H. Blanchard and Paul Hersey: *Management of Organizational Behavior: Utilizing Human Resources*, 2nd ed. (Englewood Cliffs, NJ: Prentice-Hall, 1972).

ifestations, the 1968 youth revolts in America and France as political or ideological ones. A moral revolt was really in question, in America against the so-called "organization America" or against the "establishment," in France against its "structures." In both cases it was against some aspects of civilization. According to Ugo La Malfa, it was resistance to the consumption ethics of the industrial society. Unable to explain this revolt in the midst of abundance, some called it "revolt without reasons," as Malraux put it: "irrational revolt of youth," which it indeed would have been if the moral aspect of the question were abstracted.

Arthur Miller, a competent judge of modern America, says: "The problem of youth delinquency does not belong only to large towns but to the country as well; it is not a problem of capitalism only but of socialism too; it does not appear only in poverty but is present also in riches; it is not a racial problem, or an immigration problem, or even a pure American problem. I believe that in its present form, it is a product of the technology which destroys the conception of man as a value by himself. ... In a word, the spirit disappeared. Maybe the brutality of two wars chased it away from the earth. ... Or the technological process sucked it out of the other, except as a customer to a seller, a worker to a manager, as a poor man to a rich man and vice versa — briefly, as the factors which are in a way manipulated and not as really worthy personalities."[45]

How can the fact that the number of suicides and psychic diseases is proportional to the level of civilization be explained? "A very interesting fact, from the psychological point of view, is that men become less satisfied with the betterment of their life," complains an American psychologist. That phenomenon, which is particularly evident in some developed countries free from classic social problems, shakes the very grounds of trust in progress.

In the US, 4 men per thousand are in psychiatric hospitals. In New York state, it is 5.5 per thousand. More than half of the beds in all American hospitals are held by mental patients. Hollywood has proportionately the greatest number of psychiatrists in the world.

---

[45]There is no doubt that television has its sad share too. Informing the British public on the results of a six-year study inquiring if violence on TV instigates violence in life (the inquiry was finished in 1977), William Belson declared that the answer is resolutely affirmative. Somebody calculated that an average American child sees 18,000 murders on TV before he finishes secondary school.

According to an 1978 official report of the American Public Health Service, every fifth American had a breakdown or was on the verge of it. This conclusion was based on incontestable materials: the examined persons had been chosen in a way to represent 111 million adult Americans between 19 and 79 years of age.[46] Sweden holds the record for suicides, drunkards, and mental patients while, at the same time, it leads the world in national income, literacy, employment, and the quality of social insurance. In 1967, in Sweden, 1,702 suicides were registered, an increase of 9 percent since 1966 and 30 percent more than in 1960. The World Health Organization in Geneva published, in 1968, a comparative list of the suicidal occurrences ratio in several countries. In that year, the first eight places on the list were held by West Germany, Austria, Canada, Denmark, Finland, Hungary, Sweden, and Switzerland. In these eight countries, suicide is the third cause of death for men between 15 and 45 years old, coming after heart diseases and cancer. The Organization's report for 1970 clearly stated that this phenomenon is "parallel to industrialization, urbanization, and the breakdown of the family." If we consider the said phenomenon within a country or a community, we shall find out that it increases along with the degree of development and education. In Yugoslavia, for example, in highly developed Slovenia (with a literacy of 98 percent), there are 25.8 suicides per 100,000 inhabitants; in underdeveloped Kosovo (with a literacy of 56 percent) only 3.4, rendering a ratio of 7:1. Such was the situation in 1967. According to the research made by Dr. Anthony Rail, Chief of the Health Service, the number of suicides at British universities is six times higher than the national average, while the number of suicides at Cambridge University is ten times higher than the number of suicides among British youth of the same age as a whole. This is of special concern since all British students either originate from rich families or are on government scholarships.

---

[46]Ten years later, a special commission for mental health was established by the U.S. president; in its report (September 1977), the commission concluded that problems of that kind among Americans were "worse than had been expected, and that at least one third of the inhabitants suffered consequences of serious emotional stresses." According to a study prepared by the National Institute for Mental Health (1977), more than 31.9 million Americans were treated for different mental troubles in 1976; 8 million American children out of 54 million needed help because of physical difficulties; at least 10 million people had problems caused by alcohol consumption, while the number of heroin addicts exceeded 500,000.

It would be quite wrong and unjust to conclude that the said phenomena are characteristic only of Western civilization. In fact, they are the expression of the very nature of civilization itself. All that has been said about the US, Germany, England, or Sweden is applicable to Japan as well, even though it is at the other side of the globe and in a quite different circle. The phenomena, depending on conditions, can meet certain modifications but keep the main tendency. In the case of Japan, some difference comes from the tenacity of Japanese cultural traditions and from the strength of the Japanese family.[47]

It is difficult to discover all of the reasons for the phenomena in question. However, the drug problem among the youth was traced to the parental home. Dr. Vladeta Jerotic, a Yugoslav psychiatrist, writes: "A disturbed or completely destroyed family which causes neurotic development in a young person causes him or her to look for the wrong protective mechanism against the neurosis. ... Disintegration of the patriarchal community and family, which is common all over the world, creates a climate of internal displeasure, having two ways out in the external world: as anger and revolt, or as a passive, resigned, and apathetic state resulting in the use of drugs."[48]

Roger Rewel, Director of the Harvard Sociological Research Center, suggested founding a special committee within the American Senate to research the influence of technology on man and society. "Owing to modern conditions, man's life will be prolonged for three decades, but it will be a dull and vain life," he said.

Contrary to the materialistic view, civilization and comfort are not quite appropriate to human nature. The social gap, for instance, is generally larger in Catholic countries than in Protestant ones.[49] The number of suicides and mental diseases shows the reverse situation. The "material" from which man is made is not that or only that which was held by the science and evolutionary biology of the nineteenth century. Man is not suitable for living only by his senses. "An unrealized wish causes a pain, a realized one a feeling of saturation."[50] The comfort and the corresponding mentality re-

[47]Anasaki: *The Crisis of Japanese Culture*, (n.p., n.d.).
[48]NIN, 9/11, (1969).
[49]Differences in the incomes in France, for example, are twice as high as England's and West Germany's, and three times higher than in Holland.
[50]Schopenhauer.

duce or even annihilate the devotion to any system of values.[51] Civilization, far from giving sense to our life, might be rather a part of the nonsense of our existence.

The lack of choice, that fatal feature of civilization, is nowhere so evident as in the inability to stop the production of the means of mass devastation and the horrible rhythm in which only the civilized part of mankind destroys the natural living conditions in their own environment. This is a conflict between the mechanical and the organic, the artificial and the natural principles in human life.

Because of civilization's invasion, the front line of the Brazilian woods retreats 10 – 15 kilometers every year. A desert is conquering the green spaces. More than 80 percent of the US's fresh waters are polluted by industrial waste. The smoke from Tennessee's big Ductown copper foundry has turned the rich earth to a desert covering 20,000 hectares. The concentration of copper acids and soot in London's fog in 1952 killed more than 4,000 men in a single day. Chimney stacks and vehicles in the US discharge 230 million tons of different noxious matters a year into the atmosphere. French power stations released 114,000 tons of sulphur gas and more than 82 million tons of cinders in 1960. These numbers increased twofold in 1968, in spite of many protective measures. About 27,000 tons of industrial dust falls yearly on every town in the Ruhr area of West Germany. In the English and Swiss cities which are covered by clouds of smog, the mortality caused by pulmonary cancer has increased 40 times during the last 50 years; and in the US, 50 times during the last 20 years. Research from Tokyo, at the large Yanaga crossways, has proved that 10 out of 49 examined passers had 2 to 7 times more lead than normal in their blood. The main cause: gases discharged from vehicles. Since its invention, the car has killed more people than all the wars of this century.[52]

Inside civilization, without leaving it, it is impossible to see any forces which could fight all these troubles. Moreover, on the scale of values known to civilization, there is not a single argument opposed to the inroads of pornography and alcohol. The same feeling of helplessness and resignation is found in American criminologists

---

[51]"But Thou didst bestow on them and their fathers good things in life, until they forgot the message ..." The Qur'ān 25:78.

[52]Data given by the American road expert Norbert Timan at the International Conference on Roadway Security, held in Paris, in 1976. How can we escape such "progress"?

faced with the rise in delinquency. In fact, it is the helplessness of science in the face of social ills which have an evident immoral aspect. Civilization cannot be refuted from within but only from without, namely by culture because, from the viewpoint of civilization, science cannot turn back to religion, or civilization to the classical family. The circle is closed.

The Pessimism of the Theater

It is symptomatic that an ominous philosophy is coming only from the rich and developed regions of the world (Ibsen, Heidegger, Mailer, Pinter, Beckett, O'Neil, Bergman, Camus, Antonini, and so forth). Scientists who follow the outward appearance of things continue to be optimistic. Thinkers and artists, especially the latter, are troubled.

Superficially observed, pessimism seems to follow the achievement of complete literacy, social insurance, and a 2,000 dollars per capita income for the nation. Scandinavian philosophy, from the end of the nineteenth and the beginning of the twentieth centuries, is extremely pessimistic. It considers human destiny hopelessly tragic, the final result of all human efforts and human existence as darkness and waste. Ironically, this philosophy emerged in those countries where, by the beginning of our century, there were no illiterates, while the southern part of Europe still enjoyed sweet ignorance. In 1906, Bulgaria and Serbia were 70 percent illiterate, Italy 48 percent, Spain 63 percent, Hungary 43 percent, and Austria 39 percent. We are tempted to wonder if there is a connection between Swedish social insurance, the best in the world so far, and the feeling of hopelessness. Does the feeling of material pleasure give birth to the feeling of spiritual displeasure?

Contrary to the outward activity of the economic and political life, civilization is characterized by a slow, inward living rhythm. The absurd plays are a living portrait of human life in the most developed societies of today.

Comfort is the outward and absurdity is the inward image of life in civilization. Dialectically expressed: the more comfort and abundance, the more the feeling of emptiness and despair. On the contrary, primitive societies can be poor and affected by sharp social differences, but all that we know about them indicates a life colored by strong and rich feelings. Folklore, the "literature of the primitive society," can show, in its specific way, the extraordinary living vigor of primitive man. Feelings of disaffection and hopelessness are alien to that poor society.[53]

This is the theater in which the civilized world unveils its "human tragedy." There is still some optimism in comedies and old-fashioned musicals. Serious plays emit pessimism. The theater keeps tearing down the nimbus of perfection that science puts on civilization. Science brutally intrudes with its data about the abundance of products, the indexes of mass production, energy and human power, while the arts point to human waste, intellectual and moral misery, violence, bestiality, and emptiness. In the midst of the wealth and power of a rich world, the theater discovers an aggressive, culpable, and helpless man.

The poets are the "sensors" of mankind. Judging by their fears and doubts, the world is not marching to humanism but to open dehumanization and alienation.

Yasunari Kawabata, the Japanese Nobel Prize winner for literature in 1968, committed suicide in 1971. Two years earlier, in 1969, another great Japanese novelist, Yukio Mishima, ended his life in the same way. Since 1895, thirteen Japanese novelists and writers have committed suicide, including the author of the *Rashomon*, Ryunosuko Akutagawa, in 1927. That "continuous tragedy" of Japanese culture during 70 years coincides with the penetration of Western civilization and materialistic ideas into the traditional culture of Japan. Whatever it be, for the poets and the writers of tragedies, civilization will always have an inhuman face and be a threat to humanity. A year before his death, Kawabata wrote: "Men are separated from each other by a concrete wall that obstructs any circulation of love. Nature is smothered in the name of progress." In the novel *The Snow Country*, published in 1937, Kawabata places man's loneliness and alienation in the modern world at the very focus of his reflections.

All great cultural representatives similarly see man's failure and defeat in civilization. André Malreaux wonders about the final result of the nineteenth century's hopes and optimism and he answers: "It is Europe, devastated and stained with blood, as the devastated and blood-stained figure of the man it expected to create."[54]

---

[53]Galupo's inquiry "The Whole Mankind's Opinion," made in 1976, showed that contrary to the skepticism of the developed countries' inhabitants, the poor peoples of South American and Africa look to the future in an optimistic way.

[54]At the UNESCO conference of 1964.

A similar picture was seen by Paul Valéry immediately after the First World War: "There is a lost illusion of a European culture and proof of knowledge unable to save anything; there is a science wounded to death in its moral ambitions and as desecrated by the cruelty of its applications; there is an idealism which won with difficulty, deeply tortured, responsible for its dreams; a realism, disillusioned, beaten, mashed, loaded with crimes and faults; a lust and a renunciation, both exposed to ridicule; faiths intermingled in times, a cross against a cross, a crescent against a crescent; there are some skeptics, even they are confused by the events, so quick, so vehement, so indelible, playing with our thoughts like a cat with a mouse; the skeptics lose their doubts, find them, lose them again, forgetting how to use the skills of their mind."[55]

Nihilism and the philosophy of the absurd are the fruits of the most civilized and richest parts of the world. That philosophy speaks of "the perspectiveless world," of "the psychically split and disintegrated individual, of the world of deaf mute silence." It is by no means a poisonous philosophy, as it is called by some people. In fact, it is very deep and instructive. It is an expression of man's resistance, of his nonconsent to the world that is growing in a manner opposite to the very image of his own. It is man's revolt against the one-dimensional world of civilization.[56] For the same reasons, some people found modern nihilism a kind of religion and, as we will see, such a concept is not groundless.

They both represent a negation of materialism and embrace this world with the same idea. The primeval anxiousness, the views beyond the grave, the desparate searching for a way out of the world in which man is a stranger[57] — these ideas are common to both of them. The difference lies in the fact that nihilism does not find the way out, while religion claims to have found it.

The failure of civilization to solve the problem of human happiness by means of science, power, and wealth, once understood and admitted, will exert the strongest psychological impact on mankind. That will be the beginning of the revision of some of our elementary

---

[55]Paul Valéry: *Collected Works*, ed. Jackson Mathews, vol. 10: *History and Politics* (New York: Pantheon Books, 1956).
[56]Camus: *l'Homme révolté*, Marcuse, *One-Dimensional Man* (Boston: Beacon Press, 1964)..
[57]Camus: *The Stranger* (New York: Alfred Knopf, 1946).

and generally accepted ideas so far. The first one to be revised will be the scientific misconception of man. If civilization does not solve the problem of human happiness, then the religious idea of the human origin is true and the scientific one is false. A third option does not exist.

Nihilism

Let's turn to the idea of common points between nihilism and religion, a fact which represents modern nihilism as a form of religion in civilization.

Nihilism is not a negation of God, but a protest against His absence or, as with Beckett, a protest against the absence of man, against the fact that man is not possible or not realized. That attitude implies a religious — not a scientific — conception of man and the world. Man, as conceived by science, is possible and realized, but all that is final is inhuman. Sartre's famous sentence that man is a futile passion is religious by its sound as well as by its spirit. In materialism, there is neither passion nor futility; there cannot be futility because there are no passions.

Rejecting the higher purpose of the world, materialism got rid of the risk of absurdity and futility. Its world and its man have a practical end; they have a function, be it a zoological one. The statement that man is a futile passion implies that man and the world are not congruous. This radical attitude toward the world was the beginning of all religions. Sartre's futility or Camus' absurd presume a search for purpose and sense, a searching which, as distinguished from the religious one, ends in failure. That searching is religious because it means rejecting the worldly purpose of human living, rejecting the function.

Searching for God is a religion, but every searching is not a discovery. Nihilism is a disappointment but not because of the world and order. It is a disappointment caused by the absence of good from the universe. Everything is futile and absurd if man dies once and forever.[58] The philosophy of the absurd does not speak directly of religion, but it clearly expresses the belief that man and the world are not made by the same measure. It expresses the anxiousness

---

[58]The Qur'ān 23:115.

which is, in all its degrees except the conclusion, a religious one. For both nihilism and religion, man is a stranger in this world; for nihilism he is a stranger hopelessly lost, for religion he is with a hope for salvation.

The thoughts of Albert Camus can be understood only as the thoughts of a disappointed believer:

> In a world from which the illusions and the light suddenly disappear, man feels like a stranger. It is the expulsion without any way out, as there are no memories of the lost homeland or any hope to reach a promised land. ... If I were a tree among trees ... that life would have its sense, or better, this problem would not arise because I would be a part of this world that I now resist with all my conscience. ... All is allowed since God does not exist and man dies.[59]

The last statement has nothing in common with the superficial and convinced atheism of the rationalistic thinkers. On the contrary, it is rather a silent curse of a soul tired of searching for God without finding Him. It is the "atheism of despair."

On the question of moral freedom, existentialism has the same attitude as religion. Simone de Beauvoir writes: "In the beginning man is nothing; it is up to him to make himself good or bad, depending on his acceptance or rejection of freedom. Freedom sets its aims absolutely, and no outside force, even death, is able to destroy what freedom has set up. ... If the game is not won or lost in advance, it is necessary to fight and take risks in every moment."[60] Even Sartre's duality of being (*"l'être en soi"* and *"l'être pour soi"* — "being by itself" and "being for itself") is a clear negation of materialism. Only the terms are new; the essence is old and can be easily identified.[61]

---

[59]Camus: *The Stranger.*

[60]Simone de Beavoir: *l'Existentialisme et la sagesse des nations* (Paris: Gallimard, 1970).

[61]The same applies to man's recognition of the conscience: "All that happens in the conscience cannot be explained by anything that is out of it but only by what is inward to itself," Jean-Paul Sarter, *The Emotions: Outline of a Theory*, trans. Bernard Frechtman (New York: Citadel Press, 1971). Also, what about *Huis-Clos* in Jean-Paul Sarter, *Théatre* (Paris: Gallimard, 1947), this play which tells us that everything really existing exists only as a relation between man and man?

The beatniks or the hippies are, in a way, a continuation of existentialism, especially of its practical manifestation and its application. The beatniks' protest against progress regardless of its extreme and absurd form is the great merit of that movement, making it an authentic cultural phenomenon of our time. The negation of progress could have its origin only in a philosophy which is, at least in its basic premises, religious.

This critique of civilization is not a demand to reject it. Civilization cannot be rejected even if we would like to do so. The only thing that is necessary and possible is to destroy the myth of it. Destruction of this myth will lead to the further humanization of the world, a task which by its nature belongs to culture.

Chapter 3

THE PHENOMENON OF ART

Science wants to discover laws and use them. But a work of art reflects the cosmic order without questioning it.

THE PHENOMENON OF ART

Art and Science

There is an order to an engine and an order to a melody. These two orders cannot, even in the final analysis, be reduced to a common source. The first is a spatial or quantitative combination of relations and parts in accordance with nature, logic, and mathematics. The second maintains a combination of tones or words in a melody or in a poem. These two orders belong to two different categories: science and religion, or from this point of view, science and art.

The existence of another world (another order) in addition to the natural one is the basic premise of every religion and art. If only one world existed, art would be impossible. In fact, every work of art is an impression of a world to which we do not belong and from which we have not arisen, into which we have been cast. Art is a nostalgia or memory.

Somebody once said that art is a call for the creation of man, and every science must finally conclude that man does not exist. Art is therefore in natural opposition to the world, to all of its science, its psychology, its biology, and its Darwin. Essentially, this is a religious opposition. Religion, morality, and art are on the same genealogical branch that springs from the act of creation. That is why the Darwinian negation of creation — because it renounces this act — is the most radical negation not only of religions but of ethics, art, and law as well. If man is really "made according to Darwin," if that is not solely a support, a frame for his spirit and for his "self," then art has nothing to do, and the poets and tragedians delude us and write nonsense.

Here, at this crucial point, lies the first and probably the most intimate union between art and religion and, concomitantly, the absolute and irrevocable chasm between art and science.

There are three degrees of reality known and possible in our universe: matter, life, personality. Science deals only with the first, art with the last. The rest is only an illusion or a misunderstanding because when facing life and man, science finds only what is dead and impersonal in them.

Science and art are related to each other as quantity and quality. The queen of science, mathematics, was defined by Auguste Comte as an "indirect measuring of quantities,"[1] and art by Giacometti as "a research of the impossible, a vain effort to grasp the essence of life."[2]

There is only quantity in the material world, and all quantities are comparable. Quality is here only a form of quantity. In his *Dialectics of Nature*, Engels states that "it is impossible to change the quality of a body without adding or taking away substance or motion, that is, without a quantitative change within the body."[3] This quantitative principle in nature is formulated by Pythagoras as: "the harmonious system of numbers and their relations."[4] Mendeljev, the Russian chemist who is also the father of the Periodic System of Elements, states that "the chemical properties of elements are periodic functions of their atomic weights."[5] In the world of nature, there is only this quantitative and therefore apparent quality.

No two men can be identical nor two stones alike. What makes two molecules of water different? Their position in space? However, if we assume that space is infinite, the differentiation loses

---

[1]Auguste Comte: *A General View of Positivism*, French trans. Y. H. Bridges (New York: R. Speller, 1957).

[2]Alberto Giaeometti: *Alberto Giacometti*, with an introduction by Michel Leiris (Basel: Editions Galeries Beyeler, 1946).

[3]Friedrich Engels: *Dialectics of Nature*, trans. Clemens Dutt (London: Laurence & Wishart, 1941).

[4]Frederick H. Young: *Pythagorean Numbers. Congruences, A Finite Arithmetic. Geometry in the Number Plane* (Boston: Ginn, 1961).

[5]Dimitri I. Mendeljev: *The Principles of Chemistry*, 5th ed., trans. George Kamensky, (London: Longmans-Green, 1981).

its sense. Natural science is possible because there is no quality in nature. A science of quality or a conception of quality is impossible. Nature can be beautiful or terrible, purposeful or chaotic, meaningful or meaningless — it can have a quality only in relation to a subject, and so, in relation to man. Otherwise, objectively, such qualities do not exist since nature is homogeneous and indifferent.

In a poem, melody, or picture, we are faced with a mystery: quality in the metaphysical sense of the word. How could the difference between an original painting and its copy be explained by means of quantity? The original possesses the quality of beauty and "every copy is ugly."[6] The difference does not arise from the fact that something has been added or taken away from the copy in the quantitative sense of the word; it lies in the personal touch between the artist and the work of art. Quality can only be "in touch" with a personality.

Science and art: here lies the difference between Newton, a prophet of the mechanical universe, and Shakespeare, "a poet who knew everything about man." Newton and Shakespeare, or Einstein and Dostoevski, these embody two views facing opposite directions or two completely separate and independent kinds of knowledge which neither succeed nor depend on each other. The question of human destiny, loneliness, ephemerality, death, and the way out of these dilemmas can never be the subject matter of a science. Art, even if it tried, could not evade these questions. Poetry is the "knowledge of man," as science is the knowledge of nature. These two kinds of knowledge are parallel, simultaneous, and independent in the same way as their two respective worlds are parallel, simultaneous, and independent. The first approach, by means of intelligence, analysis, and observation, conducts experiments in the material world, which is "the sum of things and processes connected by casual relations." The other looks into the inner man, his hidden corners, his secrets. Here, we understand or perhaps only guess through excitement, love, and suffering. Knowledge is not acquired here in a rational, scientific fashion.[7]

---

[6]Emile Chartier [Alain]: *Système des beaux-arts* (Paris: Gallimard, 1958).

[7]Viewed from this angle, philosophy is closer to science than to art. Although the subjects they research are different, science and philosophy use the same rationalistic method. Every reasoning, whether scientific or philosophic, leads to the same or similar conclusions. The philosopher-rationalist of the eighteenth century worked out the

This inner, "organic" character of art is reflected in another characteristic fact: there is no teamwork in an artist's creation. A work of art is always connected to the artist's personality. As a creation, as a "making of man,"[8] it is the fruit of a soul and thus an indivisible act. Teamwork is possible in science because the subject of science is composed of details and therefore is suitable to analysis, separation, and division. All of science, from the very beginning until today, is an almost mechanical continuation. This would be impossible in art. The ceiling in the Sistine Chapel could not have been painted by two artists, although it is the work of a lifetime. This also applies to poetry or music. It is a question of something unique, simple, and indivisible, of something that cannot be divided and still remain alive. The assertion that teams in architecture attain remarkable results (Bauhaus and others)[9] is mainly a misunderstanding. A building as a product of construction material, technique, and utility is the subject of teamwork, while the style, the idea, and the artistic side of architecture have always been the work of one man the artist.

Where science appears, it discovers the identical, the congruous, the immobile, and the consistent. Art is a "continuous new arising."[10] "A village potter wants the existence of one amphora from

---

so-called "geometrical" (also called axiomatic) method of explaining philosophical theories. Baruch Spinoza, considered its creator, explained his principal work *Ethics* by using the geometrical method, similar to Euclidian geometry, and then formulating definitions, axioms, and theorems arising from it. See, Benedictus de [Baruch] Spinoza, *Ethics*, trans. George Eliot (Salzburg: Institut für Anglistik und Amerikanikstik, Universität Salzburg, 1981). Nicholas Malebranche, using the same method, derived all of his teachings about the world from a small number of obvious and generally accepted principles. See, Nicolas Malebranche, *De la recherche de la vérité, où l'on traite de la nature de l'esprit de l'homme, et de l'usage qu'il en doit faire pour éviter l'erreur des sciences* (Paris: J. Vrin, 1945). Christian Wolfe derived his whole system which comprised cosmology, onthology, etiology, psychology, law, and logic by using the method of rationalistic deduction. Philosophy, even when it deals with man or morality, remains inevitably on the ground of nature, and thus, it can apply the methods used in mathematics, geometry, and rationalistic deduction. This explains why philosophy never reaches the full truth about life.

[8]Michelangelo Buonarroti: *Complete Poems and Selected Letters of Michelangelo*, 3rd ed., trans. Creighton Gilbert (Princeton, NJ: Princeton University Press, 1980).

[9]Eckhard Neumann: *Bauhaus and Bauhaus People: Personal Opinions and Recollections of Former Bauhaus Members and Their Contemporaries*, trans. Eva Richter and Alba Lorman (New York: Van Nostrand-Reinhold, 1970).

[10]Jean Cassou: *Art and Confrontation: The Arts in an Age of Change*, trans. Nigel Foxell (Greenwich, NY: New York Graphic Society, 1970).

Canossa."[11] Science discovers. Art creates. The light of a distant star that science discovered had existed before its "discovery." The light that art suddenly casts on us is created by art itself at that very moment. Without it, that light would never have been born. Science deals with the existing; art is creation itself, the arising of the new.

Science is exact; art is truthful. Look at a portrait or a landscape painting. How true are they? Still, there is more truth in them than in a photograph of that face or landscape. Science turns the soul into "psyche" and God into "First Cause" just as learned, insincere academic art makes a face-poster, an anonymous individual out of a live, free personality. Essentially, this is the same degradation caused by the elimination of the inner dimension of freedom. All biological or psychological analyses are more or less correct and, with enough time and financial resources, will turn out quite correct. Nonetheless, they are not truthful because the phenomena of capital importance — life and soul — are missing. From this point of view, these exact sciences are false sciences. Art ignores facts, even intentionally, while searching for the truth of things. So-called abstract art tends to eliminate every semblance to the outer world by giving shape and color a spiritual meaning. That is, as Whistler put it, "to deprive the painting of any outside interest."[12]

Science wants to discover laws and use them. On the contrary, a work of art "reflects the cosmic order without questioning it." Francis Bacon, the father of European science, stresses clearly the functional or utilitarian character of science: "True knowledge is the only one that increases man's power in the world,"[13] while Kant talks about the "aimless usefulness" of the beautiful.[14]

A poem is neither functional nor concerned, nor is it a "social order,"[15] as Mayakovski asserts. The French painter Dubuffet destroys this pleasant misconception without mincing words: "Art is es-

---

[11]Etienne Socrian: n.p.d.

[12]Whistler: n.p.d.

[13]Francis Bacon: *The Advancement of Learning and New Atlantis* (London: Oxford University Press, 1966).

[14]There exists proof that wars were the principal propelling force of scientific progress. Periods of intensive scientific research or technical achievements coincided with the periods of war or severe confrontation. World War II and the bitter peace that followed proved this very clearly. As for Kant's statement, see Kant.

[15]Vladimir Mayakovski: *How Are Verses Made?*, trans. G. M. Hyde (London: J. Cape, 1970).

sentially uncomfortable, useless, antisocial, dangerous. And when it is not all that, it is a lie, a mannequin."[16]

Science, no matter how deep or complex, has never felt the insufficiency of language. Art, because of its spiritual character, has always looked for other, "extra-lingual" means. Language itself is "the hand of the brain," and the brain is part of our physical whole, our mortality. Words and letters have become the most powerful instrument of science, enabling the continuation of human experience. Writing corresponds to language, language to thought, and all of them have been molded by intelligence, therefore being quite inadequate and almost incapable of expressing a single move of the soul.[17] There is no way to retell Beethoven's *Ninth Symphony*, nor can *Hamlet* be translated into the language of science or reduced to a number of questions from psychology or ethics. The failure of the analytical approach should teach us something.

While staging the tragedy *King Lear*, Peter Brook called it "a mountain, the top of which will never be reached and conquered."[18] To reach the essence of the spiritual, it is necessary to cast aside concept and language. In Joyce's works, for example his novel *Ulysses*, we come across a strange multilingual play of words.[19] Similar expressions can be found in the Qur'ān at the beginning of many chapters. Morality, metaphysics, and beliefs are passed on in tales, theatrical plays, or in the wordless language of dance. There is reason to believe that dance is older than language. In fact, perfection of very old dances went side by side with extreme imperfection and simplicity of language.

The inability to attain the level of art using rational and logical means does not apply only to certain branches or styles of art. The widespread belief that realism is closer to man and can be more easily understood than impressionism or surrealism is a mistake if art's very essence is in question. The mystery of the "Mona Lisa" is not

---

[16]Andreas Franzke: *Dubuffet*, trans. Robert Erich Wolf (New York: Abrams, 1981).

[17]"Painting is a complete absence of speech, a special visual world where a painter serves himself. It is a world unto itself, a metaphysical phase which critique cannot explain since critique is dependent on language." Camille Bryen, *Bryen, abhomme*, ed. Daniel Abadie (Brussels: La Connaissance, 1973).

[18]Peter Brook: *Peter Brook's Production of William Shakespeare's A Midsummer Night's Dream* for the Royal Shakespeare Company, ed. Glenn Loney (Chicago: Dramatic Publishing Company, 1974).

[19]James Joyce: *Ulysses* (New York: Random House, 1946).

less than that of Picasso's *Maidens from Avignon*, the painting that started the Cubist revolution in European painting. The essence of works of art is as inscrutible as the concept of piety or the sense of inner freedom, and all the attempts to determine it rationally have failed, as have the attempts to define life.[20]

Art and Religion

All these attempts, although they inevitably remain incomplete and even unsuccessful, point vaguely to the essential link between art and religion:

"Poetry is the fruit of contact between the spirit and reality, and with its source — God."[21]

"Every poem owes its poetic character to the presence, radiance, and uniting influence of a mysterious reality called pure poetry."[22]

"Poetry emerges as a direct awareness of that horrible mystery which our life, swept away by a cosmic riddle, is asking itself."[23]

"The poet is a clairvoyant who discovers the key to the festivities of the past."[24]

"Art as creation, and especially poetry as a way of existence, strive to become a kind of substitute for the holy. ... Whether it appears as knowledge or a way of life, or both simultaneously, poetry raises man above his human condition, becoming a sacred profession."[25]

"A majority of people would not have any opinion on painting,

---

[20]Hauser's definition seems to appear only to prove that any definition of a work of art is a failure: "A work of art is shape and contents, confession and illusion, a play and a message; it is close to nature and far from it, purposeful and purposeless, historical and ahistorical, personal and super-personal at the same time." See Arnold Hauser: *The Social History of Art*, trans. Stanley Godman (New York: Knopf, 1951).

[21]Jacques Maritain: *The Situation of Poetry: Four Essays on the Relations Between Poetry, Mysticism, Magic, and Knowledge*, trans. Marshall Suther (New York: Philosophical Library, 1955).

[22]Abbot Bremon: *Pure Poetry* (n.p., n.d.).

[23]Roland de Peneville: *Poetic Experience* (n.p., n.d.).

[24]Jean-Baptiste A. Rimbaud: *The Poet's Vocation: Selections from Letters of Hölderlin, Rimbaud, and Hart Crane*, trans. William Burford and Christopher Middleton (Austin: Humanities Research Center, University of Texas Press, 1967).

[25]Gaëtan Picon: *Contemporary French Liteature, 1945 and after*, trans. Kelvin W. Scott and Graham D. Martin (New Yourk: F. Ungar Publishing Company, 1974).

sculpture, or literature any more than they would have on architecture, had they not experienced through a birth, a death, or even through a certain person that vague feeling of transcendency upon which every religion is based."[26]

Many people believe that Kafka's novels can be understood only as religious parables, and Kafka himself said that he saw his questions as a kind of prayer. "The universe is full of signs we do not understand."[27] Michel Leiris, a well-known surrealist, says: "I no longer believe in anything, not in God in any case, not even in another world, but I have gladly talked about the Absolute, the Eternal ...; I vaguely hoped that the poetic miracle would make everything change and I would enter Eternity alive, having thus conquered my destiny as a man by means of words."[28]

It is a question of the same human aspiration expressed in different ways. Religion lays stress upon the eternal and the absolute, morality upon the good and freedom, and art upon man and creation. Basically, all of them are different aspects of the same inner reality expressed by language which is perhaps an insufficient means but the only one available.[29]

At the roots of religion and art there is a primordial unity. Drama is of a religious origin, from the thematical as well as from the historical point of view, and temples are the first theaters with actors, costumes, and audiences. The first dramas were ritual dramas in the Egypt of 4,000 years ago. Old Greek drama emerged from choral songs in honor of the god Dionysus. "Theaters were built near the temple of Dionysus, and performances were given during the festivities connected with the cult of Dionysus as a part of religious service."[30] The ritualistic origin of the theater and of culture as well is beyond doubt, and this is based on accurate historical evidence.[31]

Drama, not theology, is a means to express the true religion and

---

[26]André Malraus: *Voices of Silence* (New York: Doubleday, 1953).
[27]Franz Kafka: *Parables and Paradoxes in German and English* (New York: Schocken Books, 1958).
[28]Michel Leiris: *The Age of Man*, n.p.d.
[29]More about this in *La poesie moderne et le sacre* by Jules Mounerot (n.p.d.).
[30]Maurice E. Bloch: *Death and the Regeneration of Life* (New York: Cambridge University Press, 1982).
[31]See Zvonko Lesic: *Theory of Drama Throughout the Centuries* (Sarajevo: n.p., 1977).

ethical problems of man and mankind. Its dual nature is clearly reflected in the mask, which suggests both religion and drama at the same time. The early pictures, statues, songs, and dances were a part of the ritual, only later being separated from the cult and beginning to exist independently. When a "savage" painted the animal he wanted to catch (so-called "hunting magic"), that was a kind of cult, a prayer for his success. Indians draw different multicolored designs in the sand during their religious festivities. It is an integral part of the ritual. The old Japanese ballet known as *gigaku* came into existence, according to the belief of the Japanese, "when the universe was created." These ancient plays were in fact a mixture of song, dance, and mime, and they displayed in a symbolical way the metaphysical life of the souls of the dead. In pre-Islamic times, the poet was an honored person whose might was due to a magical power able to protect or destroy life.[32]

Gabriel Zaida recently published a selection of Mexican Indian poetry. In his preface, he says that: "the general and common characteristic of the poetry of Mexican Indians is a symbolizing of eternal life and that the relation to totems — a plant, an animal, or a natural phenomenon — nearly always turns into a magical or religious ritual."[33] The unity of art and religion can answer the well-known riddle of the Song of Songs, a clearly secular text of high artistic value found in the Bible. If art is strictly separated from religion, there is no explanation. If they are not separated, there is no riddle and it is no wonder that the Song of Songs found its place within a religious reading. After all, that was a riddle only for the learned interpreters of the Bible. Believers have never felt anything odd in that.

Art is a daughter of religion, just as "science is a daughter of astronomy."[34] Art, if it wants to survive, must always return to that source of its own, and it obviously does.

In all cultures, architecture has reached its greatest inspiration in the building of temples. This applies equally to the temples of ancient India and Cambodia, mosques all over the Islamic world, temples built in the jungles of pre-Columbian America, as well as the churches and chapels of the twentieth century all over Europe and

---

[32]Smailagic: *Introduction to the Koran* (Zagreb: n.p., 1975), p. xxvi.
[33]Gabriel Zaida: *Ommibus de Poesia Mexicana* (n.p., n.d.).
[34]Bergson: *Creative Evolution*.

America. None of the great builders and architects of today can resist that challenge. Frank Lloyd Wright built Beth Sholom Synagogue in Elkins Park, Pennsylvania; Le Corbusier, Notre Dame du Haut in Ronchamp (finished in 1955) and the Dominican Monastery in Evre, France; Mies van der Rohe, the Chapel of the Institute of Technology in Illinois (1952); Alvar Aalto, a Lutheran church in Vuokesniski, Finland (1959); Philip Johnson, the First Presbyterian Church in Stamford (1959) and the Temple Kneseth Israel in New York (1954); Rudolph Landy, the Lutheran Church of St. Paul in Sarasota, Florida (1959); Oscar Niemeyer, the Church of St. Francis of Assisi in Pampulha, Brazil; Eduardo Torroja, the Herald Chapel in the Pyrénées (1942); Felix Candela, the Church La Virgen Milagrosa in Mexico (1953) and so on. Architecture, although the most functional and least spiritual of all art, proves its sacred character through the tireless construction of places for worship.

Art has been repaying its debt to religion even more obviously through painting, sculpture, and music. The greatest works of art of the Renaissance deal with religious themes almost without exception, and they have found parental hospitality in churches throughout Europe. Is there a church in Italy or the Netherlands which is not a gallery at the same time? Michelangelo's paintings and sculptures represent a particular continuation of Christianity; His works could quite literally be referred to as "the Gospel in paint and stone." Handel's *Oratorios*, a kind of spiritual opera, are really great religious music: *Saul*, *Samson*, and *The Messiah*. The two greatest composers of the twentieth century, Debussy and Stravinsky, created their music on religious topics (Debussy, *The Martyrdom of St. Sebastian*; Stravinsky, *Symphony of Psalms*, *Mass*, *Canticum Sacrum*), while Chagall painted his fifteen major canvasses on biblical themes. The great piano composer Oliver Messiaen, a representative of the avant-garde music of the fifties, created a series of works inspired by religious meditations (*Twenty Looks upon Jesus' Infancy*). The most impressive ballets of Maurice Bejart, the greatest contemporary creator in this field and choreographer of *The Twentieth Century Ballet*, have been inspired by Wagnerian mythology and the mysticism of the Far East, for example, *Baudelaire*, *Bakti*, and *The Winners*. Mondrian, one of the founders of abstract painting and also a member of the Theosophical Society of Holland sees art as asceticism and sanctification, as a means to reach the "supreme truth," and Jan Torop, his no-less-famous countryman, has developed a religious and moral conception of painting through his symbolism and mysticism. Kenneth Clark writes about Rembrandt: "His mind was steeped in the Bible, he knew every story by heart down to the minutest detail. ... In his drawings, one often does not know if he is recording an observation or illustrating the scriptures, so much had the two experiences grown together in his mind."[35] Yves Klein draws his inspiration from the studies of Zen Buddhism and meditates about immaterial cosmic energy, which is in a way a painted form of Bergson's philosophy of intuition. For him, art is a pure outburst of vocation, a kind of divine announcement. He made his most audacious painting, *Cosmogony*, with the aid of rain and wind. The idea of so-called "world theater" shows clearly the sacral character of its symbols. "Our age," as a writer says, "is the age of growing symbols of sacral thought and feeling." However, as we have seen, it is neither a new nor a temporary tendency. It is a permanent state that wells out of the very nature of art. In true art (that is, if we expel the mediocre) everything is exactly like that — surrational and sacral.[36]

What art tells us and how it tells us is as incredible as the message of religion. Look at an old Japanese fresco, an arabesque on the portal of the Lion's Courtyard in the Alhambra, a mask from a Melanesian island, a religious dance of a tribe in Uganda, Michelangelo's *Last Judgment*, Picasso's *Guernica*, or listen to Debussy's *Martyrdom of St. Sebastian* or to a Negro spiritual song, and you will experience something as inscrutable and beyond logic and the sensible as in prayer. Does a work of abstract art not look as irrational or as "unscientific" as a religious ritual? In a way, a painting is a ritual on canvas while a symphony is a tonal ritual.

Art is not primarily a creation of the beautiful especially when one considers that the opposite of beauty is not ugliness but falsehood. The Aztec masks or the masks from the Ivory Coast, or Albert Giacometti's little eyeless statues cannot be called beautiful, but they are an expression of an authentic search for truth for they represent a feeling, a presentiment, an association with a cosmic event related to human destiny, simply, a feeling of transcendency.

This inner link between art and religion can be perceived in one more fact: it is the intentional or the "professional" lack of attention

---

[35]Kenneth Clark: *Civilization* (London: n.p., 1969), p. 203.

[36]The eighteenth century, the age of Bach, is not the only example of this, but it is certainly the most evident because of the sharp contrasts: thought is antireligious, life is secular, and art is clearly religious.

that artists devote to their physical appearance and the "sacred dirtiness" of certain religious orders, especially in Hinduism and Christianity. In the eyes of the common people, artists and monks are of a similar kind. However strange it may seem at first, there is the same idea at the root of monasticism and bohemianism. When Julius II "chased" Michelangelo while he was working on the frescoes in the Sistine Chapel, he only forced him to fulfil his destiny. State persecution of artists has always had the opposite aim: to force them to abandon their mission. The artists did not sense the totalitarianism of the Church in the Middle Ages, the scientists did, and it seems that the scientists in the Soviet Union sense the totalitarianism of the present government the least. At the end of the Middle Ages, when the Inquisition and the persecution of scientists were in their full swing, the famous Italian School created its best works. Under Stalin and Zhdanov,[37] Soviet science reached its highest results in the field of atomic energy and the cosmos. Soviet art bore all the pressure because, being art, it belonged to another world, to another order. The Church once tried to make science a servant of theology; in the Soviet Union, they are trying to make art a servant of politics. When a body of governmental authority declares the "truth" that "socialist realism" (according to Stalin's term) is the only proper method in Soviet art, then this is a dictate and a mistake of the same kind as the Church's. The difference is that one dictate is addressed to art, while the other is addressed to science, but that is rather a question of nonunderstanding, even of a natural nonunderstanding. Atheism will never understand the very nature of art; religion will never understand science. Picasso can go to the Soviet Union but his works cannot. The Soviet Union accepts his political attitude but not his art because art remains, regardless of the artist's conscious desires or opinions, what it is — a sacral message, a testimony against the finiteness and relativity of man, a tiding of a cosmic order of things, a cosmic perspective which as an entirety and in its every point opposes the vision of a materialistic universe without God. Fyodor Dostoievsky's Christian novels have been blacklisted in the USSR for the same reason the paintings of his compatriot Mark Chagall have been. In the suffering of Pasternak and Solzhenitsyn, there is the same tragedy but an inverse logic. In the context of Bruno and Gallileo, Zhdanovism and the

---

[37]A. A. Zhdanov, Stalin's close collaborator, the secretary of CK KPSS, is known as a protagonist of the persecution of artists, philosophers, writers, composers, and other intellectuals after World War II.

Inquisition are parallel and comparable occurrences. Zhdanovism is the Inquisition against artists and thinkers in the name of state atheism, while the Inquisition was Zhdanovism against the scientists in the name of the Church as an institutionalized religion. Zhdanovism is an inverse Inquisition.

Art and Atheism

The recession of art and the expansion of education in the sense of civilization is characteristic of "state atheism." The rate of literacy in communist countries surpasses everything that has been accomplished in this field to date. According to certain data, in the Soviet Union in 1965, there were 60 million people who were enrolled in school. However, it is mere education whose one-sided character is only being stressed by uncritical, political, and ideological indoctrination. In this typical country of civilization, culture and art are obviously lagging behind. This particularly applies to the relation between authority and citizens, or more clearly, to the question of human freedom as the essential question of culture.

According to the official opinion — all opinions are official there — literature in the Soviet Union should be a means of everyday political influence on the masses. A resolution of CK KPSS in 1932 abolished various literary groups and founded the Union of Soviet Writers. This was abolition in the literal sense of the word. From 700 writers who attended the First Congress of Soviet Writers in 1934, only about 50 were still alive at the next congress held in 1954. Most of them found death in Stalin's purges.[38] Socialist realism was declared as the only correct method in Soviet art. As a form of this engaged art, "production novels" appeared, dealing with industrialization and kolkhozes. At the congress of Soviet writers in 1965, the theory of antiheroism in Soviet literature was condemned and a conclusion was reached that "the characteristic of Soviet literature was deep patriotism and heroic deeds."

"Film is the most important of all kinds of art," Lenin said, but film is the least artistic of all phenomena called art. If art has to serve someone or something, be it ideology or government, then film is most suitable to be hired.

---

[38]Data from the *Encyclopedia*, vol.5, (Zagreb: Jugoslavenski liksikografski Savod), p. 641.

R. N. Yuryenjev, the Soviet film critic, states in one of his monographs on Soviet film comedy that Stalin did not like films on contemporary topics showing difficulties, disadvantages, and conflicts. Instead, he insisted that scenes of feasts, weddings, meetings, folk dances, and chorus songs be shown. As Stalin watched all films before their public presentation, he gave instructions which became laws. The result was a decrease in film production and the appearance of the "fear of satire."

The country was poor and half illiterate in the nineteenth century and it still gave the world Pushkin, Gogol, Chekhov, Tolstoy, Dostoevski, Tchaikovsky, and Rimsky Korsakov. Nowadays, in the second half of the twentieth century, it cannot point to a single artist or writer who could equal the great protagonists of Russian literature when it first appeared on the historical scene. If a significant name still appears in the field of literature, it is because of the mighty spiritual genius of the Russian people and is as a rule in opposition to the system like Pasternak, Solzhenitsyn, and Voznesensky. The Russian land my be fertile, but for poets and artists, the atmosphere is stuffy.

The ascent of Soviet science and the recession of the coutry's art begins after the revolution. Soviet Russia has yielded physicists, atomists, statesmen, and organizers but no poets, painters, and composers.

The lag is striking, especially in the field of philosophy. It is, in fact, a complete void unless we include here those professors of philosophy and the clerks of the philosophical institutes. There is not a single philosopher in the Soviet Union of today who could stand side by side with a Heidegger, Marcuse, or Sartre. In any case, present-day Soviet philosophers cannot be compared to their countrymen who devoted their intellectual abilities to science, engineering, or politics.

All aspects of intellectual life are oppressed by forced socialist realism. The interest of audiences is obviously decreasing, and attempts are being made to raise it by slogans such as: "How high and wonderful is the platform on which the banner of socialist realism is raised."[39]

---

[39]The slogan was put up at the retrospective exhibition of Soviet academics in Maniez in early 1974.

The writers Grigurko, Boiko, Malcev, Tarasov, and Sushinsky — more or less unknown in Europe and even in the USSR — are praised by the official critique because they take up the contemporary topics about "production." Their works deal with the construction of big industrial objects and "reflect the life of the working class and working people in the villages." Those are the works written as the "orders for the society," the *soczakaz*.[40] The academic Korzev admits: "Unfortunately, many paintings seen at the exhibitions are often only variations of forms created before." The poet Boris Oleinik complains about the black-white technique in painting life, of the grayness, superficiality, and mediocrity: "In the sky of Soviet poetry, stars of feeble and uniform light appear. There is no true poetry; there are only verses and imitations of poetry." A group of Soviet writers (Andrei Voznesensky, Bela Ahmadulina, Vasilii Aksionov, Fazil Iskender, and others) complain in a recent (1979) publication, *Almanac*, of the state of Soviet literature. In their opinion, it is suffering from a "chronic ailment that can be diagnosed as the fear of literature and as a gloomy inertia resulting in a state of stale and quiet timidity."[41]

This curtailment of art concerns architecture as well. It is true that architecture has moved toward functionalism, toward bare "texture," everywhere in the world, but the artificial towns or their new sections in socialist countries are the bleakest and the most impersonal urban entities that have ever been built. They emanate grayness and monotony.

Various explanations have been given for this: great demands, insufficient funds, construction techniques, and the like. It turns out, however, that these reasons cannot hold their ground. All beautiful objects date from a period when we were much poorer, and beautiful buildings can be built even of prefabricated elements. What we find here is a conscious or unconscious attitude which can be worded as the question: If people have no soul, then why should cities have one?

In any case, when speaking of art, it is necessary to distinguish

---

[40]*Soczakaz* a term in the USSR for the works of art on order, characterized by uniformity and lack of true inspiration.

[41]*Almanac* is better known as the object of pungent polemics between a group of American writers (Albee, Miller, Updike, and others) and the management of the Moscow Organization of Writers, owing to its suppression and the administrative measures taken against its authors. The almanac is published in the USSR and the US.

between the Russian people and the Soviet government. The first is full of religious and artistic feelings, while the other is antireligious and consequently adverse to art. The people's interest in literature is enormous, almost "hysterical," as the writer Vasilii Aksionov has said. The phenomenon is worth festering the suppressed religiousness of the Russian people, who experience through literature what is impossible for them to experience through religion in their country. In forced atheism, art becomes a substitute for supressed religion.[42]

The Material World of Art

Culture has art; civilization has science or, more precisely, sociology. Sociology is a faithful reflection of the spirit or lack of spirit of civilization. The difference between the artistic and sociological approach also reflects the primeval disunion of the world and the fact that searching aimed at two opposite directions: toward man as a personality and toward man as a member of society.

For the poet, the so-called "average man" is a fiction and a lie. For him, there is only the individual man, the particular personality. On the other hand, sociology sees in man (and in life as well) only the general and the quantitative, and it remains blind to that which really only exists: the live personality, unique and incomparable with any other one.

Art does not see people or mankind. It sees only man next to man in an infinite line, definite personalities, and portraits since a painter would say that the individual cannot be added up or made into a medium case, into an average man. What does it mean to make a portrait if not to make a face recognizable, unique, and different from all other faces? Sociology wants to find the general, the common; art wants to find the particular, the individual.

Man does not want to be systematized. People feel a spontaneous aversion to examination based on quantitative methods, to ciphers, to general characteristics, to patterns, and to standards.

---

[42]This substitution may have different causes and forms, but it is always natural and spontaneous. Kenneth Clark notices that in Catholic countries, the opera houses replaced the churches, "when these became somewhat out of fashion." In those countries, opera houses are, like cathedrals once were, the most beautiful and largest buildings in the city. Kenneth Clark, *Civilization*, p. 236.

Nobody wants to be an average Frenchman, an average citizen. The aversion to sociology is by all means strongest with poets and artists.

Rainer Maria Rilke writes: "For our grandfathers, the house, the public fountain, a well-known tower, and even their own suite, their coat were still infinitely more significant, far more authentic; almost every object had something personal in it, something human preserved in it. Nowadays, the things come from America and pile up, futile and unimportant objects that create an illusion of life. ... A house in the American style, and American apples or their grapes have nothing in common with the house, the fruit, the bunch of grapes that held the hope and thoughts of our ancestors..."[43]

W. H. Auden says:

> Thou shalt not answer questionnaires
> Or quizzes upon World Affairs,
> Nor with compliance
> Take any test. Thou shalt not sit
> With statisticians nor commit
> A social science.[44]

Science and philosophy talk about the outer world or about man but always about things in general, in principle, in the idea. Art does not see things in such a way; it sees them as they are — material. Art does not talk about man in general; it always deals with a determined man, with Oliver Twist, Eugene Onegin, Fyodor Karamazov. The limetree the poet mentions is not the tree which the botanists discuss; it is a scented, shady tree in the poet's garden under which he dreamed his boyish dreams. Art seems more real to us because all things that exist are apparently individual. Here are a few examples that illustrate this statement.

There are a lot of characters in Tolstoy's *War and Peace*, and all of them are individual personalities. The following is a description of one of the characters, the diplomat Bilibin: "He was one of those diplomats who knew how to work, and despite his laziness, he sometimes spent whole nights at his desk. ... He liked to talk just as he liked to work, but only when the talk could be elegantly

---

[43]Rainer Maria Rilke: *Letters of Miso*. See, *Briefe. Hrsg. vom Rilke Archiv in Weimar* (Wiesbaden: Insel-Verlag, 1966).

[44]W. H. Auden: *Under Which Lyre? A Reactionary Tract for the Times* (Cambridge: Harvard, 1946).

witty. In company, he was always waiting for an opportunity to say something significant and only then entered the conversation. Bilibin's talk was always brimming with originally witty and perfect phrases that were of common interest. ... His thin exhausted yellowish face was all covered with heavy wrinkles that always looked as diligently scrubbed as do one's fingertips after a bath. The movements of these wrinkles were the main play of his physiognomy..."[45]

Here is the description of Olivia Pentland from *Early Autumn*: If she had a rival in all the crowd that filled the echoing old house, it was Olivia Pentland — Sybil's mother — who moved about, alone most of the time, watching her guests, acutely conscious that the ball was not all it should have been. There was about her nothing flamboyant and arresting, nothing which glittered with the worldly hardness of the green dress and the diamonds and burnished red hair of Savine Callender; she was rather a soft woman, of gentleness and poise, whose dark beauty conquered in a slower, more subtle fashion. You did not notice her at once among all the guests; you became aware of her slowly, as if her presence had the effect of stealing over you with the vagueness of a perfume..."[46]

A thing described is not a thing in general; it is always something determined. It could even be a pencil box as in R. Llewellyn's novel *How Green Was My Valley*. Here is that description: "There is a beautiful box — it was too. About eighteen inches long and three wide, with a top that slid off and a piece cut for your thumb to press through the groove. On the bottom tray, three lovely red pencils, new, and without the marks of teeth, with sharp points, and two green pens, with brass holders for nibs, and at the end a little pit for a piece of rubber. The top tray, with five more lovely pencils, three yellows, and a red and a blue..."[47]

A situation described is always a certain unique situation: "For example, on Saturday, about four in the afternoon on the short wooden pavement of the station yard, a little woman in sky-blue was running backward, laughing and waving a handkerchief. At the same time, a Negro in a cream-colored raincoat, with yellow shoes

---

[45]Leo Tolstoy: *War and Peace*, trans. Constance Garnett (New York: Modern Library, 1940).

[46]Louis Bromfield: *Early Autumn, A Story of a Lady* (New York: Frederick A. Stores, Co., 1926).

[47]Richard Llewellyn: *How Green Was My Valley* (New York: Macmillan, 1940).

and a green hat, was turning the corner of the street, whistling. Still going backward, the woman bumped into him, underneath a lantern which hangs from the fence and which is lit at night. So there, at one and the same time, you had that fence which smells so strongly of wet wood, that lantern, and that little blonde in a Negro's arms, under a fiery-colored sky."[48]

Here's yet another very clearly shaped character from the same novel: "It is half past one. I am at the Café Mably, eating a sandwich, and everything is more or less normal. In any case, everything is always normal in cafés and especially in the Café Mably because of the manager, Monsieur Fasquelle, who has a vulgar expression in his eyes which is very straightforward and reassuring. It will soon be time for his afternoon nap and his eyes are already pink, but his manner is still lively and resolute. He is walking around among the tables and speaking confidentially to the customers..."[49]

Then there is the following description of a landscape: "It was eleven o'clock in the morning. The sun was a little on the left and behind Pierre and it lit, through the clean and rare air, the huge panorama that spread before them like an amphitheatre on the ground that was sloping up. On the top and on the left, the big road to Smolensk was winding and cut through the amphitheater and went across a village with a white church, at five hundred paces away from the top and lower. That was Borodino. The road crossed the bridge at the foot of the village, and it wound up, descending and climbing to the village of Valuyevo which could be seen at a distance of about six versts. Behind Valuyevo, the way disappeared into a forest that was yellowing at the horizon. In that birch and fir forest, on the right of the road, there shone in the distance against the sun the cross and the bell tower of the Calocha monastery. All over that blue valley, to the left and to the right of the highway, smoking fires could be seen at different places and indefinite masses of our and the enemy's army. To the right, in the direction of the river Calocha and Moscow, the ground was rocky and mountainous. The villages of Bezbovo and Zaharino could be seen between the rocks in the distance. The ground was flatter to the left. There were cornfields here and smoke could be seen coming out of the burnt village of Semionovsko."[50]

---

[48]Jean-Paul Sarter: *Nausea* (New York: French & European, 1938).
[49]Ibid..
[50]Tolstoy: *War and Peace*.

Finally, there is this description of the interior of a room: "Pierre knew this room well, divided by pillars and an arch, all upholstered with Persian carpets. A part of the room behind the pillars, where a high mahogany bed stood under the silk curtains on one side and a big icon case with icons on the other side, was lit red and clearly just as the churches were lit during vespers. Under the lighted rises of the kioto there stood a long Voltairian armchair, covered at the top with snow-white uncrumpled pillows, apparently just changed, and in the armchair there lay, covered up to the waist with a bright green blanket, the grand figure of his father Pierre knew so well, the Count Bezuhov, with the same grey mane of hair above the broad forehead that reminded one of a lion and with the same characteristically noble heavy wrinkles on the beautiful reddish yellow face..."[51]

These few examples, taken at random from novels which were at hand, are not characteristic only of the works of Tolstoy, Sartre, Bromfield, or Llewellyn. It is a phenomenon that does not relate the artist but rather the very essence of the art, and the greater an artist, the more he follows this inner law of every art — the material, the individual, the personal, the original, the unique. Intelligence and science tend to the pole of homogeneity, always discovering the same in everything that exists. Art, on the contrary, implies that only originals exist, that nothing repeats, neither a character nor a situation, and that there has been nothing throughout eternity that is the same and identical. This belief lies in the very nature of art, just as the equal, the repeatable, and the identical underlie the basic assumption of every science. In this spectrum, from the mechanical to the personal, dead matter with its laws is at one pole while life with its highest achievement, personality, is at the other. The more we move away from the mechanical, the more freedom and creativity emerge, so that on the other pole, that of the personality, there is only the original. The opposite is also true: the more we get away from the personality, the more conditionality, regularity, and homogeneity come into sight, so that the abstract, the equal, and the mechanical are only reigning at the other pole.

The Drama of the Human Face

Art is obsessed by the problem of personality. Five hundred

---

[51]Ibid.

and twenty-nine characters appear in *War and Peace*, and *The Divine Comedy* is a whole world of personalities. Each of them is a soul and exists with its sins and responsibilities so that the scene of the last judgment, with the billions of people that lived and died, seems quite real. The frescoes on the Sistine Chapel ceiling with the creation scenes represent a gallery of individualized faces — that is, characters. Individuality makes a face a character by giving it its inner life, its freedom. The character is not identical with the human face; it is a desire reflected therein. Character and nature relate to each other like mind to matter, quality to quantity, consciousness to inertia, drama to utopia. A character opposes nature by being free, unique, even immortal in a sense. Nature means uniformity, homogeneity, identity, causality. The character is individuality, spontaneity, freedom, a miracle.

Religion talks about soul, art about character, and that is nothing but two ways of expressing the same idea. Religion turns to the soul and art tries to reach it, to bring it before our eyes. Art has always expected to find it somewhere behind the human face. In primitive art, the most important part of the composition is the head, while the body is reduced to a supporting role, usually presented schematically or completely neglected. The sculptured heads found in Jerihon, dating from 6000 B.C., indicate that Neolithic man believed that the head was the abode of the spirit / soul. The makers of the huge stone figures on Easter Island concentrated their attention on the faces only, completely ignoring the body and the occiput. All the great artists from Phidias and Praxiteles to Raphael, Michelangelo and da Vinci were obsessed with one single great theme: man's face and his inner world. The fame of the "Mona Lisa" owes to the fact that it is perhaps one of the most successful attempts "to paint" the mystery of the inner life. The trend in American art during the last ten years, especially in painting, has been termed by some people as "a return to the drama of the human face. That is only one more return for art."

Thus, the subject of any work of art — regardless of what is assigned to it or what it can be used for — is always spiritual and personal, never social or political. The plot or the happening could be social, but art always deals with the moral aspects of the problem. Art is spiritual even when it "deals" with the body. Some called Rubens, misled by outward appearances, a painter of the body and Rembrandt a "painter of the soul." Any painter who paints a personality also paints a soul. Essentially, the subject of any drama — due to its religious origin — is in the last instance the relation of the human inner freedom to the determinism of the outer world. "In Shakespeare's plays, we do not care about actions. We pay all our attention only to the motives and to the hidden soul which seems so real in its perverted grandiosity, so that the crime itself becomes of minor importance."[52] "There is no need for action; characters are sufficient," says Eugene O'Neill, aiming obviously at the same idea.

The character is never an object; he exists in art only as "I and You."[53] This explains the constant tendency to wipe out the difference between the creator and the observer and to integrate the observer as a direct partaker in creation (even in painting as with the American painter Rauschenberg). When a group of African dancers comes to an African village, the spectators join them so that in the end there are no spectators. Nobody is left out; they all take part. This is the principle of the unity of the work, the artist and the audience, a principle springing from the metaphysical nature of art.

What kind of principle is that? It is, first, the relation of art toward what we usually call objective reality. This so-called objective reality, which materialistic science and philosophy have turned into a kind of absolute, is only an illusion for art, a scenery or a false deity. The only reality that art admits is man and his eternal longing to confirm himself, to save himself, to not get lost in "objective reality." Every painting is an impossible attempt at "presenting a miracle we call character." What lies at the heart of every painting is the personality in an alien world and a conflict emerging from this basic relation. Without this there is no art; what remains is only technique. That is exactly what distinguishes Rembrandt's famous portraits from cheap pictures at a fair, however skillfully they are made. Even if not particularly stressed, this conflict is inwardly present because every portrait tends to depict an authentic man who represents consciousness, individuality, and freedom, thus being in opposition to nature and the world.

This soul is not, therefore, the "psyche" that scientists discuss. It is the true soul, *ruh*, a bearer of human dignity and responsibility,[54] the soul that all religions, all prophets, and all poets have talked about. It is like the difference between Jung's *Psychological*

---

[52]Charles and Mazy Lamb: *All Shakespeare's Tales* (New York: Fredrick A. Stokes Co., Hampton Publishing, 1911).
[53]Martin Buber: *I and Thou*, trans. Walter Kaufmann (New York: Scribner, 1970).
[54]The Qur'ān 32:9.

Types and the characters in Destoevski's *Crime and Punishment*. The first are monsters, artificial two-dimensional beings; the others are real men, torn between sin and freedom, God's creatures, characters.

The Artist and His Work

Thinking about this strange, irrational, unnatural (or supernatural) nature of art, one suddenly realizes that a work of art understood as an object, a fact in the outer world, is not the primary aim of art. On the contrary, the aim of art is creation itself, and a work is its inevitable by-product. The essence of art is a longing, a desire, and it is inside in the soul, not outside in the world. Art retains its nature even without a work of art. Pollock used to paint by walking on a canvas or by waving tubes of paint above it. Rauschenberg started a new phase of this by a series of completely white empty canvases of different sizes. Yves Klein published a book of ten monochrome sheets of paper in Madrid in 1954. The American pianist John Cage in his composition *4 Minutes and 33 Seconds* sat for this length of time at the piano without playing. Hamlet's "inactivity full of action" is of the same kind. The same goes for the well-known lack of action in Anton Chekhov's plays: in some of his pieces, certain scenes consist of silence only. Nothing happens on the stage, but still, the play goes on. The action takes place inside because hope, repentance, anger, humiliation, shame, and despair are not events; they are experiences. In the Japanese Noh dramas, there are scenes when the actor does not make a single move for twenty minutes. During that time, he expresses his inner conflicts.

Such an attitude, which even though it borders on absurdity, is inwardly present in art and becomes a stress of the inner and the subjective and a negation of the exterior and the objective.

A monochrome canvas in the informal style can be understood only as an absolute negation of the outside world, a negation that could not be expressed more clearly or radically. Painting, the activity itself and not the picture, is the real sense of art. A work of art may remain unrealized, unmaterialized, in a state of longing, but it can never be turned into a mass production, a series. It must never lose its quality of uniqueness. The nonexistence of such a uniqueness does not deny the existence of "the work," whereas the copy or copies are always its negation. That is how we reach a paradox: a work of art is destroyed by multiplication.

Consequently, the artist's aspiration or his intention is the last verification of a work of art, confirmed by his signature. "Whatever an artist spits out is art," according to Schwitters.[55] That is why the parts of a bicycle put together by the hands of Picasso and authenticated by his signature becomes a work of art. Another example of this is *The Bull's Head* in the Luise Leiris Gallery in Paris. At this point, morality, art, and religion meet again. "Piety is not in turning your face toward the East or the West,"[56] and the intention or aspiration remains an irreducible value of human behavior, although it does not change its consequences in the outer world. Art is creation, the very activity, just as morality in the eyes of every man is what gives value to a failed attempt or to a sacrifice made in vain. If we remove from morality, religion, and art all that is unessential and accidental, if we reduce them to their essence, we will find aspiration, desire, intention or, in a word, "freedom" as their last and authentic content. Thus, religion, morality, and art have as their ultimate quintessence one and the same thing: pure humanity.

Even works which by nature can be reproduced are renewed through the personality of the artist. Arthur Rubinstein said once that although he had played Beethoven's *Fourth Symphony* many times, he had never performed it in the same way. Meyerhold advocated theater in which only one play would be performed: *Hamlet*. Different directors would put it on stage and always make it a new play. This is possible only because art is not in the work, but in the inner life and personality of the artist, and this personality is pure freedom. The result: both artist and audience experience a work of art in a new way.

When speaking about a work, we actually speak about its author, about the man who created it. Picasso said that looking at Cezanne's paintings always made him wonder about the enthusiasm or ecstasy the artist experienced while painting them. He said: "It does not matter what the painter does. It is important what the painter himself is."[57] In his opinion, a work is important only as a reflection of the artist's personality. It even reflects his moral

---

[55]Kurt Schwitters: *Das Literarische Werk*, ed. Friedhelm Lach (Köln: M. DuMont-Schauberg, 1973).

[56]The Qur'ān 2:177.

[57]Pablo Picasso: *Picasso on Art: A Selection of Views*, ed. Doré Ashton (New York: Viking Press, 1979).

life. Boris Pasternak said that a bad man could not be a great poet.[58] A work of art is the artist himself. That is why we often identify a work of art with the artist. Instead of saying the titles of the paintings, we say a Cezanne, a Dürer, a Rubens. When we say "Rembrandt" and not *The Night Watch*, everything is said about this painting. That is the essence, the rest is accident.

Art belongs to our inner world of truths, not to the outer world of facts. That is why we can draw the line between true art and false art or between an inspired poem and an ordered one. Why is "every reproduction ugly," as Alain (pseudonym for Emile Chartier) vehemently declared? The difference between an original and its copy exists only with the view of creation. From the objective point of view, it does not exist or exists only to an insignificant degree.

The same applies to kitsch. All the attempts to define it have failed. This is why Abraham Moles made a real breakthrough when he discovered that kitsch "is not an object but a relation between man and object; an adjective, not a noun."[59]

A painting or a style of painting is not true or false in itself. Only the artist's attitude toward the world and his own work can make it false. Repetition, perfection, and academicism are false, regardless of the style or genre to which a work of art nominally belongs. Such a work is deprived of true inspiration and freedom, the *sine qua non* of the inner life in art. "Any academicism means dying."[60] An insincere artist brings a stillborn work of art to the world. It is like our praying to God. A prayer without enthusiasm or inner presence is nonsense in any world and in any consciousness. Academicism in art is like hypocrisy and formalism in religion.[61]

The primary importance of creation as a movement of a soul, and the secondary importance of a work of art as a fact in the outside world, are also manifested in the creation of completely unintelligible

---

[58]Boris Pasternak: *Letters to Georgian Friends*, trans. David Magarshak (New York: Harcourt, Brace, & World, 1968).

[59]Abraham Moles: *Information Theory and Esthetic Perception*, trans. Joel E. Cohen (Urbana, IL: University of Illinois Press, 1966).

[60]Cassou: *Art and Confrontation*.

[61]Everything is the opposite in civilization. Things have objective value here. The railway lines and roads to the West Coast of the US, which changed the life of America to the benefit of millions of people, were built by adventurers and greedy bankers, and their motives had no effect on the projects in question.

works of art. Here we should say that completely intelligible works of art do not exist. "A work of art is primarily an inner problem, a secret, a problem of belief."[62] It is a confession only partly intelligible to others. "Only one man can understand my pictures, and that is me,"[63] says de Chirico, one of the leading Italian painters and the founder of so-called metaphysical painting. Every work of art is in a sense autobiographic. Dramas written by tragedians are only fragments of drama in their own life. "Although I never write about my personal life, all the characters in my novels speak of my life," says Ignazio Silone. Poetry is a monologue, very often a tacit monologue. It is a complete truth only for the poet and his own world. What does Alberto Giacometti want to tell us with his little eyeless figures? By defining art as an "absurd activity, as a research into the impossible, and a vain attempt to grasp the fire, the psyche, the essence of life,"[64] he partly answered this question. In this vain search, in this impossible activity, every man is alone, everyone follows his own way. Thus, a protest of the audience against an unintelligible poem, picture, or sculpture is mainly the result of their nonunderstanding of the very essence of art.

Creation thus appears to be the authentic aim of art, while the work of art is its "unfinished symbol." In the act of creation, art is complete and happiness is unspoiled; there is only a part of it in the work itself. It is sometimes difficult to grasp the meaning of a portrait or a sculpture because the work is separated from the artist and the act of creation. Visits to galleries may leave us indifferent since the "eternal fire" does not burn there anymore. "They were paintings once, but no longer,"[65] says Jean Dubuffet. A work of art is the result of the fire which once burned in a soul, but it is not the fire itself. It is rather a testimony or a trace left after it.

Style and Function

The opposition between an artist and his work can be observed in a work of art, as seen in the well-known controversy on the primacy of style or function.

---

[62]Statement made by the French Sculptor Adam.

[63]Giorgio de Chirico: *De Chirico: Essays by Maurizio Fagiolo dell' Arco*, ed. William S. Rubin (New York: Museum of Modern Art, 1982).

[64]Cf. footnote 2 of this chapter.

[65]Cf. footnote 16 of this chapter.

Style against function is man against thing. Style is personal, individual; function is impersonal, objective. Style is created; function is analyzed, examined, produced. A style may be dignified, monumental, florid, sincere, experienced; a function can be technically perfect at most. Style is inscrutable; function is reasonable. "Style is the man"[66] function is the fact, the objective reality.[67]

We can distinguish two independent and separate activities: aesthetic shaping and technical perfecting. The one tends to fulfill man's inexplicable desire for beauty; the other tends to meet man's need for function. Aesthetic designing tends toward diversity and individuality; technical perfecting tends toward uniformity and leveling.

Viewed in light of the ideas presented in the second part of this book, it would be interesting to remark that both of those tendencies, if prolonged and separated from each other, lead to a lifeless result. Architecture is the most suitable example because of its mixed character. Sheer aesthetic design, regardless of function, soon becomes a degenerate decor and makes the building appear as artificial and empty as stage scenery. On the other hand, sheer technical perfection and sheer functionalism results in cold and impersonal buildings that are uniform and monotonous.

"If we build honestly," says Mies van der Rohe, one of the advocates of functionalism, "a church must not be different from a factory."[68]

All primeval divisions of the world are reflected once again in the opposition of style to function.

Art and Critique

The said facts can explain the failure and the limits of

---

[66]Georges L. Buffon: *Oeuvres choisies, précédées du discours qui a obtenu le prix d'éloquence décerné par l'Académie française*, ed. Félix Hémon (Paris: Delagrave, n.d.).

[67]It is difficult to give a satisfactory definition of style. Here is an interesting one by Werner Nihls: "There is a causal connection between the system of shapes and the spiritual currents of a period. ... Every shape is an expression of the prominent spiritual and emotional currents, the materialization of spiritual needs and historical analysis." Werner Nihls, *The End of the Functionalist Era*, n.p.d.

[68]Ludwig Mies van der Rohe: *Mies von der Rohe*, ed. Martin Pawley (New York: Simon & Schuster, 1970).

critique. Critique is an attempt to explain a work of art, but it is a priori incapable of doing so because of its rationalistic method. It wants to "think" something that is not basically a fruit of thought.[69] For an artist, the work is an inner vision aroused through suffering and experience, not a result of analysis and logical reasoning, but a "daughter of sorrow and pain."[70] This is why critics bring more confusion than light to interpreting a work of art; "Critique kills the work." Having read a book by Franz Kafka, Einstein complained in a letter to Thomas Mann: "I could not read it. A human mind is not complicated enough to understand him!" All the same, the critics managed to outdo Kafka himself. Alfred Casim wrote that it was easier to read Kafka than most of his interpreters. "Kafka would cite their books as one more example of his remoteness from mankind." Dostoevski was admired by his readers but tormented by his critics and interpreters. In 1876, he wrote in his diary: "I have always had the support of my readers, not my critics."[71]

Art needs an uncritical audience. A critically disposed spectator will reduce a work of art to a series of facts and morals, but he will disregard the artist's intention. It is therefore possible to assume that it would be easier for the average spectator or reader to understand the true message of the work than it would be for a learned critic. By not trying to "understand" a work of art, they will succeed in "experiencing" it. The different appreciation of a play or a poem by critics and an audience could result from these two completely different approaches.

Critique and art do not go together, just as theology and religion do not. After all, Faulkner compared critics to priests. Ethical questions may be adequately expressed in a drama, at the theater, or in a novel. The Bible and the Qur'ān are not theological books. This is another point where religion and art meet each other or where they even prove to be interdependent. Christianity can exist truly

---

[69]André Marchand says: "A painter is not an intellectual. In painting, intelligence is of no use. It is the light in the soul that is necessary"; and Bissier: "Painting appeals to human emotions. One should always return to the sources. They are the purest and the truest. Our civilization is intellectualistic, and an intellectual is far from understanding figurative art." See Julius Bissier, *Brush Drawings*, trans. Oliver Bernard (London: Thames & Hudson, 1966).

[70]Picasso: *Picasso on Art*.

[71]Feodor Dostoevski: *The Diary of a Writer*, trans. Boris Brasol (New York: C. Scribner's Sons, 1949).

only as a history of Jesus, not as theology. Jesus and the Gospels are one aspect of it, Paul and the Church are another.

To conclude this discourse on the common points between religion and art, we ought to say that art, in its search for the human, becomes a search for God. The fact that there are artists who are nominally atheist does not change anything because "art is a way of doing and not a way of thinking."[72] There are unreligious pictures, sculptures, and poems, but there is no unreligious art. The phenomenon of the artist-atheist, very rare indeed, could be ascribed to the inevitable contradictions in man and to the relative independence of conscious logic from the spontaneous, yet so much more authentic, general attitude that is man's answer to all the pressures of heaven and earth. If there is no religious truth, then there is no artistic truth either!

---

[72]Chartier [Alain]: *Sustène des beaux-arts.*

only as a history of Jesus, not as theology. Jesus and the Gospels, [illegible] Paul and the Crucifixion [illegible]

[illegible] between [illegible] and [illegible] we ought to say [illegible] The [illegible] that there are artists who are [illegible] not change anything because [illegible] a way of [illegible] and not a way of [illegible] There are [illegible] pictures [illegible] [illegible]

Chapter 4

MORALITY

There are moral atheists, but there is no moral atheism

MORALITY

Duty and Interest

The features of the two different orders out of which all reality emanates are still not discernible. Creation with its freedom, spontaneity, consciousness, and individuality is on one side; evolution with its causality, entropy, inertia, and anonymity (homogeneity) is on the other. Duty and interest are two more links in these chains; the former is the central term of morality, while the latter plays a similar role in politics.

Duty and interest, opposed to each other, are the two moving forces of every human activity. They can in no way be compared; duty is always beyond interest, and interest has no connection with morality. Morality is neither functional nor rational. If one risks one's life by entering a burning house to save a neighbor's child and comes back carrying the dead child in one's arms, can we say that the action was worthless since it was unsuccessful? Morality is what gives value to this apparently useless sacrifice, to this attempt without success, just as "architecture is what makes the ruins beautiful."[1]

The sight of defeated justice, which even if defeated wins our hearts, appears not to be a fact "of this world." After all, what reasons of this world (natural, logical, scientific, intellectual, or otherwise) can justify the action of a hero who falls because he remains on the side of justice and virtue? If this world exists in space

[1]A Perret: n.p.d.

and time only, and this nature is indifferent to justice and injustice, then the sacrifice of a hero is senseless. Nevertheless, as we refuse to consider it senseless, it then becomes a revelation of God, tidings of another world with meanings and laws opposite to this world of nature and all its laws and interests. We approve of this "absurd" act with all our heart, without knowing why nor asking for any explanation. The greatness of a heroic deed is not in success, as it is very often fruitless, nor in reason, as it is very often unreasonable. Drama retains the brightest trace of the divine in this world. Here lies its unsurpassed and universal value and its significance for all people in the world.

The existence of another world should appear to us even more possible since we cannot consider tragic heroes defeated but as winners. Winners? Where, in which world have they been winners? Those who lost peace, freedom, or even life — in what way are they the winners? Obviously, they are not winners in this world. Their lives and their sacrifices in particular induce us to always ask the same question: is there another meaning to human existence, a meaning different from this relative and limited one, or have these great and courageous men only been failures?

As a phenomenon of real human life, morals cannot be rationally explained, and as such, in them lie the first and perhaps the only practical argument of religion. Moral conduct is either meaningless, or else, it has its meaning and sense in the existence of God. A third option is not possible. We should either discard morality as a heap of prejudices or introduce into the equation another value that we could call the figure of eternity, provided that life is eternal and that God as well as a world, different from the natural one, exists, in which man's moral conduct can be meaningful and justified.

There are not many people who work according to the law of virtue, but this small minority is the pride of mankind and every human being. There are not many moments in our own life when we act according to the law of duty. However, the rare moments when we rise above ourselves by neglecting interests and benefits are the only undying essences of our life.

A man is never morally neutral. That is why he is always either morally true or false, or both, which is the most frequent. People have acted and behaved differently, but they have always spoken in the same way about justice, truth, equality, and freedom: the wise men and heroes out of sincerity because of truth, and the politicians and demagogues hypocritically and out of interest. Still, the false morality of demagogues and hypocrites is no less significant to the topic we are discussing. Their feigned morality, their moral mask, their centuries-old campaigning with the words "justice," "equality," "humanity," and so on confirm the reality of morals as do the noble sufferings of heroes and saints. Political history, especially that of recent times, is full of examples of how enemies of freedom, while maintaining the apparatus for repression and spying, maintain at the same time another one for speaking incessantly and loudly of freedom and justice. Hypocrisy, as false morality, proves the value of true morality, just as the temporary value of forged money is owing to the fact that there is legal tender. Hypocrisy is a proof that everyone expects or requires moral conduct from everyone else.

Intention and Deed

Things exist objectively in the world of nature. The earth revolves around the sun whether we know it or not, whether we like it or not. We can even hate it, but we can neither ignore nor change it. From the moral point of view, the facts are meaningless. They are neither good nor bad, and they are nonexistent as far as morals are concerned. On the contrary, in our inner world, things do not have an objective existence. Here we are direct partakers, and the look of that world depends directly on us. That is the field of human freedom.

In distinction from the outer world, where we do what we have to do, where there are the rich and the poor, the clever and the stupid, the educated and the primitive, the weak and the strong (all those states which do not depend on our will and do not express our authentic self), our inner world is made up of freedom and equality of chance. This freedom is complete for there are no material or natural limitations.

It expresses itself in intention and desire. Every man may aspire to live in harmony with his conscience — according to certain moral laws. This may not be easy for some, but every man admires righteousness. Many people have no way to remove an injustice, but every man can hate injustice and condemn it in his mind and in this very fact lies the meaning of repentance. Morality is not in the very act; it is in the desire to live righteously, in the strain of the will, in the struggle for salvation. It is not human to be perfect and therefore sinless. To sin and to repent is to be man. Think of

Alyosha and Misha Karamazov. Alyosha is wonderful, almost perfect, while Misha is fully human; yet, in spite of all of Misha's passions and sins, can one tell with certainty which one of them is nearer to God's grace?

How many things have we done which we did not really want to do? How many things are there which we intend or desire to do but never do? So, there are two worlds: the heart and nature. A desire of ours, although never fulfilled, has come true in the world of our heart, where it becomes a complete reality. In the same way, an accidental action, a deed that was unintentional, happened completely in the world of nature and did not happen at all in the other, inner world.

This contact between a desire and a deed reflects the primeval opposition between man and the world and appears in a similar way in ethics, art, and religion. Intention, artistic desire, and piety belong inwardly to each other and are in the same relationship with their material, worldly projections: behavior, a work of art, and a ritual. The former are experiences in the soul, the latter are happenings in the world.

The question then arises whether deeds should be judged by their intentions or their consequences. The first is the message of every religion, while the other is the motto of every ideology or revolution. These are two opposite logics. One reflects the negation of the world; the other reflects the negation of man.

Science and materialism inevitably had to call into question the authenticity of intention in human behavior. They found that intention is not primeval or authentic but something that could not be readily explained, something that is a consequence rather than a cause. According to them, the source of human action is not in intention but somewhere beyond consciousness, in an area of general determinism.

On the contrary, according to religion, there is an inner center in every man which is essentially different from the rest of the world. It is the bottom of every being — the soul. Intention means an inner step into the depths of one's inner self, to this bottom. In this way, an action is adopted, verified, or inwardly confirmed. It can then be done or not done. In the inner world, it has been done once and forever. Without this "consultation with himself," a man's action is a mechanical act, a pure coincidence in an outer and transient world.

A man is not what he does but what he wants, what he earnestly desires. A writer does not limit himself to the plot; he penetrates into the soul of his hero and describes his hidden motives. If he does not do so, he is writing a chronicle and not a literary work.

According to Arnold Geulincx, our true being consists only of cognition and will, a combination which makes us incapable of action beyond the limits of our consciousness. Deeds are almost beyond our power; they are completely in the hands of God. Thus, morality is not in the honest act but only in the honest intention.

Hume expresses a similar thought: "An action has no moral merit in itself; to learn the moral value of a man, we have to look inside. Since we cannot do it directly, we pay attention to actions; but they have been and remain only signs of inner will, therefore of moral appraisal as well."[2]

An intended act is an act already performed in eternity. Its outward performance bears an earthly and therefore a conditional, unauthentic, accidental, and even meaningless aspect. Intention is free; the performance is subject to limitations, laws, and conditions. The intention is completely ours; the performance has something alien and casual in itself.

Man is good if he wants to be good as he understands it. However, this "good" may be bad in somebody else's opinion. Man is evil if he wants to do evil, even if that were "good" for others or from the point of view of others. The question is always of the man himself and of the world that belongs solely to him. Within that relationship, which is definitely inward and spiritual, every man is completely alone and equally free. This is the meaning of Sartre's statement that every man is absolutely responsible and that "there are neither innocent victims nor innocent convicts in hell."[3]

Drill and Upbringing

The most striking and wonderful things that old books can offer us are the stories about conversion and moral revival. The worst sinners and tyrants turned overnight into humble martyrs and defenders of justice. It is always a spontaneous event; there is no process

---

[2]David Hume: *Treatise on Human Nature* (London: J.M. Dent & Sons, 1926).
[3]Jean-Paul Sartre: *Huis Clos in Theatre* (Paris: Gallimard, 1947).

of reforming or influencing. The question is one of a move in the depths of the soul, of an experience existing together with an energy of a completely inward nature which by its own force completely changes a man. This transformation belongs to man and that is why there is no process, casualty, conditionality, causes, and consequences, or even a rational explanation. The essence of this drama is freedom and creativity.

Good and evil are within man. There are no drills, laws, forces, or any outside influences by which a man can be "improved." It is only his behavior that can be changed. Virtue and sin are not "products like sugar and vitriol" as Taine and Zola hold.[4] In his novel *Resurrection*, Tolstoy shows how the "reeducation" of prisoners in reality means manipulating them and results only in the deprivation of people.[5] Revival and conversion are spontaneous. They are a result of the soul's being moved. From the religious point of view, every outside influence to remove evil is fruitless. This is the correct meaning of the Christian and Buddhist "nonresistance to evil."

Also, this is why drill has no influence on the moral attitude of man. You can drill a soldier to be tough, skillful, and strong, but you cannot drill him to be honest, dignified, enthusiastic, and brave. Those are spiritual qualities. It is impossible to impose a belief by means of decree, terror, pressure, violence, or force. Every pedagogue can give a number of examples of how children resist persistent guidance in one direction and how they can consequently develop an interest in completely opposite behavior. This is due to the "human quality" of man. Man cannot be drilled like an animal. The inefficiency of drill and the uncertainty of education are the "palpable" proof that man is an animal endowed with a soul — that is, with freedom.[6] This is why every true upbringing is essentially self-upbringing and a negation of drill. The aim of true upbringing is not to change a man directly (because, strictly speaking, that is not possible) but to incite an inner stream of experiences and to cause an inner decision to the benefit of good by means of

---

[4]Such as in Emile Zola: *Le ventre de Paris* (Paris: Fasquclk, 1953) and in Hippolyte Taine, *Notes on Paris* (New York: H. Holt and Company, 1879).

[5]Leo Tolstoy: *Resurrection*, trans. Louise Maude (New York: Norton, 1966).

[6]The result is that materialists believe in the omnipotence of breeding in the sense of drill (for example Laude Helvetius in *De l'Homme*), while Christians claim that it is completely inefficient.

example, advice, sight, or the like. Beyond that, man cannot be changed; only his behavior may be changed, and that could be feigned or temporary. Behavior which does not engage our deepest will is not an upbringing but rather a drill. Upbringing includes our participation, our effort. This is why the result of upbringing is always different and cannot be foreseen.

Individualists believe in man's conversion, in inner renewal; positivists believe in the change of his behavior. The philosophy behind these views is clear: if a crime is a result of free choice or of an evil will, then reeducation by some outside measure has little chance of success. On the contrary, if the offense is the consequence of bad conditions and habits, the offender can be reeducated by changing these conditions or forming new habits. This is the difference between an inner conversion and a drill. Every re-education technique enforced by clerks and government officials, and especially by the army or the police, always consists of drill and never of upbringing. Upbringing is an immeasurable and subtle influence upon man's soul. It is completely indirect through love, examples, forgiveness, and punishment with the intention of initiating an inner activity in man himself. Drill, being essentially bestial, is a system of measures and action taken to force a certain behavior, the so-called right behavior, upon a human being. Upbringing belongs to man; drill is designed for the animal. By means of drill, it is possible to form citizens who obey the law not out of respect but out of fear or habit. Their insides may be dead, their feelings withered; yet, they still do not break the law because they have been drilled. The stories about so-called blameless citizens who are morally empty and trespassers who are essentially good and noble very often appear in literature. Hence, there exist two kinds of justice: man's and God's, the first looking at deeds and the other at the essence of being.

The inner span of man is huge, almost infinite. He is capable of the most abominable crimes and the most noble sacrifices. The greatness of man is not primarily in the doing of good deeds but in his ability to choose. Everyone who reduces or limits this choice debases man. Good does not exist beyond one's will, nor can it be imposed by force: "There is no force in faith." The same law applies to ethics. Drill, even when it imposes the correct behavior, is essentially immoral and inhuman.

Morality and Reason

The concept of human freedom is inseparable from the idea of ethics. Despite all the changes this idea has undergone, freedom has remained the constant of any turning point or development throughout the history of ethics. What space and quantity are for physics, freedom is for ethics.[8] Reason comprehends space and quantity, but it does not understand freedom. This is the dividing line between reason and ethics.

The function of reason is to discover nature, mechanism, and calculus, in other words, to discover itself in everything. This is why reason constantly rotates in place, for in nature it can find nothing but itself — the mechanism. Hence the paradox of some ethical theories which end their complex reasoning with conclusions such as unselfishness equals selfishness and negation of pleasure equals pleasure — the paradox, which caused Voltaire to establish his famous *reduction ad absurdum* (sacrifice of one's own life out of one's own interest).[9]

Reason's (logical) analysis of morality reduces it — perhaps to the observer's surprise — to nature, selfishness, and egoism. In nature, the mind discovers general and omnipresent causality. In man, it discovers nature again: the instincts (the power of two masters — pain and pleasure) which reflect man's slavery, his non-freedom. It is this very same mechanism of thinking which reduces God to the First Cause (the Immovable Mover), the soul to the psyche, and art to work and technique. The attempt to base ethics on reason cannot take us further than so-called social morality, the rules of behavior necessary for the maintenance of a certain group, in reality, a kind of social discipline.

Morals, for that matter, also cannot be called a product of reason. Reason can only examine and determine the relations between things; it cannot give a judgment of value when the question is of moral approval or moral renouncement. For instance, every man understands the principle that the spiritual uniformness of people could not be admitted, but this very principle could not be rationally

---

[8]The essence of spirit is freedom, in the same way that the essence of matter is weight. See Georg Hegel, *Sämtliche Werke*, ed. Hermann Glockner (Stuttgart: F. Frommann, 1961).

[9]François Marie Arouet de Voltaire: *Oeuvres complètes de Voltaire*, vols. 17-20: *Dictionnaire philosophique* (Paris: Garnier frères, 1885).

justified and proved. It is impossible to prove scientifically that something is not good in the moral sense of the word, just as it is impossible to draw the exact, scientific distinction between art and kitsch or between the beautiful and the ugly. Nature or reason (since it is the same) does not distinguish between right and wrong, good and evil. These qualities do not exist in nature. Then, what does man as an unrepeatable individuality mean to science? A scientist must be more than that — he must be a man — to understand that premise. The famous ethical maxim that a good man is always happy and a bad man unhappy cannot be understood rationally. Christian ethics do not lend themselves to a teaching in scientific terms. All of their moral demands are portrayed in one ideal personality: that of Jesus Christ. The three famous principles of the French revolution (equality, freedom, and brotherhood) cannot be derived from science, nor can they be obtained in a scientific way. Science would rather establish three opposite principles: inequality, absolute social discipline, and anonymity or alienation of human units into a perfectly organized society.

Could Jean Valjean[10] resort to science to solve the moral problems he faced? Should he have sacrificed the interest of so many people to save a simple and innocent man? What kind of answer would that have been? Would not science have taken the side of so-called common interest? The problem in question cannot be the subject of science, nor would the answer to it, if possible, reflect the wish of any man. What Victor Hugo described in so exciting a way in [*The Storm Under a Skull*] "*La tempête sous un crâne*"[11] is not a conflict in the reason of a man but a conflict between reason and the soul, the destructive clash of arguments that belong to different sides of the human personality. Essentially, it is a dialogue between reason and conscience, one in which two opposite kinds of argument alternate. However, this discussion is only apparently logical, and no definite conclusion is to be expected. The arguments are of two different qualities, of two different categories, and they consequently cannot be compared. They are from two different worlds from heaven and earth. Only man can make a choice for himself and in himself when facing this dilemma. The decision that Jean Valjean makes is the defeat of reason but the victory of man, a victory which

---

[10]Victor Hugo: *Les misèrables* (Paris: Garnier - Flammarion, 1972).

[11]See, more specifically, *Livre septième: l'affaire Champmathieu* in *Les misérables*, vol. 1, pp. 247-264.

cannot be rationally explained or justified but one with which all people side with a silent and unanimous approval.

All of us may have an inner certainty of our freedom, but let us prove and explain in a scientific way this certain but still undefinable feeling. All of us agree that it is right to castigate the man who caused an offense by accident; however, this clear and logical attitude cannot be scientifically justified. What the heart simply accepts, science cannot prove or explain. Shall we renounce fulfilling our duty because reason cannot justify or support that inner voice? If not, then we maintain an attitude without knowing why, against our reason, because of a *sui generis* certainty — because we believe.

What does reason have to do with moral decisions? Hume answers this question clearly and precisely: "To our mind, a crime is nothing but a number of motives, thoughts, or actions related to a given personality and a certain situation. We can investigate that relationship, explain the origin and performance of the deed, but only when we let our emotions talk does the disapproval appear, characterizing that deed as morally evil." He resumes: "All that our mind is capable of is displaying relationships among things; on the other side, in a value judgment, a completely new moment emerges, one which does not exist in a factual judgment, and it can be explained only by the productive power of feelings."[12]

Francis Hutcheson writes in his *System of Moral Philosophy* that: "As a higher value of pleasure in art and science is perfectly clear in comparison to pleasure in eating, so it is with the difference between 'good' and all other perceptions."[13] According to him, the ability to discern morals does not depend on intelligence or education. Moral judgments are not mediated by reason; they are immediate.

The contrast between science and ethics is also reflected in everyday life. Science, for example, accepts artificial insemination to conceive babies in a test tube as well as euthanasia or mercy killing. These procedures cannot be imagined without science as they are its product. On the other hand, every ethic, regardless of its nominal attitude toward religion, rejects those acts as contrary to the

---

[12]Hume: *Treatise on Human Nature.*

[13]Francis Hutcheson: *A System of Moral Philosophy* (New York: A.M. Kelley, 1968), vol. I, part VI.

[14]Lucien Cuenot: *"l'Eugénique," Revue d'Anthropologue*: 1935-36.

very principle on which human life is based. Ethics, religion, and art share the same opinion in this regard, although they explain it differently. Religion cannot accept artificial life and violent death because life and death are in the hands of God, not of man. From the point of view of ethics, artificial insemination and euthanasia are an offense against humanity for they degrade man to an object, which leads to his manipulation and misuse. To an artist, birth and death are mysteries and should remain so. Hamlet's three most famous monologues are dedicated to death. To science, death is banal, a physical fact — just remember the scientific definition of death: a biological event in the material world. The chasm is complete; no comparison is possible.

Eugenic sterilization, experiments on man, artificial insemination, and euthanasia are completely rational and logical. There are no rational and scientific arguments against them. How, then, can science prevent its own misuse? The French Academy of Moral and Political Sciences came out against artificial insemination with a quite unscientific argument: "...artificial insemination is an offense against the grounds of marriage, family, and society." Cuenot expresses a similar thought about artificial death: "The feeling of respect for life and maternity has nothing in common with logic, and I do not believe that euthanasia, which imposes itself in certain cases, can ever be legalized."[14]

Euthanasia, artificial insemination, sterilization, transplantation of organs, abortion, and the like are the domain of science only in so far as technique is concerned. Their application is a matter of morality, and science can make no decision here. "The plan to treat people as cattle appears disgusting and at the same time it offends our feeling of personal dignity."[15] Artificial insemination came to medicine through veterinary surgery. The question again lies in the conflict between humanism and biology or individualism and materialism. This is the same primeval dilemma that man has faced from the very beginning: interest or spiritual imperative. Biology offers him progress in exchange for his soul and his human dignity. "Man refuses the progress which is at hand if he has to achieve it by means disgusting to him, but will he refuse it

---

[14]Lucien Cuenot: *"l'Eugénique," Revue d'Anthropologue*: 1935-36.

[15]Jean Rostand: *Humanly Possible: A Biologist's Notes on the Future of Mankind*, trans. Lowell Boir (New York: Saturday Review Press, 1973).

tomorrow? Will he always refuse it?"[16]

It is only natural that Christians, poets, and artists have the same attitude toward this kind of progress. For Christians it is "luciferian naturalism" and for poets a "bulk of programmed brutality."[17] It is also natural that materialists are delighted with the prospectives which new developments in biology offer.

The progress of science, no matter how great and spectacular, cannot render morality and religion unnecessary. Science does not teach people how to live, nor does it establish value standards. Those values which raise biological life to the level of human life would remain unknown and incomprehensible without religion. Religion is an initiation to the nature of another superior world, and morality is the meaning of it.

Science and Scientists or Kant's Two Critiques

There is pure reason and practical reason.

Thought denies God; man and life confirm Him. This explains the often-encountered difference between the belief of the scientist and science as a method or sum of results.

All that a scientist says, thinks, and believes is not necessarily science. Science is only a part of his complete impression of the world, a part that is a result of the critical, comparing, and classifying function of his reason. In so doing, reason rejects all that which requires a supernatural explanation, and it retains only that which is based on the chain of natural causes and consequences and which if possible, can be proved by experiment and observation. What remains after this rigorous selection is science. Thus, science always finds in its hand only nature, for everything else slips through its fingers. These are the natural limits of science.

Science usually stops at these limits, but a scientist, because he is a man, goes on. Oppenheimer did not need Indian philosophy when making the A-bomb; he possibly needed it concerning the moral problem of its use. Later in his life, he completely

---

[16]Ibid.

[17]Rémy Çollin: *Plaidoyers pour la vie humaine* (n.p., n.d.), and Voznesensky in his poem "Oza" respectively.

abandoned atomic science and devoted himself to the study of Indian philosophy. Einstein took a great interest in Dostoevski's works, especially in his novel *The Brothers Karamazov*. The novels of this great Russian writer evidently have little in common with the relations of mass and energy, the speed of light, and the like. It was not Einstein the scientist who was concerned with the moral problems of Ivan Karamazov; it was Einstein the thinker, the man, or the artist since every man is an artist to a certain extent.

There is a difference between scientific research and the use of its results. The motive of the first is to understand the world, while that of the second is to conquer it. For this reason, a scientist does not look at science with the same eyes as do other people. To the public, science is only a sum of results, mostly of the quantitative and mechanical kind. For the scientist as a doer, it is a search, an experience, an effort, a desire, a sacrifice in a word, life. Moreover, science is for him the joy of learning, a sublime feeling of the highest ethical value. In this joy, the scientist surpasses himself and becomes a thinker, a philosopher, an artist. Thus, the difference between what the scientist discovers for himself and what he discovers for the rest of the world arises spontaneously. Only when science grows detached from the scientist and his life, when it "cools" and becomes a sum of knowledges and results, does it become indifferent and, in its final result, an unreligious function. Through its innate rejection of metaphysics and its inevitable silence on "ultimate questions," science contributes to the formation of atheistic opinions — maybe not with the scientist — but certainly with the public.

The classical example of this duality, the conflict between thought and life or between nature and freedom, are two of Kant's critiques. In his second critique, Kant resurrects the religious ideas about God, immortality, and freedom which he destroyed in the first one. Kant, the logician and the scientist, speaks in the *Critique of Pure Reason*; Kant, the man and the thinker, speaks in the *Critique of Practical Reason*.[18] The first critique shows the inevitable conclusions of any reason and logic; the second shows the feelings, experiences, and hopes of every life. The first critique is the result of an objective view on reality, the result of the analysis and

---

[18]Immanuel Kant: *The Critique of Pure Reason*, trans. J. M. D. Meiklejohn (Chicago: Encyclopedia Brittanica, 1955); and idem, *The Critique of Practical Reason*, trans. Thomas Kingsmill-Abbott (Chicago: Encyclopedia Brittanica, 1955).

atomization of reality. The second critique is the fruit of the inner knowledge and certainty formed in the soul as an answer to the questions of the world observed and experienced as a whole.

These two critiques did not cancel each other. They stand side by side, grandiose as they are, confirming in their own way the universal dualism of man's world.

Morality and Religion

Morality can be based only on religion, but morality and religion are not one. Morality as a principle does not exist without religion even though morality as a practice, as a particular case of behavior, is not dependent directly on religiousness. A common argument that connects them both is the other, superior world. Because it is the other world, it is a religious world; because it is a superior world, it is a moral world. This shows both the interdependence of religion and morality as well as their independence of each other. There is a certain inner consistency that is not automatic, mathematical, or logical but rather practical; divergencies are possible but sooner or later the dependence is reestablished. Atheism, after all, ends up as a negation of morality, and every true moral transformation starts with a religious renewal. Morality is a religion transformed into rules of behavior — that is, into man's attitude toward other men in accordance with the fact of God's existence. To have to fulfill our duties regardless of the difficulties and risks we face (this being moral behavior as distinguished from behavior motivated by interest), such a demand can be justified only if this world and this life are not the only world and the only life. This is the common starting point of morality and religion.

Morality was born by prohibition and has remained a prohibition until today. A prohibition is religious by nature and by origin. Out of the Ten Commandments, eight of them are prohibitions. Morality is always a restrictive or prohibitive principle which opposes the animal instincts in human nature. The Christian ethic can serve here as an example — not as the only one but as the most famous and the most evident.

The history of religion is full of seemingly meaningless prohibitions. However, from the point of view of ethics, there are no meaningless prohibitions. Of course, a prohibition can have a rational meaning too, but utility is never its primary aim.

Morality is not "life in harmony with nature" as the Stoics defined it.[19] It is rather life against nature, provided that the word "nature" is understood in its true sense.[20] Like man, morality is also irrational, nonnatural, supernatural. Natural man and natural morality do not exist. Man within the limits of nature is not man; he is, at best, an animal endowed with reason. Morality within the limits of nature is not morality but rather a form of selfishness, a form of wise and enlightened selfishness.

In the Darwinian "struggle for survival," the best (in the moral sense) do not win; only the strongest and the best adjusted do.[21] Biological progress also does not lead to human dignity being one of the sources of morality. A Darwinian man may reach the highest degree of biological perfection, a "superman," but he will remain without human quality and, therefore, without human dignity as well. The latter could have been given to him only by God.

Social progress as a prolongation of the biological progress has the same effect on morality. The English moralist Mandeville asks: "What is the significance of morality for the progress of society and the development of civilization?" and answers very simply: "None. It may even be harmful."[22] According to him, the means that are usually blamed as sinful have the most stimulating effect on a society's progress since "what increases man's needs promotes his development the most." To be more definite: "The so-called moral and physical evils of this world are the main driving forces that make us social beings."

If all progress, biological as well as technical, is to be found in Darwin's theory of natural selection where the stronger suppresses and even destroys the weaker, morality must be in opposition to this essential point of progress. Morality has always demanded protection, compassion, and regard for the weaker and less capable. Thus, morality and nature have been in opposition with each other

---

[19]Whitney Jennings Oates, ed. *The Stoic and Epicurean Philosophers: The Complete Extant Writings of Epicurus, Epictetus, Lucretius, Marcus Aurelius* (New York: Modern Library, 1957).

[20]Somebody said that the word "nature" is used with 52 different meanings. In this discourse, the word nature means all the reality beyond the human essence, therefore man and his worldly parts: his body, instincts, intelligence, and so on.

[21]Charles Darwin: *On the Origin of Species by Means of Natural Selection or the Preservation of Favoured Races in the Struggle for Life* (London: Oxford University Press, 1925).

from the very beginning. "Get rid of the conscience, compassion, forgiveness — those inner human tyrants. Oppress the weak, climb over their corpses..."[23] The parting with morality is very evident. Destroy the weak versus protect the weak — those are the two opposite demands that separate the biological from the spiritual, the zoological from the human, nature from culture, and science from religion. Only Nietzsche consistently applied biological laws and their consequences to human society.[24] The result was the rejection of love and forgiveness and the justification of violence and hatred. For Nietzsche, Christianity, especially Christian ethics, was "the most poisoned poison that had ever been instilled into the vigorous body of the ardent mankind."

In *Phaedo*, Plato expounded a genuine ethic: ordinary courage is only a kind of cowardice, and ordinary moderation is only a hidden lust for pleasure. That kind of virtue is only a commercial business, a shadow of virtue, a virtue of slaves. A true moral man has only one desire: to be away from the physical and closer to the spiritual. The body is the grave of the soul. In its earthly existence, the soul never reaches its aim, and true knowledge comes only after death. That is why an ethical man is not afraid of death. To truly think and live means constant preparation to die. Evil is the force that rules the world, and morality is neither a natural possibility of man, nor can it be based on reason.[25]

Established ethics have never been rationally proved and, of course, they cannot be proven by this method. Plato referred to metaphysical proofs instead of anthropological ones, which made him the forerunner of theologically based ethics. This development was lawful. It is well known that Plato proponed a teaching about preexistence which stated that every item of knowledge is only a remembrance. An integral part and necessary presumption of such a teaching is the idea of immorality.[26]

Plato's meditations on ethics led him directly to the religious

---

[23]Friedrich W. Nietzsche: *Thus Spake Zarathustra: A Book for All and None*, trans. Thomas Common (London: Allen and Unwin, 1967).

[24]If Nietzsche's ideas were a philosophical continuation of Darwin, Hitler and his national-socialism were a political derivative from both doctrines.

[25]Plato: *Phaedo*, trans. R.S. Bluck (London: Routledge and Paul, 1955).

[26]The great Islamic thinker, ibn Rushd (Averroës) dealt with the same question. According to him, morality is the essense of the universal religion. See *Averroës on Plato's Republic*, trans. Ralph Lerner (Ithaca, NY: Cornell University Press, 1974).

position.[27] Two other ancient thinkers, Epictetus and Seneca, were led to a specific religion (Christianity) through similar meditations. There are very certain indications that Epictetus was a clandestine Christian, and that Seneca corresponded with Paul. In his *De viris illustribus*, Jerome includes Seneca in the list of church writers.[28]

Christianity is a striking example of a perfect harmony, a strong mutual affinity, and almost a unity of a great religion and great ethics. The art of the Renaissance, completely inspired by biblical themes, proves that great art joins them.

From a historical point of view, moral thought is one of the oldest human thoughts. It is preceded only by the idea of the divine which itself is as old as man. These two thoughts have been closely connected throughout history. In the history of ethics, there is practically no serious thinker who has not decided about religion, either by borrowing the necessity of religion for moral principles or by proving the opposite. The whole history of ethics is a continuing story of the reciprocal permeance of religious and ethical thought. Statistics cannot be proof in this matter, but it can be pointed out that religious moralists prevail, while atheists almost never do.

The so-called laic (secular) ethical movements which stressed the independence of ethics from religion[29] showed that every moralistic thought or activity naturally tends to approach or even to identify with religion. Notwithstanding the contradictory course of these ideas and their oscillation between religion and science, their development is of great importance. Schoolbooks in French state schools, where moral instruction replaced religious instruction, followed the catechism format of teaching religious doctrines in Christian churches. This trend had a permanent tendency to maintain an independent position against religion which all the while continued to approach it unconsciously.

Therefore, it is possible to imagine a truly religious but immoral man and vice versa. Religion is one kind of knowledge, and morality is a life lived in accordance with that knowledge. There remains, however, a certain discrepancy between knowledge and

---

[27]Pierre Abelard considered Plato a Christian.

[28]Saint Jerome: *Hieronymi De viris illustribus liber* (Leipzig: B. G. Teubner, 1879).

[29]These appeared in France, England, America, Germany, and Italy during the nineteenth and twentieth centuries. In the Anglo-Saxon world, they were known as Societies for Ethical Culture, Settlements, Ethical Societies, and so on.

practice. Religion is the answer to the question of how to think and believe, while morals are the answer to the question of how to desire and aim or how to live and behave. The tidings of the other world also imply a demand to live in accordance with this wide and infinite vision, although the demand itself is not identical with the vision. Jesus' sublime ethics were a direct consequence of an equally strong and clear religious consciousness. However, the inquisitors' devotions were also sincere, even though this assertion sounds paradoxical. "Believe and do good deeds" — this sentence, which is repeated in the Qur'ān more than fifty times, points out the necessity of uniting something that people tend to separate. It expresses the difference between religion ("believe") and morality ("do good") as well as the imperative that they should go together. The Qur'ān uncovers a reverse relation and shows how religion can find a strong incentive in morality: "You will not believe until you give amply of what is dear to your heart." It is not: "Believe and you will be a good man," but the reverse: "Be a good man and you will believe." To the question of how one can strengthen his faith, the answer is: "Do good and by so doing you will find God."

So-Called Common Interest and Morality

Morality has also been negated by rationalism. Rationalistic negation arises with the removal of the duality between duty and interest and reducing morals to utilitarianism or pleasure. This eliminates the independent position of morals.

This tendency has been present throughout the whole history of ethics, from Aristotle to Russell. Dietrich von Holbach, one of the first materialist writers of the West, explained this tendency in a very clear way. Having stressed a well-known motto that only interest motivates human conduct, he developed the following scheme: "Among the sensations and impressions that man receives from objects, some are pleasant and some are painful. He approves of some and wants them to last longer or to reappear again, while he disapproves of others and avoids them as much as possible. In other words, he likes certain sensations and impressions and the objects that cause them and hates other sensations and impressions and all that cause them. As man lives in society, he is surrounded by beings both similar to and as sensitive as himself. All those beings are looking for pleasure, and all of them are afraid of pain. They call 'good' all that causes them pleasure, and they call 'bad' all that causes them pain. They call 'virtue' all that is permanently useful to them, and they call 'sin' all that is harmful to them in the character of their neighbors." According to Holbach: "A conscience is the awareness of the influence which our conduct can have on the people that surround us as well as upon us, and remorse is 'the fear we feel at the thought that our conduct can make other people hate us or be angry with us.'"[30]

Jeremy Bentham, the ideologist of utilitarian morality, is equally clear and logical: "Nature has submitted mankind to the rule of two sovereigns: pain and pleasure. Only they govern our actions."[31]

According to the eighteenth-century French philosopher Helvétius, every human behavior is always directed toward the point of least resistance, and no man does anything unless he believes that he will by such activity either increase his pleasure or lessen his pain. Just as water cannot flow uphill, man cannot go against this law of his nature.

From that point of view, morality is only a refined egoism, a well-understood interest of an individual. Reason intervenes to transform a desire for pleasure into a moral demand. Man's intellect and memory enable him to see the past and the future in addition to the present. Thus, his conduct is not motivated solely by his present interest but also by the whole eudaemonistic[32] result. By calculating in such a way, he transforms his sensations of pain and pleasure — those biological, zoological, Darwinian facts — into the concepts of good and evil. Good and evil are nothing but pleasure and pain increased for an intellect, a reflection, a calculation. The morality of utility thus remains within the limits of nature and of this world. It never advances beyond the limits of interest to become morality in the authentic sense of the word.

All human experience in the field of morality contradicts the preceding materialistic opinion since people have generally defined as moral what is unpleasant to them: asceticism, celibacy, material sacrifice, fasting, different forms of renunciation and restraint, sacrifice

---

[30]Paul Henry Thirty [Dietrich von Holbach]: *The System of Nature, or Laws of the Moral and Physical World*, new ed., trans. H. D. Robinson (Boston: J. P. Mendum, 1889).

[31]Jeremy Bentham: *An Introduction to the Principles of Morals and Legislation*, ed. J. H. Bujrns and H. L. A. Hart (London: Athlone Publishing, 1970).

[32]This adjective is derived from the theory of eudaemonism which defines moral obligation by reference to personal well-being through a life governed by reason.

for principles or for the well-being of others, and so on. Utilitarian morality is contrary to civilized man's concept of morality just as it is to primitive man's. It was primitive man who invented a whole series of prohibitions, taboos, deprivations, obligations of an apparently nonutilitarian character. Thus, every useful, rational, or purposeful meaning behind these "innovations" is usually missed by civilized man.

Morality is not profitable in the common sense of the word. Can we say that the maxim "Women and children first!" is useful from the social point of view? Is it useful to do justice and to tell the truth? We can imagine numerous situations in which injustice or falsehood are profitable. For example, religious, political, racial, and national tolerance are not useful in the usual sense of the word. To destroy the adversaries is more profitable from the pure rationalistic point of view. Tolerance, if it exists, is not practiced out of interest but out of principle, out of humanity, out of that "aimlessly purposeful" reason. The protection of the old and decrepit, or the care of the handicapped or the incurable patient is not useful. Morals cannot be subjected to the standards of usefulness. The fact that moral behavior is sometimes useful does not mean that something has become moral because it has proved useful in a certain period of human experience. On the contrary, such coincidences are very rare.[33] Optimistic belief in the harmony of honesty and usefulness has proved naive and even harmful. It has a destructive effect on people, for they are continually witnessing the opposite. A truly righteous man is one who accepts sacrifice and who, when facing the inevitable temptation, will remain true to his principles rather than his interests. If virtue were profitable, all intelligent crooks would hurry to become examples of virtue.

The experiences of criminologists are instructive and bitter. According to a report from the Chicago police, more than 90 percent of all burglaries and thefts committed in 1951 have not been solved. The Kefauver questionnaire shows that American criminals snatch hundreds of millions of dollars and usually enjoy their booty undisturbed. Crime is profitable, criminologists conclude, especially to those who organize it and do not commit it themselves like the

---

[33]people have concentrated their experience in the characteristic saying: "The honest and the mad are brothers." However, it should be pointed out that popular wisdom never preaches dishonesty or corruption, although it is well aware of the nonutilitarian character of morality.

Mafia or other gangs. "It seems that the more profitable the murder, the less chance the murderer has of being arrested and punished," asserts an American criminologist. Also, what about the profitability of legal crimes such as pornography, strip shows, crime stories, and the like? The making of a porno film is ten times cheaper than a feature film, and the profit is ten times greater.[34] The most striking examples of "legal crimes" are those of great scale: aggressive wars, occupation of foreign countries, persecution of minorities, and so on. Can we say that the Spaniards did not profit from the extermination of the Mexican and Central and South American Indians, or that the white settlers didn't from the systematic extermination of the North American Indians, or that all colonial powers by exploiting and ravaging occupied countries didn't derive material benefit? We can, therefore, conclude that crime is profitable, provided there is no God.

The morality of utility can be based upon reason, at least as a theoretical model. However, with reason only — without God — it is impossible to establish the morality of unselfishness or of sacrifice, the true morality.

Aristotle's inconsistency in Nichomachus' ethics is well-known. He derives altruism from egoism because "altruism begins from one's own personality," and then he says that "... the ethical man will do a lot for his friends and his country; he will sacrifice money and property and will gladly surrender positions and honors to the others. Moreover, if necessary, he will even die for others and for his country."[35] It is evident that these attitudes are not coherent in themselves and that they do not all come from the same source. Many have noticed the contradiction. Schleihermacher reproaches Aristotle's "heap of virtues,"[36] and Jodl observes that Aristotle is evidently inconsistent when he derives even heroic conclusions from the principle of a reasonable ethical egoism "which certainly cannot be derived from this principle."[37] When Aristotle says that "... even with a heroic attitude, we do not leave the field of

---

[34]According to a 1976 questionnaire in Paris.

[35]Aristotle: *The Nicomachean Ethics*, trans. David Ross (London: Oxford University Press, 1954).

[36]Friedrich Schleiermacher: *On religion: Speeches to Its Cultured Despisers*, trans. John Oman (New York: Ungar, 1955).

[37]Friedrich Jodl: *Leben und Philosophie David Humes* (Halle: C. E. M. Pfeffer, 1872).

egoism because those who die for the sake of others choose the great and the beautiful only for themselves," he enlarges the concept of selfishness and egoism beyond its meaning in the consciousness of every man. If somebody runs into a burning house to save a neighbor's child, can wc say that he does that out of selfishness — because of himself? We can say so, but only in a particular sense, namely if the fulfilling of duty for the sake of good is the supreme interest and also the interest of the one who sacrificed himself (the hero). In such a case, the sacrifice and the interest are not in collision because it is not a question of interest in the usual sense of the word but interest in the absolute sense of the word: a moral interest. The distinction between common and moral interest (if we can accept this expression) supposes the distinction between the two worlds: the transient and the eternal. Only if there is this other supreme world can we talk about a sacrifice as an act done in one's own interest. Without this, there is a limit which cannot be exceeded: life.

We define authentic morality as a conduct which may be opposed to one's own interest. Yet, there is another phenomenon here which seems similar, although in its essence it is completely different: it is so-called "social behavior." In his social life, man does not always behave according to his social interest. His social behavior aims at fulfilling his personal needs, though on a larger social basis. Society becomes the expression of all personal interests which can now be fullfilled more effectively. This new situation creates different duties for the members of society, which remind us (because of their name) of moral demands, "duties." Activities aiming at the fulfillment of personal interests appear now as duties, as social obligations. As they can sometimes be disproportionate to personal interest (requiring inadequate sacrifice or giving) or contrary to the momentary desires and wishes of the individual members of the group, the illusion is formed that the individual acts not in his own interest but in the interest of a supreme principle. In fact, society is a specific form of fulfilling personal interests. The essence is not changed; only the form has been changed to attain the same aim. The so-called common interest is a personal interest, equally selfish and immoral. Collective action is created by means of intelligence and not by means of heart or soul that will lead, if the account is well prepared (if we provide for possible error in the account or the abuse of those who define social action) to the fulfillment of the greatest personal interest of the majority of the group or to what has been termed the "Greatest Principle."[38]

That which is provided in human life imperfectly by means of intelligence is provided in the animal kingdom perfectly by means of instincts, for example, the social behavior of ants and bees or wild animals in a pack. The examples of social conduct within some animal species prove that here we are not faced with a moral phenomenon at all. The difference is evident: social behavior is motivated by interest; moral behavior is not. Behavior in the name of selfishness is one thing; behavior in the name of duty is another. The first is based on interest, need, discipline, and reason. The latter is possible only in the name of God.

There is another point that helps to make this distinction. Moral behavior is always based on spiritual perfection and is in harmony with the ideal of good, truth, and justice.[39] On the other hand, collective behavior is based on discipline and may even be criminal, but most often it is immoral or amoral. The common interest is never the interest of mankind; it is always the interest of a limited, closed group, be it political, national, or a class one. Tolstoy spoke of "state blasphemy" or the "blasphemy of common welfare."[40] The common interest of a group or a nation may require exploitation, enslavement, and even extermination of members of another group or nation. The modern history of nations, especially the history of imperialism, is full of examples of how so-called "common interest" can have an openly criminal character.

Recent times offer a striking example of how the logic of common interest can lead to a general confusion and deceit with tragic consequences. *The Communist Manifesto* declared that proletarians renounced morality as a bourgeois fraud. The Second International revised that point to reaffirm the principle of justice and to reject the approach of the ends justifying the means. Nonetheless, Lenin returned to the position of *The Communist Manifesto* by asserting that:

---

[38]The author of this famous formula is Jeremy Bentham, a well-known English jurist, philosopher, and materialist. Also, see footnote 31 of this chapter.

[39]"A true moral action is the one which aims at man's perfection." See, Gottfried W. von Leibniz, *New Essays Concerning Human Understanding*, ed. Karl Gerhardt, vol. 5: *Die Philosophischen Schriften von G. W. Leibniz* (LaSalle, IL: Open Court Publishing Company, 1949).

[40]Leo Tolstoy: "The Christian Teaching," ed. Leo Wiener, vol. 22: *The Complete Works of Count Tolstoy* (New York: AMS Press, 1968).

"Morality is only what helps the victory of the proletariat,"[41] reestablishing in this way the criterion of the aim. By applying Lenin's rule, Stalin came to the conclusion that it was in the interest of the proletariat's victory, and therefore, it was permissible and moral, to strengthen the government and police apparatus to an extent unheard of until our time; to prevent any criticism of the government and its officials and to maintain the idea of their infallibility; to establish the cult of a leader who is infallible and omnipotent; to maintain a state of permanent fear to discourage or prevent any attempt at resistance; to organize from time to time mass purges of undesirable persons, groups, or whole nations; to corrupt by high salaries and other privileges the army, the police, the political apparatus, and the obedient part of the intelligentsia; to establish the ministerial and similar warehouses for the privileged governing caste; to monopolize all channels of information such as the press, radio, and television, and to make them talk incessantly about democracy, freedom, humanism, welfare, "bright future," leaders' and officials' virtues; to occupy foreign countries" on the grounds of their own free will," and so on. It was necessary to repeat incessantly all that is in the interest of the victory of the proletariat since it was permissible and even moral.[42]

While religious morals declare the principle of resistance to evil, a principle that can be found in an explicit or implicit form in all morals based on religion, utilitarian morality declares the opposite principle, that of reciprocity. The utilitarians clearly assert that anyone who obeys the moral norms at a time when nobody obeys them works against reason, which is the consistent conclusion from the utilitarian point of view. Moreover, this fact also shows very clearly that utilitarian morality is not a true morality and that it belongs to politics rather than to ethics. To establish reciprocity as a

---

[41]Vladimir I. Lenin: *The Proletarian Revolution and Renegade Kautsky* (New York: International Publishers, 1934).

[42]In a manual for Soviet citizens, it is stated that one's supreme duty is to be faithful to the working class. This supreme duty is also politically and not ethically determined. When an authority declares itself the representative of the interest of the working class, the next step is to claim that faithfulness to this authority is the supreme duty of every citizen. Stalin's abuses began and were performed exactly in that way. There is also the following example from more recent times: in the schoolbook of Marxist ethics for a secondary school in Hungary (published in 1978), it is said that a child (son or daughter) "should on no condition kill his mother unless she becomes a class traitor." The schoolbook raised bitter polemics and the authorities promised that it would be withdrawn.

principle in moral behavior means to relativate morality and to separate it from the very principle upon which its binding force is based.

Utilitarian morals were also called in English literature the morals of consequences. Something is moral or immoral according to the good or bad consequences it brings about. Still, as we have seen, an authentic morality does not really care about the consequences at all, to the point of completely negating deeds as the outward expression of one's behavior. Authentic morality is interested only in intentions, in motives. To desire and to work is human, and here the scope of ethics ends. The results and consequences are in God's hands.

Morality Without God

Practical moral experience offers many examples of morality in people who are indifferent to religious teachings or do not believe in God. There is often an inconsistency, a discord between nominal, declarative conviction and real behavior. There are many people who consider themselves strictly religious and even preach religion but still behave as hardened materialists. The opposite is also true: there are many doctrinaire materialists who are very honest and ready to suffer and fight for other people. From this confusion and inconsistency, a strange human comedy arises that baffles even the most clearsighted and honest thinkers.

There is no automatism[43] between our belief and our behavior. Our behavior is neither exclusively nor primarily one of our conscious choice. It is more a result of education and attitudes formed in childhood than the result of later conscious philosophical or political beliefs. If someone has learned to respect his elders, to keep his word, to judge people by their character, to love and help others, to speak the truth, to hate hypocrisy, to be a simple and proud man, then that would be the characteristic of his personality regardless of his later political opinion and formally accepted philosophy. All the same, this morality also owes to a religion: this time to a transmitted one. Education transmitted certain authentic religious views concerning the relations between man and man, but it did not transmit as well the religion from which that morality was

[43]Automatism is a theory which views the body as a machine and consciousness as a noncontrolling adjunct of the body.

derived. In this case, there is only one step between abandoning that religion and abandoning its morality. Some people never make this step, and thus they remain "split" between a religion they do not follow and that religion's morality which they continue to follow even though they no longer believe in the basis of its morality. This gave rise to the appearance of two phenomena which complicate the research: the moral atheists and the immoral believers.

The question of whether morality without God is possible will probably remain the subject of theoretical discourses as it cannot be tested in practice nor referred to by a certain historical event. No case of a completely irreligious community has ever been known throughout history, nor have we countries where generations are brought up in complete indifference or hatred toward religion to give us a sure answer to the question of whether there is morality without religion, or whether an atheistic culture and society are possible. Such societies, regardless of the walls with which they surround themselves, cannot remain beyond space and time. All the past is present here, radiating in innumerable ways; the rest of the world is also present, influencing it either intentionally or spontaneously. I dare to assert that the behaviors, laws, human relationships, and social order of a community in which the members were brought up in complete ignorance of religion would be drastically different from everything we know or encounter today both in the religious societies and in those which live under the predominant influence of atheistic ideas.[44] Many nonreligious people would probably be shocked if they knew the views or laws of a truly atheistic society or if they were suddenly faced with the image of a consistently atheistic world.[45]

There are moral atheists, but there is no moral atheism. The morality of the nonreligious man also has its source in religion, but in an earlier, forgotten religion which still influences and radiates from all surroundings, family, literature, film, architecture, and so

---

[44]This applies even to the language. By reducing human relationships to functions only, language could be reduced to a one-hundredth of the present vocabulary. This impoverishment of language can be observed already today in the so-called specialistic (or functional) languages of technical and social sciences. Impoverishment of language is also due to urbanization — that is, to the disappearance of the village, the constant source of a language's renewal and enrichment.

[45]George Orwell's cheerless visions relate, no doubt, some aspects of such a society! See, George Orwell, *Nineteen Eighty-four*, ed. Irving Howe (New York: Harcourt, Brace & World, 1963).

on. The sun has set, but the warmth that radiates in the night comes from the sun. The warmth is still felt in the room, although the fire in the hearth is out. Morality is past religion in the same way as coal is the sum of past centuries. Only by the complete destruction and elimination of the spiritual inheritance of the ages would it be possible to create the psychological conditions for the complete atheistic education of a generation. Mankind has been living for thousands of years under the influence of religion. Religion has pervaded all aspects of life: morality, laws, beliefs, and even language. It is therefore appropriate to ask whether it is possible today to "produce" a pure atheistic generation. The attempt would have to be made in complete isolation. The people of such a generation would have to be kept away from the Bible, the Qur'ān, and all other religious texts. They could not be allowed to see a single work of art, to hear a single symphony, to see any drama from Sophocles to Beckett. All the famous architectural works that man has ever built and all the literary works that he has ever written would have to be hidden from sight. These people would have to grow up in complete ignorance of everything we call the fruits and expressions of human culture. Because of man's natural inclination toward religion, even one of Hamlet's monologues about death, a glance at Michelangelo's frescoes, or the knowledge of the legal principle *nullem crimen...* could bring before them the vision of another universe completely different from the atheistic one. This, however, is not the case with science. There is no danger in future atheists acquiring all mathematical and technical knowledge or studying some revised and simplified sociology or political economy. The Chinese Cultural Revolution of the 1960s is too recent an event to judge its true aims and consequences. Nevertheless, it is beyond doubt that one of its aims was the elimination of China's spiritual inheritance which was seen as being quite contrary to the official Maoist philosophy and ideology.[46] The very idea of the Cultural Revolution, as distinguished from the political or social one, shows that the problem has been spotted, namely that it is not possible to form a consistent atheistic system while all cultural traditions radiate a quiet and unobtrusive religion. Something similar can be said about Marx, too. It is not quite certain which spiritual or intellectual sources inspired him, but the influence of humanistic education

---

[46]The Cultural Revolution prohibited, among others, the works of Tolstoy, Shakespeare, and Beethoven, which is only logical.

and literature is evident in his early works.[47] His theory of alienation is almost entirely a moral, humanistic theory and therefore quite unexpected from a materialist philosopher. It seems that Marx himself, as the years passed, became aware of his youthful delusions. There is a clear difference between, as the critics term it, "the early" and "the mature" Marx. This inner process of maturation is in fact a shedding of the idealistic heritage (which is basically religious and moral) and an increasing acceptance of the consistent materialistic outlook.

The present generation, nominally nonreligious or even atheistic, did not grow up in ignorance of religion but rather in opposition to it. Not having accepted Jesus' principles of love, brotherhood, and equality in the name of God, it could not reject them either. In a kind of strange delusion, it retained them in the name of science. Therefore, we have no right to take the present generation and its world as a proof that an atheistic culture is possible. In fact, the present generation and its culture are growing up imperceptibly and constantly influenced by religion and its great ethical principles. Strictly taken, the new generation has only a new ideology; the education and moral standards are old. The builders are old, only the design is new. In living practice, every system resembles the people who carry it out more than the ideas and declarations to which it refers. If the essence of man is his morality (and not his ideology or political choice), we can say that the present world has been created by earlier people with new ideas. Those people introduce idealism and sacrifice into the realization of the ideas which expressly deny idealism and sacrifice. The use of a "moral stimulative" (instead of a material one) for work compensation in Communist China and the Soviet Union is considered by some people as the exploitation of the deeply hidden religious feelings of the masses. What does it mean, from the point of view of atheism, to reject material stimulatives and accept moral ones? It is natural to attain religious aims out of idealism and materialistic ones out of interest. All else is inconsistent.

---

[47]Marx himself said that Aeschylus, Shakespeare, and Goethe were his favorite writers. Every year, he read Aeschylus in Greek again. He often recited Homer and Ovid. Rousseau's influences (for example his ideas about the origin of social inequality and property) are very recognizable in Marx's early works. See, Jean Jacques Rousseau, *On the Origin of Inequality. On Political Economy. The Social Contract.*, trans. G. D. H. Cole (Chicago: Encyclopedia Britannica, 1955).

The question of whether there is morality without religion can be posed in the same sense as the question of whether a man, in the name of man, can be required to do what his religion demands from him in the name of God. When attempting to establish ethics, materialists gladly refer to this formula, although it is an obvious example of inconsistency or forgetfulness. They suggest man's conscience, instead of his fear of God, as one motive behind man's righteous behavior. An atheistic philosopher, in line with this formula, once presented the following thought: "I would dare to assert that just atheism means the elevation of man and human morality. If I, as a free human being, hear an inner imperative voice, without anybody's command, which tells me not to steal or not to kill, if I feel it in myself, if I do not derive it from any kind of absolute, the social or the divine, then that is not a degradation of man. ... That means on the basis of insight into my own consciousness and conscience."[48]

After all that, we cannot but ask ourselves who has mistaken the concepts. Are conscience and consciousness parts of the real world? Is not belief in man instead of God only a lower form of religion? The materialists' references to man instead of to God sounds even stranger, as it was Marx himself who correctly asserted that hope in the abstract humanity of man was no less an illusion than the pure religious illusion. This would be concomitant with the formula "If there is no God, there is no man either." Lenin's assertion that scientific socialism has no relation to morality and the statement of the *Communist Manifesto* that workers reject morality are well-known facts. It is alleged that Communism arises out of a necessity of historical development and not out of moral or human reasons. The classical Marxist works, as distinguished from present Marxist writings for everyday use, clearly state that the law of exploitation has the capacity of natural law in human relations and that every man will exploit another as long as he can — that is, until he is stopped by force. Here, there is no room for the conscience's "inner voice," tolerance, natural humanism, and the like. Exploitation will exist until it is eliminated as a result of changes in objective relations. It depends neither on the will of people nor on their moral or similar subjective qualities (education, character, opinion, and so on), nor on their mutual relations (national, familial, or

---

[48]Professor Vuko Pavicevic at The Belgrade Dialogue of Atheists and Theologists held during May 1971.

others). When Marx offers in *Das Kapital* examples of child exploitation "on the part of their hungry mothers," he obviously wants to draw our attention to the absolute effect of the law of exploitation on human society.[49] That is why it is strange that some Marxists today try to establish so-called ethics by referring to man and abstract humanity.[50] Marx always stressed that references to man, humanism, consciousness, and the like constituted idealism going along with religion. We can agree with Marx on that, but the present Marxists cannot agree with him for practical reasons. From the British Library, Marx could say that morality did not exist, but people who try to realize Marx's ideas and establish a society cannot declare that with the same ease. To establish a society and to maintain it, they have to ask the people for more idealism and self-sacrifice than any prophet ever asked in the name of religion. This is why they sometimes have to forget some very clear materialistic postulates. Therefore, the real question is not whether an atheist (materialist) may preach morality or humanity; the point is whether he can do that and remain what he is — that is, within the limits of materialism.

The well-known controversy connected to Epicurus' philosophy shows that peace between materialism and ethics cannot be maintained for long. This famous Greek philosopher (342-270 B.C.), although a materialist when explaining the world, retained a specific attitude toward ethics. He taught that happiness was to be found in pleasure, but he advised enjoyment in *ataraxia* (the calmness of the mind), and he himself appreciated spiritual joys more than sensual ones. His disciples removed that inconsistency and made his ethics eudaemonistic. Epicureanism is today a synonym for sensual pleasure as the ideal life. There is a logical connection or an inner conformity between eudaemonism and Epicurean materialistic teaching, according to which the universe and all the variety of phenomena in it are only a product of the mechanical moving of material particles

---

[49]Karl Marx: *Capital* (Moscow: Progress Publishers, 1965).

[50]Engels too has no better opinion of ethics "on the basis of insight into one's own consciousness and conscience." He wrote: "In fact, every class and even every profession has its own morality, and they break it whenever they can do so and go unpunished. The love which should unite everything manifests itself in wars, conflicts, family quarrels, divorces, and in the greatest possible exploitation of people on the part of other people." See, Friedrich Engels, *Ludwig Feuerbach and the Outcome of Classical German Philosophy*, ed. C. P. Dutt (New York: International Publishers, 1941).

in empty space. That conformity does not exist between Epicurus' materialistic teaching and his *ataraxia* or priority of spiritual values. The accusation that "Epicurus' disciples distorted the teaching of their teacher" has no grounds. They only brought them into concord. Materialism had to deny ethics in the end.

So, we have come to two conclusions. First, morality as a principle does not exist without religion, whereas practical morality does. However, practical morality exists by inertia and is very weak, being further from the source that gives it its initial force. Second, moral order cannot be based on atheism. Atheism, however, does not abolish morality, at least not in its lower form: social discipline. Besides, if atheism is put into practice when trying to form a society, it will even be interested in maintaining the existing forms of social morality. The socialist practice of our century confirms these facts. Atheism, however, has no means to preserve or to protect the very principle of morality once this principle is called into question. Atheism is quite helpless against the rush of purely utilitarian, selfish, and immoral or amoral claims. What can be done against this crippling logic? If I live only today and have to die tomorrow and be forgotten, why should I not live as I like and without obligations, if I can? The wave of pornography and the "new morality" of sexual freedom is stopped at the frontier of socialist countries only by force and by censor — that is, artificially. No moral order approves of that wave of the immoral kind, and even if certain arguments are heard in favor of it, they are an example of inconsistency and can endure only due to the lack of open and free criticism. In fact, only inherited old moral norms still exist in the consciousness of people, or the state maintains them out of necessity. Still, strictly speaking, this inherited moral order is in contradiction with the official ideology, and there is no room for it in the system.

Having taken the liberty to simplify the matter, we can conclude that morality is nothing but another "state of aggregation" or religion.

Chapter 5

CULTURE AND HISTORY

Culture has no development and man is a constant of world history.

CULTURE AND HISTORY

Initial Humanism

Both rationalists and materialists are characterized by a certain linear understanding of history. According to them, the development of the world starts from zero while history, regardless of some zigzag movements and temporary regressions, displays a continuous forward movement. The present is always something more than the past and something less than the future.

We can understand such an attitude if we recall that for the materialists, history is the material development of human life. They deal with the history of things or of society, not with the history of man himself. This is not the history of human culture but the history of civilization.

The history of man and culture does not start from zero, nor does it flow in a straight, ascending line. After its first emancipation from nature, human society was hardly above the herd found among animals. However, at the same time, it displayed certain specific human features and ethical values which puzzle us. Man entered history with a tremendous initial moral capital which he had not inherited from his alleged animal ancestors. Science has found and acknowledged but has never explained the nature of the authentic and simple humanity of human communities from those times when human and zoological societies were still adjacent. Rejecting a priori the religious assumptions, science has hindered the understanding of this phenomenon.[1]

Describing old gentes (clans) which apparently were cells of prehistoric societies all over the world, Lewis Morgan quotes the following characteristics of these communities' social and moral life:

— A clan chooses a chief and dethrones him. A dethroned chief becomes a common warrior again, thus becoming like the other men.
— Conjugal relations and sexual intercourse are forbidden within a clan. This prohibition is adhered to consciously and is almost never broken.
— Mutual help and protection among the members of a clan is so strong that they sometimes go to the level of self-sacrifice.
— Bravery of warriors and chivalrous treatment of captives (the prisoners of war are not killed).
— All members of a clan are free, equal, and bound by relations of brotherhood.
— Accepting new members into the clan by a religious ceremony. Religious rites are mostly in the form of dances and plays. Idols are unknown.
— A gens council consists of representatives of the clans (sachems). The council decides matters of common interest in public, in the presence of the clan members. The decisions are adopted unanimously.[2]

Delighted by such a description, Engels exclaims: "And a wonderful constitution it is, this gentile constitution, in all its childlike simplicity! No soldiers; no gendarmes or police; no nobles, kings, regents, prefects, or judges; no prisons; no lawsuits; everything takes its orderly course. All quarrels and disputes are settled by the whole of the community affected, by the gens of the tribe, or by the gentes among themselves. ... There cannot be any poor or needy — the communal household and the gens know their responsibilities

---

[1]The vague memory of that period of initial humanism is reflected in the legends and fairy tales of almost all nations as a classical myth of the Golden Age of the Patriarchs in the Bible. "The common belief that the past had been bad appeared only with the theory of evolution," asserts Bertrand Russell in his *History of Western Philosophy and Its Connection with Political and Social Circumstances from the Earliest Times to the Present Day* (New York: Simon and Schuster, 1945).

[2]Lewis H. Morgan: *Ancient Society* (Chicago: C. H. Kerr, 1907). His description refers to the gens (clan) of the Iroquois in North America, which is considered to be a classical paragon of the first gentes.

toward the old, the sick, and those disabled in war. All are equal and free — the women included. There is no place yet for slaves, nor, as a rule, for the subjugation of other tribes. ... And what men and women such a society breeds is proved by the admiration inspired in all white people who have come into contact with unspoiled Indians, by the personal dignity, uprightness, strength of character, and courage of these barbarians."[3]

The situation described in Morgan's book was depicted in the novels of one of his countrymen, J. Fenimore Cooper, through vivid and impressive pictures.[4] There is no doubt that Ralph Waldo Emerson also had in mind the American Indians when he wrote: "I have seen human nature in all its aspects. It is the same everywhere, only the more wild it is, the more virtue is in it."[5]

The social idea for Tolstoy was the state that he found in the life of uncorrupted primitive Russian peasants.[6] Here, and everywhere else, the moral and human values went along with a very low level of material and social development.

In the *General History of Africa*,[7] we come across very impressive facts about the culture of primitive African peoples. It is known, for example, that in the old African kingdoms, all foreigners — whether white or colored — enjoyed hospitality and had the same rights as the native people. At the same time, a foreigner in ancient Rome or Greece usually became a slave. Such and similar facts have probably made Leo Frobenius, a well-known German ethnologist and a great connoisseur of Africa, write: "The Africans are civilized up to their bones, and the idea of their being barbarians is a European fiction."[8]

We have to ask here about the nature of the similar values found

---

[3]Friedrich Engels: *The Origin of the Family, Private Property, and the State* (New York: International Publishers, 1972), p. 86.

[4]James Fenimore Cooper: *The Complete Works of James Fenimore Cooper* (New York: G. P. Putnam's Sons, 1893).

[5]Ralph Waldo Emerson: *The Conduct of Life, Nature, and Other Essays* (London: J. M. Dent, & Co., 1908).

[6]Leo Tolstoy: "My Confession," *The Complete Works of Count Tolstoy*, trans. Leo Wiener, vol. 13 (New York: AMS Press, 1968), p. 81.

[7]Edited by UNESCO (2 volumes out of 8 already published).

[8]It is easy, of course, to understand that Frobenius used here the term "civilized" when he was talking about being "cultured." See, Leo Frobenius, *The Childhood of Man*, trans. A. H. Keane (New York: Meridian Books, 1960).

among the American Indians, or native tribes in Africa or Tahiti, or primitive Russian peasants, and even among the lowest social orders in India. What is their origin? Why do they appear at the very beginning of history and why do they "quantitatively" decrease with historic development? The Iroquois idea of protecting the old and invalid — where does it come from? Is it of animal origin? The various forms of "care" which we find with some animals are always based on utility — there is no humanity there.

Morgan ends his well-known book with the words: "Democracy in government, brotherhood in society, equality and general education will bring forth a higher level of society to which experience, mind, and science have always aspired. That will be the renewal — but in a much higher level — of the freedom, brotherhood, and equality of the old gentes."[9]

According to Morgan, freedom, equality, and brotherhood of future civilized societies are to be brought about by three forces: experience, mind, and science. At this moment, at least two things are certain: (a) the freedom, equality, and brotherhood of primitive communities did not result from experience, mind, and science, and (b) the period of experience, mind, and science that followed Morgan's book (first published in 1877) has by no means confirmed his predictions.

History is being written by the civilized peoples and not by the "barbarians," and to this fact we should probably attribute the widespread prejudice that in barbarianism and civilization we see not only the extreme poles of social and technical development but also the opposites of good and evil. If somebody destroys a culture or performs genocide, we may call it a barbaric deed. On the other hand, if we ask for tolerance and humanity, we request the other side to behave "as a civilized nation." It is strange that these prejudices stubbornly live on in spite of so many facts that deny them completely. The history of the American continent alone could allow us to draw the opposite conclusion. Did not the civilized Spaniards (conquistador) destroy in a most disgraceful and unheard-of way not only the culture of the Mayans and the Aztecs but also the very peoples of the region? Did not the white settlers (should we say from the civilized countries?) systematically destroy the native Indian tribes and the gentes which Morgan wrote about, in a way

---

[9]Morgan: *Ancient Society*.

unprecedented in modern history? Even in the first half of the nineteenth century, the American government paid a certain amount of money for each Indian scalp. During three hundred years, the shameful Atlantic trade of black slaves went on, together with the development of Euro-American civilization as its constituent part, ending not earlier than 1865. During that period, about 13 to 15 million free people (the exact number will never be known) were captured in a literal man hunt. Here again, civilized atrocity was faced with free and tame primitive man.

In this context, we could also mention modern imperialism, meaning the encounter between European civilization and the so-called underdeveloped, uncivilized or less civilized people, but which has really manifested itself everywhere as violence, fraud, hypocrisy, enslavement, and the destruction of the material, cultural, and moral values of weaker, primitive peoples.

Our prejudice concerning the Middle Ages is mainly of the same kind. Were the Middle Ages really the age of darkness and general unhappiness? This is a question or point of view. By civilization's standards, it certainly was. For Helvétius, one of the first materialistic philosophers in Europe, the Middle Ages was the time in which "people were turned into animals" and the time whose laws were "a masterpiece of absurdity."[10] It goes without saying that Nikolai Berdgaev, a Christian philosopher, and Jean Arp, a painter, had completely different opinions of the same period.[11] We usually have a simplified and one-sided image of the Middle Ages. Although poverty and the lack of comfort and hygiene were everywhere, the medieval societies had, nevertheless, much more inner compactness. That was the age of an intense inner spiritual life, without which we could not understand the powers and aspirations of Western man. The Middle Ages created grandiose works of art and realized a synthesis of a great philosophy — the Greek one — and a great religion — Christianity. The Gothic style, "one of the most important human creations,"[12] is the product of the Middle

---

[10]Claude Adrien Helvétius: *De l'homme.*

[11]The painter states: "I am against mechanized things and chemical formulas. I like the Middle Ages, its tapestries and sculptures." See, Jean Arp, *Arp on Arp: Poems, Essays, Memories,* ed. Marcel Jean, trans. Joachim Neugroschel (New York: Viking Press, 1972). For the philosopher, see Nikolai A. Berdyaev, "Man and Machine," *The Bourgeois Mind and Other Essays* (Freeport, NY: Books for Libraries Press, 1966).

[12]Kenneth Clark: *Civilization: A Personal View* (New York: Harper & Row, 1970).

Ages. This age, without scientific and technical progress, had created something which Alfred North Whitehead called "qualitative progress."[13] If there is something Faustian in Western man, it was created and prepared in the great spiritual and political clashes of the Middle Ages. Without the Middle Ages, there would be no Modern Age, at least not in the form that we know it.[14]

Art and Science

Culture is in a way outside of time, outside of history. It has its rises and falls, but it has neither development nor history in the ordinary meaning of the term. In art, there is no accumulation of "knowledge" or experience as there is in science.[15] From Paleolithic times up to now, we cannot perceive any increase of the expressive power in art encompassed by development.

Civilization, however, has its Stone Age and its Atomic Age. There is no similar development in culture. From civilization's point of view, the Neolithic Age is progress; from art's point of view, it is regression. Paleolithic art, although several thousand years older, is both more impressive and more authentic than Neolithic art. Poetry has everywhere preceded prose. People sang before they narrated. Poetry needed neither experience nor model. We will see further that a similar independence of time can be found in the main moral and religious ideas. There is evidence that each religion, at its beginning, was pure and simple, and that only later on it underwent deterioration in practice (the "Theory of Premonotheism" as advanced by authors such as Lang, Schmidt, Preus, Coppers, and so on).[16] We come to the conclusion that the history of culture would be a conceptual contradiction and that only

---

[13]Whitehead: *The Future of Religion* (n.p., n.d.).

[14]Here we think, of course, of the Middle Ages in Europe. The Middle Ages, in this sense, did not exist in large areas of the world, from Muslim India to Muslim Spain for example, where Islamic civilization was at that time flourishing.

[15]In science, everything is different. Science is based on continuity, or if it is not provided by means of memory or writing, there is no science and no civilization. Progress consists of the ability to remember and to continue.

[16]See Andrew Lang: *The Making of Religion* (New York: AMS Press, 1968); Wilhelm Schmidt: *The Origin and Growth of Religion: Facts and Theories*, trans. H. J. Rose (New York: Cooper Square Publishers, 1972); and James S. N. Preus: *From Shadow to Promise: Old Testament Interpretation from Augustine to the Young Luther* (Cambridge: Belknap Press of Harvard University Press, 1969).

the chronology of cultural occurrences can be written.

Jacques Risler says: "As soon as they were discovered, and that was not long ago, the Egyptian reliefs and sculptures 4,000 to 5,000 years old, were acknowledged to be of true value. Many contemporary artists find inspiration for their work in the old reliefs engraved in tomb walls and in the tender figures of clay, marble, gold, or alabaster. This art is sometimes tender and refined (time of Thotmose II and Thotmose III), sometimes monumental and powerful (time of Cheops) and sometimes realistic and less symbolic (time of Akhenaten)."[17]

Civizationally, at the time of its discovery, America was 5,000 to 6,000 years behind the Old World. It had not even reached its Iron Age.[18] However, this measurement of time obviously cannot be applied to American art. In Bonampak, the temple which houses the oldest paintings of the American continent, we come across frescoes of outstanding beauty. A big exhibition of Mayan sculpture, held in Paris in 1966, provided a good illustration of a wealthy culture which did not have "time" to become a civilization. One visitor to this exhibition made the following comment:

> This serious refined art, whose span of expression goes from admirable simplicity to a highly baroque ornamental style, has remained a mystery up to these days. Nobody has managed to explain how it sprung up, somewhere around the fourth century, in the forests of Peten and Chiapas, already perfected, with its architecturally imposing centers for religious rites, its temples on pyramids, its ornamental sculpture, its hieroglyphic writing. The Paris exhibition of Mayan sculptures is comprised of some beautiful examples: there are bas-reliefs and statuettes of hard stone and masks of artificial marble which display the whiteness of apparition and which seem to want to give us the message of the old by-gone centuries. ... We could notice two almost completely opposite trends in the sculpture of the Mayas: the one in which bas-reliefs and stelae were made, and the other one in which heads dominate. In the first case, this is a ceremonial art

---

[17]Jacques Risler: *La civilisation arabe* (n.p., n.d.).
[18]H. G. Wells: *Short History of the World*, Rev. ed. (New York: Pelican Books, 1946).

> based on a whole set of conventions. ... This ceremonial art is in sharp contrast to the utmost simplicity of heads, especially those made of artificial marble. Such a mask, painful and calm at the same time, surpasses realism to a great extent; however, it seems to be a portrait. Two other heads with more expressionistic elements, made in a baroque style of 'grotesques,' brings a lively note to this unique collection of beauty.[19]

To Nietzsche, the Hellenistic drama — tragedy — represents the highest achievement in art, and human culture in its highest form can be understood only in what we call Hellenistic culture.[20] "None of the modern poets has reached the greatness of Homer or of the classical Greek tragedists."[21] The riddle is complete: in the dawn of human civilization, art achieves its climax. For Hegel, ancient Greece was the "golden age of philosophy,"[22] and Roger Caillos writes: "As to philosophy, I often come to the conclusion, as many others have done, that after Plato it did not make any progress whatsoever. The reason may lie in the fact that it is in the nature of art not to continue: it seems that it always starts anew."[23] Cicero's ethical writings, for example *De finibus bonorum et malorum* or *De amicitia*, are presently relevant, while his works on labor organization or state systems — topics typical for civilization — are a

---

[19]From a review of the above-mentioned exhibition in Paris, published in the *Nouvel Observateur*.

[20]See the first work in Friedrich Wilhem Nietzsche, *The Birth of Tragedy from the Spirit of Music and the Genealogy of Morals: An Attack*, trans. Francis Golffing (Garden City, NY: Doubleday, 1956). A similar statement is given by Marx, for to him the pieces of anciet art represent "unreachable norms and models." Overwhelmed with his delight, Marx seems not to understand the real meaning of his statement. Is not culture a reflection of civilization and its superstructure? If so, how can we talk about "unreachable models" already existing in the slave-holder society?

[21]André Maurois: *The Art of Writing*, trans. Gerard Hopkins (New York: Dutton, 1960).

[22]Georg W. F. Hegel: *Lectures on the History of Philosophy*, trans. E. D. Haldane and Frances H. Simson (New York: Humanities Press, 1963).

[23]Roger Caillois and Gustave Edmond Von Grunebaum, *The Dream and Human Societies* (Berkeley: University of California Press, 1966). This publication was based on the proceedings of the International Colloquium on "Le reve et les société humaines," sponsored and organized by the Near Eastern Center, University of California and held at the Cercle Culturel de Royaumond, Abbaye de Royaumond, Arnières-sur-Oise, June 17 to June 23, 1962).

complete anachronism.[24] The book of an unknown Roman writer, *De rebus bellicis*, which contained some interesting drawings of military equipment, is only of historical value, but we cannot say the same for Seneca's *On Happiness*, or for Virgil's verses. The harp, or a direct forerunner of this instrument, dates from the third millenium B.C. *Manyōshū*, an anthology of Japanese poems from the seventh and eighth centuries, which contains 1,000 poems (mostly lyrical), is considered even today as one of the masterpieces of world poetry.[25] Already in the tenth century (the starting or the "lowest point" of the night), art reached perfection and created works of unsurpassed beauty and harmony. "These huge hills of stone emerged in the middle of a group of small houses."[26] The tragedies of Sophocles and Aeschylus can be situated in any time, only the costumes must be changed. Euripides wrote *The Trojan Women*. Sartre wrote a play of the same name. So, in art, two artists separated by twenty centuries can be coauthors of the same work; we write: *The Trojan Women* by Euripides/Sartre.[27] That is not possible in science. What remains of Aristotle's physics, of Ptolemy's astronomy, or of Galen's medicine? Talking about two of Aristotle's books in the field of science, *Physics* and *On the Heavens*, Russell says that in light of modern science, not one sentence written in either of these books is valid today.[28] In the book *On the Heavens*, for example, Aristotle explains that the things which are below the moon are subject to coming into life and decaying, while everything that is above the moon is unborn and indestructable. Or,

---

[24]Marcus Tullius Cicero: *De finibus bonorum et malorum*, trans. H. Rackham (London: W. Heinemann, 1914) and idem, *De senectute, de amicitia, de divinatione*, trans. William Armistead Falconer (London: W. Heinemann, 1964).

[25]*The Manyōshū: The Nippon Gakujutsu Shinkokai Translation of One Thousand Poems with the Texts in Romaji*, ed. Donald Keene (London: Columbia University Press, 1965).

[26]"For historians, the tenth century is as dark and barbaric as the sixth century. The reason is that they consider it from the point of view of political history and the written word. If we read what Puskin called the "Book of Art," we shall get a quite different impression because, contrary to all expectations, the tenth century created works which were equally as brilliant and technically succcessful, even equally as beautiful, as any other century. ... The number of pieces of art is surprising." Kenneth Clark, *civilization*, p. 34.

[27]*The Trojan Women Adapted by Jean-Paul Sartre*, trans. Ronald Duncan (New York: Knopf, 1967).

[28]Bertrand Russell: *A History of Western Philosophy and Its Connection with Political and Social Circumstances from the Earliest Times to the Present Day* (New York: Simon and Schuster, 1945).

for example, Aristotle's explanation of gravity namely that everything has its "natural position" and a "borrowed position." When a stone falls, it tends to take the natural position of a stone — the earth's surface.[29] How does this theory stand compared with Newton's?

Art flows from the undeveloped toward the developed part of the world. It goes from the East toward the West, or from the South toward the North. Science follows the opposite direction. Things move from the direction of higher charge toward that of the lower one. Eastern music, Hindu folk music, African dances and songs, the art of Oceania penetrate the West.[30]

The art of Oceania, a region which is considered to be one of the most underdeveloped in the world, has found its place in the galleries of Europe and America along with similar pieces of art from the so-called cultural regions of the world.

Western civilization is quite "unprotected" against the epidemic of this original art. The discovery of African art has strongly affected the development of modern European and American art and can be considered to be, to some extent, a source of the revolutionary art movement in the West. At the same time, a serious comparison between European and, for example, African science, economy, technology, or social organization is almost irrelevant. Elie Faure says that an African mask from the Ivory Coast and a fresco on the ceiling of the Sistine Chapel provoke the same "sensory" excitement.[31] The International Festival of African Art, held in Dakar in 1966, and in which groups and ensembles from 39 countries attended was a first-class event in the field of culture. At the same time, an industrial and trade fair from the countries of the

---

[29]Aristotle: *On the Heavens*, trans. W. K. C. Guthrie (London: W. Heinemann, n.d.).

[30]The same is indicated in the following excerpt from a travelogue through Africa: "The best-known art galleries in the world have started lately to consider as remarkable exhibits the imaginative compositions carved in ebony which are spontaneously made by both young and old people from the Makonde tribe who live under the cane roofs of their modest houses along the roads around Dar es-Salaam. ... With unprecedented ingenuity, these artists depict in their figures of ebony the fight between good and evil, close connection between birth and death, joy and sorrow, conflict and harmony. ... Other people from Tanzania respect them very much both for their art and for a deeply rooted belief that people from the Makonde tribe possess the terrible craft and power of ancient sorcerers."

[31]Elie Faure: *History of Art*, trans. Walter Pach, vol. 5: *The Spirit of the Forms* (London: Harper & Brothers, 1930).

African continent would not even have been noticed. If Africa is underdeveloped from the point of view of science and technology, it is by no means so in the field of art because art does not know "developed" or "underdeveloped." Black Africa is a true superpower in the field of folk music, art, and dance.

The inland jungles of Irian-Jaya are probably the best preserved natural museums of prehistoric human culture. Civilization here did not advance beyond the Stone Age, but what about culture? The answer to that question is given by a missionary who spent more than 20 years there: "The feeling for beauty is strongly developed among these primitive people and their artistic works are of outstanding quality. There are some books on that subject, but they are far from comprising all the variance and richness of ideas and forms. There are marvelous sculptures in stone and wood, paintings, engravings, and statuettes of exceptional beauty. Their complicated choreographed dances in fantastic costumes represent incredible spectacles."

Scientists belong to their time only; poets belong to all times.

Ethics and History

Culture is a static topic of why we live; civilization is a continuous progress of how we live. One is the question of the meaning of life, the other is the issue of the way of it. Civilization can be shown by an ever-ascending line starting from the discovery of fire, through water mill, iron, writing, and engine to atomic energy and cosmic travel. Culture, however, is all in the search, going back, starting anew. Man as a subject of culture, with his typical faults and virtues, doubts and blunders, with everything that makes his inner human being, proves his outstanding permanence and, we could say, almost unchangeability.

All the dilemmas and questions of today were known in ethics more than 2,000 years ago. All the great teachers of mankind whether prophets such as Moses, Jesus, and Muhammad or non-prophets such as Confucius, Gautama Buddha, Socrates, Kant, Tolstoy, and Martin Buber, covering a period from the sixth century B.C. up to the present (Martin Buber died in 1965) have taught *essentially* the same morals. As distinguished from rules about social orders and ways of production, moral truths are constant.[32] The reason for this lies in the fact that the riddle had been established at the moment of creation in the "prologue in heaven," in the act preceding the whole of human history. Intelligence, education, and experience do not in themselves help us to approach or better understand all of that. Jesus pronounced his truth when he was a child and was slightly more than thirty when he was condemned. He needed neither knowledge nor experience for his great, capital truths about God and man because these truths could not be reached by knowledge or experience. Are they not "hidden from the wise and the learned and revealed to the little?"[33]

Essential moral commandments are not influenced by time, place, or social circumstances. Contrary to great differences in various social and political systems' degrees of development, even in their beliefs and religious symbols, we come across an amazing conformity of moral principles all over the world.[34] Epictetus and Marcus Aurelius, one a slave and the other a king, preached the same moral teachings and in almost the same words.[35] The differences in understanding of good and evil, the permitted and the forbidden, we find only in less important questions. The examples usually offered to show the dependence of moral standards on historical and other circumstances never concern the major moral principles but only the things related to formal morals or behavior. In the most important questions, however, we can find remarkable concordance and even identity.[36]

---

[32]In the "real" world, everything is contrary: "Change is the law of economic life." John Kenneth Galbraith, *The New Industrial State* (Boston: Houghton-Miffin, 1967).

[33]Luke: 10:21.

[34]"Although people talk differently about what God is, they nevertheless always equally understand what God asks from them," Leo Tolstoy, "Thoughts on God," *The Complete Works of Count Tolstoy*, trans. leo Wiener, vol. 16 (New York: AMS Press, 1968).

[35]Marcus Antoninus Aurelius: *Meditations*, trans. A. S. L. Farquharson (London: Dent, 1967); and Titus Lucretius Carus, *The Discourses of Epictetus*, trans. George Long (Chicago: Encyclopaedia Britannica, 1955).

[36]Some of these principles are: speak the truth; suppress hatred; be simple and modest; look at other people as your equals; aspire to freedom; defend your rights and the rights of others; earn your own bread; respect other people's works; respect parents and elders; fulfill your promises and obligations; protect the weak; be friends with people; do not enjoy the unhappiness and failure of others; do not envy other people's happiness and success; do not be conceited and do not behave arrogantly; be patient in pain; do not flatter the powerful; do not oppres the weak; do not respect people for the color of their skin, their property, or their origin; have yuour own opinion; be moderate in pleasures; do not be selfish; and so on. Do these principles vary "according to the circumstances of the economic system"?

This assertion can be well verified by Kant's famous "Categoric Imperative." This principle, which can also be found among ancient thinkers, was first defined by Kant in his *Foundations of the Metaphysics of Morals* in the following way: "Work only according to the principle which you may want to become a general law," and then later on, in the *Critique of Pure Reason*: "Work in such a way that the principle of your will can serve at any time as a principle of general legislation."[37] Thales, one of ancient Greece's "Seven Sages" (born 624 B.C.) when asked how to live a most righteous life, answered: "When we do not what we rebuke other people for."[38] Pittacus of Mytilene, another of the "Seven Sages," expressed the same principle in the following words: "Do not do what you scold others for,"[39] and ancient Rome's Cicero said: "Everything you criticize in others, you should avoid doing yourself."[40] The Jewish thinker Hillel, who lived in Palestine at about the same time as Jesus, when asked by a polytheist to explain in short the essence of religion, answered: "What you do not want to be done to you, do not do to your neighbors. The whole Torah relates to that, everything else is just commentary."[41] The same wisdom was taught in China by Confucius, the contemporary of Buddha and Pythagoras: "What I do not want to do myself, I do not do to others."[42] The principle was expressed by Jesus in his famous words: "Do unto others as you would have them do unto you."[43]

This short history of the "Categoric Imperative" proves that this major moral principle has no history at all. There are variations in form, but the essence is the same.

Artist and Experience

There is no evolution in the life of art, nor is there any

---

[37]Immanuel Kant: *Foundations of the Metaphysics of Morals*, trans. Lewis White Beck (Indianapolis: Bobbs-Merrill, 1969); and idem, *The Critique of Pure Reason*, trans. J. M. D. Meiklejohn (Chicago: Encyclopaedia Britannica, 1955).
[38]Diogenes Laertius: *Lives of Eminent Philosophers*, trans. R. D. Hicks (London: W. heinemann, 1959), I. 36.
[39]Ibid.
[40]Cicero: *De finibus bonorum et malorum*.
[41]"Part Sabbath," *The Babylonian and Jerusalem Talmud*, trans. A. Ehrman (Jerusalem: El'Am, 1965).
[42]Lun-yu: *Thoughts and Talks of Confucius* (n.p., n.d.).
[43]Matthew: 7:2 and Luke: 6:31.

evolution in the life of an artist. Each artist starts fresh, as if no man had ever created anything before him. He simply uses no one's experience but his own. Other people's experiences — the accumulation of experience — all that is a condition or a presumption of science. Other people's experiences used in art, however, means imitation, repetition, academism — in a word, the death of art.

Picasso painted for seventy years, and in that period, he went through his cubistic, neo-cubistic, impressionistic, surrealistic, and neo-realistic phases. However, we cannot talk about any evolution, any improvement from good to better, or from less perfect to more perfect. As all culture, this was also a drama of continuous search and wander.

As for this creative, unexperienced or unhistorical, specifically human character of art, we might consider some interesting facts. There is, for example, a science for adults and a science for children. The understanding of science and its reproduction and use in practice depends upon education, age, and experience. There is, however, no music for adults as opposed to music for children. Tests carried out with works by Bach, Mozart, Beethoven, Debussy, and Chopin showed that children, as well as adults, either understand or do not understand classical music. Beethoven's famous cycle of 32 sonatas, the best of its kind in the history of music, is used both as a concert teaching tool for young students and as a piece of music played by most serious pianists. Picasso painted at the age of two, before he could even talk properly. Ovid was talking in hexameters when other children started uttering their first words. Mozart had concerts at the age of six. So, art is not a knowledge; it is understanding, but by the heart, love, and simplicity of the soul. "Many a peasant when he has finished his daily work takes a piece of wood and carves sculptures. He does not need ten years of academic learning for that. I want to say that art is accessible to everybody, that some special talent or education is not necessary."[44] Such thinking reminds us of Tolstoy and his school in Yasnaya Polyana, where he used to discuss exclusively with children the most profound religious and ethical questions.[45] The understanding of art, religion,

---

[44]Andreas Franzke: *Dubuffet*, trans. Robert E. Wolf (New York: Abrams, 1981).

[45]"With groups of children from Yasnaya Polyana, Lev Nikolaevich Tolstory discussed the most important questions of human life which, having been discussed with his disciples, became clear to everybody. ... Each thought was discussed, worked out, explained, simplified, and then written by L. Nikolaevich. In such a form, it was accessible to the reason of every man" Petrov, *Tolstoy* (n.p., n.d.).

and ethics does not come from intellect and logic but from the inside. One reason is not standing here against another reason but a heart and a soul against another heart and soul.

The preceding facts invert our established comprehension of the "development" of human culture. Culture has no development and man is a constant of world history.

Chapter 6

DRAMA AND UTOPIA

Not a single utopia, including the so-called scientific socialism, deals with moral question. Utopia is beyond good and evil. Everything is a scheme.

DRAMA AND UTOPIA

Ideal Society

Does evil come from inside, from the dark depths of the human soul, or does it come from outside, from the objective conditions of human life? This question divides all people into two large groups: believers and materialists. For believers all evil and good is in man. Hence denying violence, because it is directed toward the outside, is a fight with an imaginary, nonexistent evil. Violence should be directed toward ourselves, inside, in the form of repentance or asceticism. To assert that evil is outside, that a man is evil because the conditions in which he lives are bad, that changes in these conditions would bring changes in man, to insist that man is a result of outside circumstances, is from the religious point of view the most godless and the most inhuman idea which has ever appeared in the human mind. Such an opinion degrades man to a thing, to a helpless executor of outside, mechanical, unconscious forces. Evil is in man versus evil is in the social environment. These are two mutually exclusive statements. They correspond to two other opposite and incompatible phenomena: drama and utopia.[1]

Drama is an event happening in the human soul, while utopia

---

[1]The term "utopia" is used here in its original meaning: as a vision of an ideal system of human society according to the paragon of a perfect animal community: beehive, swarm, anthill, and so on.

is an event happening in the human society. Drama is the highest form of existence that is possible in our universe. Utopia is a dream or a vision of a paradise on earth. There is no drama in a utopia and, vice versa, there is no utopia in a drama — that is, antagonism between man and the world or between an individual and society.[2]

In Plato's *Republic*, we can read:

> Let us imagine the foundations of the Republic. These foundations will be our needs. ... But how is the Republic going to satisfy all these needs? Should not some people work in agriculture, some of them be builders, others weavers? ... Everyone should perform for others the job which only he can do. ... Warriors should be severe toward the enemy and kind toward their friends. In order to have these two qualities — rudeness and kindness — they also have to be philosophers because they should be able to make a difference between friends and enemies. In order to be good protectors of the state, these warriors are to be educated. ... The beginning is the most important in that education ... usually starts with fairy tales, and the state should therefore censor authors who write them. ... Rulers are allowed to lie in the interest of the state, but others are not allowed such a thing. ... Since the subjugated should obey their superiors, all passages in books saying the opposite should be thrown out, while gods and heroes should be depicted as very noble. ... All tunes that are sad, soft, and lazy should be forbidden and substituted with masculine and marching songs. ... Drinking is forbidden. ... A citizen should not be ill or on a medical treatment because in this way he causes damage to the state. He should either work or die. ... It is good therefore for a man who is ill for a long time or who has a sick posterity to commit suicide. ... Education should help in the choice of rulers and warriors, and their sons, unless able for such jobs, should be returned to the class of

[2]This antagonism between drama and utopia is not theoretical. During the Chinese "Cultural Revolution," theater almost completely died out for what was shown on the stage was by no means drama. Plays showing personal or family life were forbidden. The heroes were depicted as perfect beings without any defects or faults. This black-white representation excluded any inner conflict and drama.

> producers. With such a system of education, each future generation will be better than the previous one, in the same way as we get a better breed of plants and animals by selective growing ..."[3]

The mechanism of a utopia is inhuman but perfect. If freedom is the essence of a drama, order and uniformity are the two essential things in a utopia.

At the beginning of the sixteenth century, Thomas More published his small but epoch-making book about the ideal state on the island of Utopia. The second part of the book is more interesting to us, and we shall therefore quickly summarize its contents. The island of Utopia was shaped like a half-moon, with 54 big towns identical in size and life style. The towns are surrounded by rural districts with houses and agricultural tools. Agricultural workers are organized in communities of 40 members each, with a host and a hostess at their head. Every community is given two slaves. Twenty members of each community return to the towns after they have spent two years on the land, and twenty new members go from the towns to the land, where they will spend a period of two years. So, there are no regular agricultural workers. Chickens are hatched without hens, in a kind of incubator. Everybody makes an effort to produce more than what is necessary for their town so that the surplus might be shared among other towns. A great number of citizens help during harvest, to make it as quick as possible. Their capital, Amaurotu, is on a river near the sea. It has a water-supply system and is fortified. The houses are perfectly clean and in rows on either sides of the streets that are of the same width (30 feet). Doors are not locked because there is no private property, and dwellings are changed every ten years by a system of ballot. Citizens take care of their gardens and some blocks of houses compete in gardening. All men and women must learn some craft — the main ones being bricklaying, smithing, woodworking, and the processing of wool and flax. Each family makes its own clothes which are the same all over the island and which differ only by age and season, by sex and marital status. All inhabitants of Utopia follow the trade of their fathers. They have a six-hour workday: they work three hours in the morning and then three hours in the afternoon after lunch, a rest for two hours. They go to bed at eight o'clock and

[3]Plato: *The Republic*, trans. Paul Shorey (London: W. H. Heinemann, 1946).

sleep eight hours. At work, they have leather clothes that last for seven years. Every town has 600 families, each of 10 to 16 members, with the magistrate, usually the oldest member of the family, at its head. Families take care not to become too large or too small. If they have too many members, the surplus is distributed to families with a smaller number of members. Every 30 families have a huge home in which the phylarch lives and where they all come, summoned by a trumpet, to eat together. They are allowed to have meals at home, but this is considered to be dishonorable, and besides, preparing food is considered to be a waste of time. The citizens of Utopia can travel around Utopia only with permission of the government.[4]

The resemblance to occurrences in some present societies is more than evident: limited freedom "in the interest of the society," leadership cults, social discipline, abolition of family and parental relationships, art at the service of the state, Darwinian selection, euthanasia, social (not family) education, the supremacy of the state over the individual, the acceptance of technical progress, the equality of sexes in the social division of labor, property leveling, voluntary mass physical labor, competition, collectivism, uniformity, censorship, and so on.

Drama deals with man, utopia with the world. In utopia, the immense inner world of man is reduced to a fictitious auxiliary point. Since people have no soul — and that is the presumption of each utopia — there are no human or moral problems in Utopia. In it, people function; they do not live. They do not live because they have no freedom. A citizen has no character here; instead, he has the "psychology" which depends on his function in the labor process, that is, in the reproduction of his own life. "Good" and "evil" are meaningless to him. Not a single utopia, including the so-called scientific socialism, deals with moral questions. Utopia is beyond good and evil. Everything is a scheme.

The final issue of history, according to Marx, is communism, the abundance of products for everybody — a complete material fulfillment.[5] According to Hegel, however, the ultimate meaning of

---

[4]Sir Thomas More: *Utopia*, trans. Paul Turner (Baltimore: Penguin Books, 1965).
[5]*Marx and Engels on Malthus: Selections from the Writings of Marx and Engels Dealing with the Theories of Thomas Robert Malthus*, ed. Ronald L. Meek, trans. Dorothea L. Meek (London: Lawrence and Wishart, 1953).

history is the triumph of the idea of freedom, or in other words, drama.[6] Socialism is a projection of the laws of the physical world upon human and social life. In the communist vision of eternal peace (or a classless society), the end of development is shown in pictures of the physical world, of its far future in the state of entropy. A classless society — that is Clausiuss' law of entropy projected on social life. Religion, on the contrary, sees at the end of everything not entropy or eternal peace, but the last judgment, not total equality and general equilibrium but drama.

Drama is therefore, both essentially and historically, a sequel of religion, while utopia is a kind of science. Lambert Quetelet wrote a book on sociology and gave it quite a logical title: *Social Physics*. Each teaching on society is a sequel either of physics or of zoology.

There are political utopias, starting with Plato, and going on to Thomas More, Tommaso Campanella, François Fourier, Saint-Simon, Robert Owen, and Marx.[7] However, we should include here science fiction as well, starting with Bacon's *New Atlantis*.[8]

Technology and so-called progress build up every day a tremendous scientific and technical mechanism in which man inevitably loses his individuality, becoming a part of that mechanism. Aldous Huxley perceives future man as an artificial man, a product of technology created by man himself. Owing to achievements in genetics, a human embryo will be processed in huge laboratories in accordance with a predetermined model plan. Science will help to create completely identical human beings, human beings "in copies." They will have no personality, but they will have "optimal properties" instead.[9] Dr. David Klein, Director of the Institute for Medical Genetics at Geneva University, has been carrying out

---

[6]Georg Wilhelm Friedrich Hegel: *Lectures on the Philosophy of History*, trans. G. Sibree (London: H. G. Bohn, 1944).

[7]Sir Thomas More: *Utopia*, in *Ideal Commonwealths*, ed. Henry Morley (New York: Kennikat Press, 1968); Tommaso Campanella, *Civitas solis*, in *Famous Utopias*, ed. Charles M. Andrews (New York: Tudor Publishing Company, 1937); François Marie Charles Fourier, *The Utopian Vision of Charles Fourier: Selected Texts on Work, Love, and Passionate Attraction*, trans. Jonathan Beecher and Richard Bienvenu (Boston: Beacon Press, 1971); and Robert Owen, *A New View of Society and Other Writings* (London: J. M. Dent and Sons, Ltd., 1927).

[8]Francis Bacon: *The Advancement of Learning and New Atlantis* (London: Oxford University Press, 1966).

[9]Aldous Huxley: *Brave New World* (London: Chatto and Windus, 1932).

experiments in which the nucleus from a cell of a frog's egg is removed and changed with a nucleus from another frog's cell, thus giving a new embryo the desired genetic properties. When the process becomes perfected, in about 40 to 50 years, it will be possible, according to Dr. Klein, to produce animals and also human beings with predetermined properties. These ideal examples can be identical to one another. Aldous Huxley brings the prospects of the technical utopia to the level of absurdity: "In the year of 2500," he remarks ironically, "the Earth will be governed by the 'brave new world,' the principles of which will be Equality, Identity, and Stability. Biology will be the main science in this world and it will enable one to obtain from incubators similar, standardized people, thousands of twins who will be working on the same machines, performing the same functions ...," and so on.[10]

In this "marvelous world," there will be no sinful people. There may be some defective individuals, but they will neither be responsible nor punished for it; they will be simply dismounted from the mechanism. In this world, there will be no good or evil, and consequently, there will be no aspirations, dilemmas, doubts, or rebellions. Drama is eliminated, and so is man and his history. Utopia is established.

Utopia and Morals

Contrary to an almost generally established opinion, man does not aspire to a functional world, but rather to an unfunctional one. That man is a social animal is very dubious. Sociability — if by it we mean a sense for living in a herd, swarm, flock, or beehive — is more an animalistic, zoological, and biological feature than a human one. What can be compared to the social life of a bee or an ant, or with the "socialness" of a cell in an organism, which is in perfect harmony with itself and with others? "Man is antisocial by nature," says the materialist Hobbes with bitterness.[11] In fact, man is an incorrigible individualist, being disgusted with and "incapable" of life in a herd. Only those who are less human than others advocate function, order, regularity, uniformity, and the supremacy

---

[10]Ibid.

[11]Thomas Hobbes: *De homine — Man and Citizens*, trans. Charles T. Wood, T. S. K. Scott-Craig, and Bernard Gert (Garden City, NY: Anchor Books, 1972).

of the state over individuals. As that type of person is more effective, they manage to impose their opinions over those of the less effective. Corporals have always been more effective than poets — and this tragic fact shows the strength and weakness of everything that is human and humane.

In his barracks, a soldier has all his basic needs satisfied: dwelling, food, clothes, work. We find here also order, safety, discipline, hygiene, and even some kind of equality or uniformity. Most of us will nevertheless agree that barracks, with all their "benefits," represent the worst prototype of a society we can imagine. Some societies that are being created nowadays are nothing else but huge barracks or are very close to being so. Beautiful slogans which ornate them change little or nothing of their essence.

Humanism and morality are connected to the name of man, to the human "calling." A member of a society or an inhabitant of a utopia is not a man in the true meaning of the term; he is a "social animal" or an "animal endowed with reason." Man has morality or immorality; a member of a utopian society has only function.

Morals have always been represented by norms. If our activity is not conscious or willing, if we do what we have to do as is the case in a utopia, then each norm, including morality, is meaningless. Even the most "humane" behavior of a communist cannot be considered as moral. This is the meaning of the Marxist assertion that there are no morals in communism. Communism abolishes morals because people relate to each other directly and not by means of norms. The fact that each ant perfectly performs its job in an anthill is not a question of morality. Ants simply cannot behave otherwise. When the bees throw out of the beehive a sick bee, they do nothing immoral, in the same way as a "sacrifice" of a bee for a swarm and its "devoted work" cannot be taken as a form of morality. The mere function of a social mechanism is in question here. This is the real meaning of Lenin's statement that in the whole of scientific socialism, "there is not a grain of morality," a statement which has aroused so many misunderstandings, but which really was the clearest admission of the connection between communism and utopia.[12]

---

[12]Howard Selsam, David Goldway, and Harry Martel, eds., *Dynamics of Social Change: A Reader in Marxist Social Science, from the Writings of Marx, Engels, and Lenin* (New York: International Publishers, 1970). Compare the following text by a well-known Soviet legal theoretician between the two world wars, Eugene Pashukanis:

Marxism is a utopia because it is scientific — that is, in the part in which it is scientific. Each utopia is what it is because it considers human life as an exclusively external occurrence (or a question of production, consumption, and distribution) and because it can be settled through science and by the application of its methods: schemes, relations, equilibrium, pressures, resistance, factors, averages, institutions, laws, prisons, and regulations.[13]

A materialistic postulate applied to society leads to a kind of socialism or communism. The same postulates, if consistently applied to the life of an individual, lead to what we usually call Epicurianism. An Epicurean is a materialist in practice. This is so because man is only conditionally and theoretically a member of a society, while in real life he is an independent individual, inclined more to a personal than to a social life.

Epicurianism is therefore individualistic, while socialism is a social result of a materialistic philosophy. "If I have just one life, then it belongs to me only" — this is more logical than any sacrifice for present or future generations. Man in a society constantly aspires to live, think, and act as an individual. Moreover, he displays a tendency to constantly break social standards and laws. Each system which does not take into account the individuality of human beings, which wants to see him only as a member of the society in spite of all these contrary facts, starts from wrong presumptions. There is no use quoting the example of bees and ants. If a bee was able to think, if it was not bound by its instincts, it would avoid work and would try to eat up the nectar which its fellow bees had collected. A termite does not go to death willingly in order to save the life of its community. If it had a choice, it would surely choose life instead of death. As for man, he most often talks about the interest of society, while in real life he works for his own benefit, a fact from which practical difficulties in socialistic systems arise (the

---

"If the relation between an individual and the class is so alive and strong that the boundaries of 'self' are almost nonexistent, so that the advantage of a class really becomes identical with an individual advantage, then there is no sense in talking about the fulfillment of moral obligations, then the phenomenon of morality does not exist at all." Eugene Pashukanis, *Algemeine Rechtslehre und Marxismus* (n.p., 1929), p. 141.

[13]The main motto of both socialism and communism is given in the function of production and consumption: "Produce according to abilities, spend according to work (according to needs). "Or, Lenin's well-known formula: "Communism equals Marx plus electrification."

well-known problem of the lack of responsibility in all states of this type). Such discord is not possible in animal communities because animals have no choice to act in their own interest, regardless of the interest of their community. Man has such a choice and this fact should by no means be ignored. People, therefore, are in a position to either invent a social order suitable for beings endowed with the ability of choice, or to destroy this ability by force or by drill. They always take one of these two directions. Socialist thinkers have always felt that the psychology of individuals, the so-called individualistic psychology which is in fact the inborn human desire for individuality and freedom, is the main obstacle to their prospect of a social, collective paradise. This is why they always talk about society, production, distribution, masses, classes, and so on, while avoiding problems of people as individuals. They oppose the "rights of people" to the "rights of man," the "social rights" to the "human rights."

For man, each decision for a more inconvenient alternative, each preference of social benefits to individual benefits, is carried out through the inner fight of motives assuming a form of morality. Faced with these facts, materialists started talking about consciousness, explaining that the term means social consciousness — that is, the feeling in an individual of belonging to a community, of fulfilling his life as a member of the community. Still, consciousness is nothing but a synonym for morality, and so, the materialists ended by introducing a completely alien element, which had never before been in the inventory of materialism. If man really were, or could only be, a member of a society, then socialism would be possible. Such a view of man is one-sided and therefore presents an untrue picture of him. In fact, since man is an independent individual, since he can choose, since he is a moral being capable of doing good and evil, since, in a word, he is a man, socialism in its consistent form is not possible.

Dependents and Heretics

There is a kind of people who admire strong power, who like discipline, who adore the outer order similar to that of the army, "where it is known who gives orders and who obeys them." They like the new parts of a town where all the houses are the same, in straight rows, and with identical facades. They like uniforms, military music bands, spectacles, parades, and other lies that "embellish" life and make it easier. They particularly like "everything to be according to the law." These are the people with the mentality of dependents. They simply like being dependents; they like safety, order, establishment; they like being praised by their heads; they like being recipients of mercy. Moreover, they are honest, peaceful, loyal, conscientious citizens. Dependents like having authority, and authority likes having dependents. They go together, as parts of a whole.

On the other side, there are those who are unhappy, damned, or cursed, who are always in revolt against something, who always want something new. They talk less of bread and more about freedom, less about peace and more about human personality. They do not accept the idea that the king gives them their salary; on the contrary, they claim that they feed the king ("it is not government that supports us, but we support the government"). These external heretics do not like authority, nor does authority like them. In religions, dependents adore people, authorities idols; lovers of freedom and rebels, however, praise only God. In fact, idolatry does not hinder slavery or subjection, and true religion does not hinder freedom.

Society and Community

A difference should be made between society which is an external group of individuals gathered on the basis of interest, and community which is an internal group of people brought together on the basis of the feeling of belonging. A society is based on material needs, on interests; a community is based on spiritual needs, on aspirations. In a society, people are anonymous members connected or divided by interests; in a community, people are brothers, connected by common thoughts, trust, and simply by a feeling that they are one. Society exists because it makes it easier to acquire benefits or to ensure our survival. A child cannot survive without other people's help, while adults cannot love well without associating with people — that being the source of a society in its external sense (the source of the social idea). We can conclude that man's aspiration to life in a society does not stem from his real being but from a necessity. Socialization is not looked for as such, but for the benefits that result from it.[14] A society is ruled by the laws of the

---

[14]Thomas Hobbes: *De cive — Philosophical Rudiments Concerning Government and Society*, ed. Bernard Gert (Garden City, NY: Anchor Books, 1972).

fittest, laws of subjection, exploitation, or, at its best, laws which share the interest. It is only a community that knows justice, mutual help, solidarity, and brotherhood. Many misunderstandings result from the unconscious confusion of these two terms.[15]

Jesus talks about love among people and he is right. Hobbes talks about a war of all against all (or Marx about external exploitation) — and he is right too. While Jesus has in mind a community of people, Hobbes and Marx think of a society. Adam Smith discovered that an affinity for and impulse of revenge are forces that regulate relations among people, but an affinity for and an impulse for revenge are forces that exist in a community, not in a society.[16]

By creating society, civilization destroys the internal, personal, direct contacts among people, establishing instead relations that are external, anonymous, indirect. The former were represented in family relations, celebrations, or birth, marriage, and death ceremonies shared by everybody, or in direct mutual help and care of one man for another. Instead of such relations which make man a human being, civilization creates institutions for taking care of people and

---

[15]To illustrate the difference that we talked about (between society and community), we would like to direct the attention of readers to a quite new and therefore not well-known or studied phenomenon in America. A strong wave of ethnicity and cultural pluralism has spread over modern America. The deepest urge of this wave is, according to Victor Turner, the search for community and the need for a spontaneous togetherness — "communitas." Communitas is, as Turner says, by its origin a spontaneous and self-developing community. It is an "anti-structure" and "hypothetically opposed to anti-substance and substance." "Togetherness is in the core of religion, literature, drama and fine arts, but its traces, deeply impressed, can also be found in laws, ethics, relationships, and even in economics." Victor Witter Turner: *Dramas, Fields, and Metaphors: Symbolic Action in Human Society* (Ithaca, NY: Cornel University Press, 1974). The Secretary of the Smithsonian Institute explains: "There is no successful countermeasure against the standardization of mass culture, but nevertheless, festivals of folk art help in maintaining the structure of cultural pluralism and brilliant variety. They reveal and revive communities which are a powerful rampart protecting individuals against the world of mega-states and mega-corporations." Sidney Dillon Ripley, *The Sacred Grove: Essays on Museums* (New York: Simon & Schuster, 1969). It seems that it was necessary to reach the American level of development to realize some essential relations between society and community and to understand that the development of a society does not lead to a community but away from it. This mass movement for the search for one's roots, as witnessed by Alex Haley's novel, *Roots* (Garden City, NY: Doubleday Press, 1976), and revival of traditions and folklore which sprung up spontaneously in the sixties is strongly supported by their protagonists who even managed to make authorities pass a law encouraging ethnicity.

[16]Adam Smith: *The Theory of Moral Sentiments* (New York: Garland Publishers, 1971).

a bare society, a utopia, for it starts to show a human dimension and becomes to some extent a community, and vice versa. The first Christian community could serve as the best example of spiritual communities in the real meaning of the term, but even in it we come across common meals which gave it a certain social note. This and other similar things made some people see in early Christianity a social movement, and in Christian equality a kind of primitive communism, which is of course wrong, a misunderstanding of the essence of occurrences.

Personality and the "Social Individual"

The first idea of a utopia in European history came from Christianity,[17] a tragic fact in its history. Campanella's *City of the Sun* is a typical anti-Christian vision, for it advocates an earthly kingdom instead of the heavenly one, and it consequently deals with society instead of man. The *City of the Sun* is a denial of the essential aims of Christianity. It marks the beginning of the economic and social theories in Europe and elsewhere.

Religion does not tend to put the outside world into order. It is passion and obligation, not a comfort or a way for better living. Jesus is not a social reformer, just as the French Revolution and scientific progress are not ways to achieve Christian ideals of peace and love. Jesus was preoccupied with the destiny of the human soul and salvation, while utopia is only a naive human dream about an ideal society of eternal harmony and peace. There is nothing in common between religion as a history of human martyrdom and the naive and illusory "success" of a utopia. One belongs to the Kingdom of Heaven, the other to the Kingdom of the Earth — "Civitas dei" and "Civitas solis." These two kingdoms do not belong to the same order of things.

Drama does not know the idea of "social safety," while utopia does not know the idea of human dignity. Marx therefore speaks about the exploited, and Dostoevski about "the humiliated and the insulted."[18] "Social utopia depicted relationships in which people

---

[17]Tommaso Campanella: *Civitas solis [The City of the Sun].*

[18]Feodor Dostoevski: *Sabrānye Sachinyénye* [Collection of Treatises], vol. 3: *Oonizhénye e Askarblyénye* [The Humiliated and the Insulted] (Moscow: Goc iza vo Choodoj, 1956).

ceased being tortured and exploited; natural law built up relations in which they are not the humiliated and the insulted."[19]

When Campanella was writing his vision of the ideal society, he was no doubt inspired by Christian "love for neighbors," but in all his sympathy, the poor monk did not see that in his vision they were neither neighbors nor remote friends. They had disappeared, vanished, into relations of production, consumption, and labor distribution. His neighbor neither loved nor hated; he was neither good nor evil; he had no soul; he was an anonymous but perfect individual who had his position in the scheme of the City of the Sun and who continually performed his function from birth to death.

If approached in this way, utopia reveals itself as an image of one side of reality, with drama as its other side. Shakespeare or Dostoevski are examples of the latter, revealing the world as a drama. In Dostoevski's novels, the human soul is emerging in all its tantalizing immensity; inner problems and inner happenings being so great that the outside world, with all its richness and poverty, its states and courts, its successes and failures, seems unreal and irrelevant. Images of the world from the perspective of drama and utopia have nothing in common. They are at extreme poles and stand against each other as quality against quantity, man against society, freedom against necessity. In utopia, we can see the world; man is only an auxiliary point which helps to perceive the outline, the scheme. In drama, man in his greatness inundates the whole world, turning it into a vision, a scenery — almost an illusion.[20]

Utopia is as true as the idea that man is an animal endowed with reason. Utopia is the result of two facts, both proceeding "from the world": man's needs (and these are always natural needs) and his intelligence (the aspiration to satisfy his needs in an intelligent way). Having needs, man must always tend to live in a society, but, as an intelligent being, he will aspire to the best arranged society — that is, the society in which a "war of all against all" is eliminated. The principles of that ideal society are not freedom or individuality, but order and conformity.[21]

The preceding facts show a direct connection between utopia

---

[19]Ernest Bloch: *Natural Law and Human Dignity* (Beograd: n.p., 1977), p. 7.

[20]Religions adhered to the astronomy which recognized the earth (and man) as a center of the universe. Hence, the bitter antagonism of the Church to Copernicus.

[21]We should remember here that Epicurus' social ideal was not freedom but safety.

and evolutionary theories about the origin of man. This fact was noticed by the biologist Rudolf Virchow as well.[22] Darwin in a sense conditioned the later socialistic ideas. To be suitable for various socialistic experiments, or to be a good citizen of any utopia, man had to be "tailored" according to Darwin. The real man is too much of an individualist and incurable romantic to fit into a utopia or to become a good member of a society. Elimination of everything that is specifically human, particularly of individuality and freedom, seems to be the basic condition for utopia.

Therefore, utopia is a creed of atheists and not of believers, but, if man is an individual and not a "perfect animal," this creed is an illusion. The possibility of an ideal society became impossible from the moment of creation, the moment of the "humanization of man." From that moment on, man has been faced with eternal conflict, disquiet, dissatisfaction, drama. "Get you down, all (you people) with enmity between yourselves."[23] The ideal society is a monotonous and infinite succession of depersonalized generations which bring forth, produce, consume, and die, and so on to the "wrong" eternity. The fact of creation and of God's interference in the human existence made this "mechanism" impossible and illusory; hence, the fanatic opposition of all utopias to God and religion. So, while prophets of utopia proclaimed society and its interests to be the supreme value, God wanted that role to be man's. He gave freedom in order to make this world a temptation and to affirm man and his soul as the highest value.

Belief in the possibility of a utopia is therefore a naive optimism, based on the negation of the human soul. Only those who ignore the human spirit and human personality can believe in the possibility of "taming" man and making him a member of a society suitable to become a part of a mechanism.[24] Conversely, to believe in the human soul means practically to be aware of an insurmountable ocean of disobedience, doubt, fear, and rebellion; to know that man is an incurable individualist who cannot be uniformed, tamed, or "calmed," and that once he acquires the comfort of abundance,

---

[22]Rudolf Ludwig Karl Virchow: *Disease, Life, and Man: Selected Essays*, trans. Lelland J. Rather (Stanford: Stanford University Press, 1958).

[23]The Qur'ān 2:36.

[24]Practice has shown that societies which did not pass through monotheism are more suitable for utopia. In them, it is easier to impose standards of obedience, uniformity, manipulation, leadership, cult, and drill, without which utopia is impossible.

he will push it all away with scorn and ask for his freedom, for his human right. "Man is an animal that refuses to be so." This is the point which connects theism with all ideas on the ideal society. Atheism is the belief that such a society is possible at all.

Utopia and Family

The family is not the basic cell of a society, as some old constitutions declare.[25] Family and society are disparate to each other. The linking principle in the family is love or emotion; in society, it is interest or intellect, or both of them.

Every development of society means the proportional abolition of the family. Social principle carried out to its ultimate consequences, to a state of utopia, does not recognize the family anymore. The family as a hearth of internal, romantic, and personal relations is in collision with all the premises of utopia. Having in mind other aims, Engels acknowledges the said fact: "Thus this history of the family in primitive times consisted in the progressive narrowing of the circle, originally embracing the whole tribe, within which the two sexes have a common conjugal relation. The continuous exclusion, first of near, then of more and more remote relatives, and at last even of relatives by marriage, ends by making any kind of group marriage practically impossible. Finally, there remains only the single, still loosely linked pair, the molecule with whose dissolution marriage itself ceases."[26]

As everything else in a utopia, the bearing of children is also free from anything that is sentimental because it is only a function or a form of production. We read in Plato's *Republic*: "Women between the ages of 20 and 40 should be confined in special rooms with men of 25 to 55 years of age. The children born in this way should be raised and educated in state institutions, without knowing their fathers or mothers. Women younger than 20 and men older than 50 are allowed to have sexual intercourse, but the result of such love should be either removed or, if a child is born, it should be

---

[25]In the new constitution of the USSR (1977), that is now "the working collective."

[26]Friedrich Engels: *The Origin of the Family, Private Property, and the State, in Light of the Researches of Lewis H. Morgan* (New York: International Publishers, 1942), p. 41.

left to die of hunger. Family life and love are to be removed."[27]

Engels is even clearer: "According to materialistic conceptions, the determining factor in history is, in the final instance, the production and reproduction of the immediate essentials of life. This, again, is of a twofold character. On the one side, the production of the means of existence, of articles of food and clothing, dwellings, and of the tools necessary for that production; on the other side, the production of human beings themselves, the propagation of the species."[28] Further on he states: "It will become clear that for the liberation of women, the first condition is to introduce again all women into public activity, and that means the abolition of the isolated family as a socioeconomic unit. ... With the transfer of the means of production into common ownership, the single family ceases to be the economic unit of society. Private housekeeping is transformed into a social industry. The care and education of children becomes a public affair; society looks after all children alike, whether they are legitimate or not."[29]

According to Marx, the abolition ("dying out") of the family means the socialization of man, his turning into a "total social being." All the fundamentals of human existence — social, material, and moral — shift from the family to society.

The French writer Simone de Beauvoir, a famous activist in the women's liberation movement in France and other countries, is very categorical: "Until the myth of the family, the myth of motherhood and maternal instinct is destroyed, women will continue to be subjugated."[30]

Civilization does not abolish family only in theory; it does it in reality as well. "Man was the first who abandoned the family, then

---

[27]Utopia, rejects love because it means personal and not "social" relations among people. One of the aims of the "Cultural Revolution" in China, which up to now has been the greatest practical attempt to achieve utopia, was to reeducate the young people to reject love as a "bourgeois tendency." Love can exist only as love for the country, socialism, and Mao, while in its natural form it is the "poisonous weeds" of the old society that should be exterminated. Even in literature, the love between a man and a woman was a taboo topic for a long time, and books describing such love were "withdrawn not only from bookshops, but also from libraries." After Mao's death, when Tolstoy's *Anna Karenina* reappeared in bookshops, people made queues that sometimes were more than 100 meters long.

[28]Engels: introduction to the 1884 edition of his *Origin of the Family*.

[29]Ibid., p. 67.

[30]An interview in the New York magazine *Saturday Review*, September, 1975.

it was women, and finally children." We can trace the abolition of the family in many aspects: the number of marriages is increasingly less, the percentage of divorce is increasing, the number of employed women is becoming greater, there is an increase in the number of illegitimate children, there are more and more single person households, and so on.[31] We should also add here the number of households of relatively young widowed people due to frequent accidents and the high increase of heart and malignant diseases which are also closely connected with civilization.

In 1960, the number of newly concluded marriages in California was equal to the number of divorces. This "Californian proportion" was rapidly reached by other centers of the highly civilized world. The number of divorces as opposed to the number of newly concluded marriages is everywhere in constant and sudden growth. In 1960, there were 26 divorces in America for every 100 new marriages. By 1975, that number had reached 48. In the Soviet Union, the percentage of divorces compared to new marriages was 10 percent in 1960 and reached 27 percent in 1973. The number of divorces in Switzerland in the last 10 years has doubled,[32] while in Poland it has increased four times in the last 20 years. In three decades (1945-1975), the number of divorces in Czechoslovakia has increased three times. In Prague, every third marriage ends in divorce. In a questionnaire carried out among schoolgirls in France, the wish for independence and an easy life was first place, while family came in last.[33]

The Stockholm Institute for Sociological Research published the results of a 1972 survey according to which women who go in for prostitution are in most cases well-off, and that they become addicted to prostitution only because of the wish for the "sweet" life.

According to the data of the Economic and Social Council of the UN (ECOSOC), the share of women in active economic life in the last 25 years grew much faster than expected. In 1975, women accounted for 35 percent of the total number of employed people in the world. Relatively speaking, the greatest number of employed

---

[31]In number of marriages (about 5 in 1,000 people), Switzerland and Sweden are at the bottom position on the world scale.

[32]With 14.1 percent of divorces among 10,000 inhabitants, Switzerland is at the top of the European list of divorces (data obtained from the Government Statistics Department for 1976).

[33]Report by B. Jazzo at the International Congress in Bonn, in 1960.

women is registered in the Soviet Union (82 out of 100 women capable of work), then in East Germany (80 percent), Bulgaria (74 percent), Hungary (73 percent), Rumania (73 percent), and Poland (63 percent). These countries are followed by Finland, Sweden, Czechoslovakią, Denmark , and Japan. In the group of countries including England, Switzerland, Austria, America, and West Germany, about half of the total number of women are employed (between 49 and 52 percent). The high ratios found in the communist countries, although they are not the most developed among the countries mentioned here, is evidently due to the influence of ideology and its attitude toward the family and toward employment of women. Another similar fact that cannot be explained only by technological development is that the Soviet Union and America have the same (and the highest) number of illegitimate children (10 percent). The Soviet Union has "reached" the status of the most developed country in the world in this respect because the general civilizational trend has been combined here with the negative ideological attitude toward marriage and family.

The phenomenon of separated families in China, Korea, and now in Cambodia results from the same reasons. Millions of families in China live separately: the father in one part of the country, the mother and children in another part, meeting each other once a year only. The reason for that is "the need of the state economy," the common interest. The family unit does not represent such an interest.

According to a survey, the number of children who run away from home in America has doubled in the last five years, reaching two million in 1976.

In such a situation, elderly people are in the worst position. In fact, the world belongs to both, to the young and to the old, but civilization, devoid of moral standards and knowing only rationalistic motives, tailors this world to the measure and taste of the young people. "On the hedonistic stage, there is the most room for those who are the most active — and these are the young and the healthy," says a Yugoslav psychiatrist. An attitude which placed sex on top of all values quite naturally reserved all the compliments for the young and mockery for the old. Respect for old age has been proclaimed as the greatest of our prejudices. If the human soul does not exist, then an old man is the most needless thing in the world. The scale of values is in question. Neither religion nor civilization can have a different attitude.

All religions have advocated the family as man's nest and the mother as the first and irreplaceable teacher. All utopias, on the other hand, have always talked with delight about social education, nursery schools, kindergarten, children's homes, and the like. Regardless of what we call these institutions, one thing is common to all of them: the absence of the mother and the committing of children to the care of employees. Plato, the first to concoct a utopia (*The Republic*), was also the first who systematically described the idea of social education. This idea culminated in the socialistic writings of the nineteenth and twentieth centuries. This phenomenon is quite lawful. If man is a "social animal" (what he really is with one part of his being), then drill, social education, nursery, and the so-called ideal society are the right solution, while parental love, family, artistic and religious education, individuality, and freedom are nothing but superfluous romanticism. In an ideal society, everybody performs his function without fault, perfectly. Mother and family could only disturb this perfect order and this "idyll" based on complete uniformity and depersonalization.

A mother gives birth to and raises a man, while a nursery raises a member of a society, a future inhabitant of a utopia. The nursery is a factory, an educational machine. A Soviet academician and high official of the Soviet government for a long time, Stanislaw Gustravovich Strumilin (1887-1974), wrote in the sixties: "Having given to social forms of education the absolute advantage over all other forms, we shall have to spread these forms in the near future with such speed that in 15 or 20 years we can make them accessible to all citizens from cradle to maturity." Then the learned academician, with pride, works out his terrifying vision: "Every Soviet citizen after leaving the maternity hospital will go to a nursery, then to a kindergarten or to an all-day children's home, then to boarding school, and from there — with a pass for an independent life — to a factory or to a higher educational institution." We see no mother or family here, for we cannot see that which does not exist. Instead of education, the raising of man, we are faced with a technological process as if it were chicken production. The climax of this "civilizing" attitude toward the family can be found in the well-known Marxist sentence from *Das Kapital*: Children of both sexes should firstly be protected from their own parents."

There are some indications that the Soviet Union is changing its attitude toward the family, but that is a deviation. Talking about principles, the essence does not lie in the question of whether Engels' (or Strumilin's) anathema to the family is right or wrong, but whether Engels could have had a different attitude toward the family at all. Engels was only drawing the ultimate conclusions from a consistent civilization (or utopia, which is the same thing), and civilization will never be completely realized until it destroys man as a personality. Such a man cannot fit into its mechanisms, structures, institutions, collectives, general interests, state justice, discipline, and so on. That is why there is this ceaseless war between man and this "programmed atrocity" as Andrei Voznesensky put it.[34]

Our attitude toward marriage, family, education, parents, or the aged depends on what we see in man — that is, on our philosophy of man. The marriage contract (for example, the new Swedish marriage) is at one pole and the marriage sacrament (Catholic marriage) at the other. Leaving aside the question of which of the two concepts of marriage is right, we just want to emphasize the fact that rationalistic philosophy had to consider marriage as a contract, and the Christian one had to see it as a sacrament. Therefore, when Engels announced the "dying out" of the family, he was not wrong; however, from the point of view of official philosophy, those Soviet sociologists who want to reestablish the "good old family" (for example) Dr. Urlanis and others) are wrong, for if man is only a perfect animal, the recipe of the academician Strumilin is the only correct solution.

We do not know what the inner value of human beings produced in this unique industry is, but we know that the quantity is decreasing nowadays in troubling proportions. A woman is not willing to have a child only to lose it at once. In all civilized countries, we can note either a stagnation or a decrease in the birth rate due either to the position of mothers or to the wish for an easy-going life without obligations, which again is the direct consequence of the abolition of religious and cultural values.

In many European countries, we find a negative demographic growth rate. Pierre Soni, a professor at the Sorbonne University, claims that the white race is in danger of dying out. According to him, the decrease in the birth rate among the Germans is such that even in the next century they might practically disappear. Demographic estimates show that the population of France, which is now about 52 million, will come down to 17 million in the first half of the twenty-first century. These estimates might seem exaggerated,

---

[34]Data obtained from the Federal Institute of Statistics in Wiesbaden.

but data make us draw such conclusions. The number of inhabitants in West Germany decreased in 1976 by 0.33 percent as compared with 1975 (more than 200,000 people), and by 0.56 percent in 1975 as compared with 1974. The decrease registered in West Berlin was as high as 1.7 percent.

The Swedish Parliament found it necessary to include on its agenda the problem of the increase in the number of mentally disturbed people — and this in the country which has the lowest death rate among children, where the average life span is the longest, where education at all levels is free, where peace has reigned for more than 150 years, where there is no problem of population density, where labor productivity is the highest in the world and income per capita one of the highest, and so on. Dr. Hans Loman, a well-known psychiatrist who was entrusted by the Swedish Parliament with investigating the reasons for such an occurrence, has so far only stated that in Sweden, as most married women are employed, the vital field of the family has been seriously affected. In Sweden, more than 50 percent of mothers with children up to the age of 3 are employed and about 70 percent with children up to the age of 17. "We have managed to create for our children an extraordinarily cold, anti-children society," says Loman in one of his reports.

In the statistical annual report for 1976, we can read that almost every second child in Sweden is the only child. A similar situation exists in Czechoslovakia. Married couples in this country consider families with three or more children as "luxurious" and "irrational." In such a situation, demographic estimates indicate that by 1990, Sweden will not be able to sustain any longer even the "ordinary reproduction" of its population.

Civilization has made woman an object of admiration or use, but it has deprived woman of her personality, the only thing that deserves appreciation and respect. Such a situation is seen very often, but it becomes most evident in various beauty pageants or in some specifically female vocations such as modeling. In this field, a woman is no longer a personality, or even a human being, and hardly more than a "beautiful animal."

Civilization disgraced motherhood in particular. It preferred the calling of a salesgirl, model, teacher of other people's children, secretary, and cleaning woman to that of mother. It was civilization that proclaimed motherhood to be slavery and promised to free woman from it. It boasts about the number of women that it has separated (it says "freed") from the family and children so that they could be employees. Contrary to this, culture has always glorified the mother. It made her a symbol, a mystery, a sacred thing. It dedicated to her the best verses, the most stirring music, the most beautiful paintings and sculptures. While the agony of the mother continues in the world of civilization, Picasso painted his magnificent painting *Motherhood* — and with his exalted hymn to the mother, he declared that for culture, the mother is still alive.

Homes for the aged go together with children's homes. They belong to the same order of things, and are in fact, two states of the same solution. Children's homes and homes for the aged remind us of artificial birth and artificial death. Both are characterized by the presence of comfort and by absence of love and warmth. Both are opposed to the family and are the result of the changed role of woman in human life. Their common feature is the elimination of parental relationships: in a nursery, children are without parents; in homes for the aged, parents are without children. Both are the "marvelous" products of civilization and ideals of each utopia.

The family, along with the mother, belongs to a religious concept of things, in the same way as a nursery, along with its employees, belongs to that other one.

PART II

ISLAM — BIPOLAR UNITY

Chapter 7

MOSES — JESUS — MUHAMMAD

Religion can affect the world only if it itself becomes worldly.

MOSES — JESUS — MUHAMMAD

Here and Now

There are two histories of Islam: the one preceding and the one following Muhammad, upon whom be peace. The latter one, the history of Islam in the narrower sense, cannot be fully understood if one has insufficient knowledge of the former, particularly of the period which covers Judaism and Christianity.

These three religions have played a major role in human history. Through them, man has become the axis of history and has learned to perceive humanity as a whole. Through them, he has known the meaning of external and internal life, external and internal progress, their mutual relations and their limits. The historical successes and failures of both Judaism and Christianity have culminated in a decisive Islamic experience of mankind. Moses, Jesus, and Muhammad are thus the personifications of three primeval possibilities of all that is human.

Among religions, Judaism represents the "this-world" tendency. All the ideas and theories of the Judaic mind are concerned with a paradise on earth. The Book of Job is a dream of justice which must be realized on earth — not in the afterlife but *here and now*.

The Jews have never entirely accepted the idea of immortality. The Sadducees still rejected it in the time of Jesus.[1] Maimonides, the

---

[1]The Sadducees, followers of Zadok, constituted an ancient Jewish political-religious

greatest Judaic thinker of the Middle Ages, states that immortality is impersonal which is almost a negation of its very concept.[2] Another great Jewish philosopher, Benedict de Spinoza, goes further and claims that the Old Testament says nothing on immortality.[3] Renan, and after him Berdyaev, noted correctly that Jews were unable to accept the idea of immortality because it was incompatible with their "this-sided" view of the world.[4] Hasdai Crecas teaches that matter is God's body. It is easy to follow, through Spinoza's example, the birth of a new materialistic philosophy in the bosom of Judaism, or at the source of its tradition, where religious essence remains shallow and thin when compared to national, political, and earthbound concerns — a situation entirely different from that of Christianity. In Spínoza's writings, it is possible to replace the term "God" with "Nature" wherever it occurs; he even gives explicit instructions to this effect. By eliminating any personal, individual, or conscious characteristics from the concept of God, he brings these two concepts immeasurably close. Regardless of his excommunication, Spinoza was an authentic Jew.[5]

The Kingdom of God which the Jews were predicting before Jesus' appearance was to materialize on earth, not in heaven as the Christians believed. In apocalyptic Jewish literature, a Messiah — an avenger or an executor of justice — is glorified. The Messiah — as expected by the Jews — would not be a prophet who suffers and dies but a national hero who will establish the kingdom of the chosen people. A world in which the just are unhappy is a senseless one. This is the basic principle of Judaic justice and every "social" justice. The idea of a paradise here on earth is essentially Judaic in its character as well as in its origin. "The Jewish pattern of history, past and future, is such as to make a powerful appeal to the oppressed and unfortunate at all times. Saint Augustine adapted

---

party which represented the ruling hierarchy and formed the core of the priestly aristocracy during the last period of the Jewish state (second and first centuries before Christ). They relied entirely on the Law of Moses, rejecting the oral or traditional law.

[2]*Moses ben Maimon [Maimonides], The Guide of the Perplexed*, trans. Shlomo Pines (Chicago: University of Chicago Press, 1963).

[3]Leo Strauss: *Spinoza's Critique of Religion*, trans. E. M. Sinclair (New York: Schocken Books, 1965).

[4]Ernest Rénan: *Oeuvres Complètes*, ed. Henriette Psichari, vol. 7: *Etudes d'histoire religieuse — Le livre de Job* (Paris: Calmann-Lévy, 1961); and Nikolai Berdyaev, *The Beginning and the End*, trans. R. M. French (New York: Harper, 1957).

[5]Bertrand Russell: *History of Western Philosophy* (New York: Simon and Schuster, 1945), pp.363-364.

this pattern to Christianity, Marx to Socialism."[6] All revolutions, utopias, socialist ideologies, and other ideas pleading for a paradise on earth are essentially Judaic, coming from the Old Testament.

The Freemasons' idea of an ethical renaissance of mankind through science is positivistic — and Jewish. It would be interesting to explore the internal and external relations between positivism, Freemasonry, and Judaism. The links and influences are not only spiritual but also quite concrete.

The history of Judaism, according to Sombart,[7] is the history of world commercial development. Nuclear science was first known as "Jewish science." Political economy could also bear this title. It is no coincidence that the greatest names in atomic physics, political economy, and socialism are almost without exception Jewish.

Jews have not always shared in culture, but they have always shared in civilization. It seems as if they have been constantly migrating from a civilization on the wane to one on the rise. This also happened in the history of the West. "Throughout the Middle Ages, the Jews had no influence on the culture of the Christian countries," says Russell.[8] The moment the city predominates in a culture, the Jews emerge. Jewish colonies have been created in every major city throughout history. Tyre, Sidon, Antioch, Jerusalem, Alexandria, Carthage, and Rome in the ancient world; Cordova, Granada, Toledo, and Seville in Muslim Spain; Amsterdam, Venice, and Marseille at the beginning of the Renaissance, and today all the great cities of the world, particularly those of America — these are the footsteps making the history of the Jews. There is something symbolic in the fact that it was the Jews who financed Columbus' journey and that they even directly participated in the discovery of a world which began to experience civilization from its very start (there is even a strongly defended theory that Columbus himself was a Jew). The father of the newest "atomic age" was also a Jew: Einstein. The Jews have in all cases been the bearers of external progress, just as the Christians were the bearers of internal progress.

---

[6]Werner Sombart: *The Jews and Modern Capitalism*, trans. M. Epstein (Glencoe, IL: Free Press, 1951).

[7]Sombart: *Les Juifs dans la vie economique.*

[8]Russell: p. 342.

Pure Religion

Jewish materialism (or positivism) oriented man's mind toward the world; throughout Judaic history, it stimulated interest in external reality. Christianity has turned the human spirit in upon itself. The explicit realism of the Old Testament could be overcome only by the equally decisive idealism of the New Testament.

According to Christianity, human energy must not be broken down into two opposed directions: toward heaven and toward earth. "No man can serve two masters, for either he will hate one and love the other, or he will hold to one and despise the other. You cannot serve God and mammon."[9] Tolstoy picks up on this thought and carries it further: "One cannot care for one's soul and for worldly goods at the same time. If one hopes for goods, he gives up his soul; if one hopes to save one's soul, he gives up worldly goods. Otherwise, one could be torn and would have neither one nor the other. ... Men wish to attain freedom through avoiding all that which might restrict them and their bodies and keep them from obtaining what they desire. The means man uses to fulfill his body — riches, a high position, a good reputation — do not result in the wished-for freedom; on the contrary, they restrict it all the more. To attain greater freedom, men build a prison out of their sins, passions, and superstitions and shut themselves up in it ..."[10]

All major church authorities have remarked an essential difference between the spirit of the Old and the New Testament. According to some authors, the Marcionian gospel, which served as a model for Saint Mark, holds that Jesus abolished the Law of Moses and that he contrasted Jehova, the God of justice and savior of the visible world, to the God of love who created the invisible world. According to Couchoud, this gospel contains, even more clearly than the others, the principles of asceticism, nonviolence, and nonresistance to evil.

Religion, therefore, from the outset gives up any intention to change or to make the outside world perfect. Pure religion would judge every human belief that exterior organization and alteration of the world would lead to an increase in the genuine good as sin —

---

[9]Matthew: 6:24

[10]Leo Tolstoy: "The Christian Teaching," ed. Leo Wiener, vol. 22: *The Complete Works of Count Tolstoy* (New York: AMS Press, 1968).

actually, a form of self-deception. Religion is an answer to the question of how to live within oneself and face oneself, not one of how to live in the world and with other people. It is a temple on a mountain top, a shelter one must climb to in order to leave behind the emptiness of an unrepairable world governed solely by Lucifer. That is pure religion.

"Take no thought for your life, what ye shall eat, or what ye shall drink." ... "If thy right eye offend thee, pluck it out, and if thy right hand offend thee, cut it off." ... " Whosoever looketh on a woman to lust after her hath committed adultery with her in his heart."[11] "For it is written, I will destroy the wisdom of the wise and will bring to nothing the reason of the prudent. Where is the wise? Where is the scribe? Where is the disputer of this world?"[12] ... "And the people asked him, saying: 'What shall we do then?' He answered and saith unto them:' He who hath two coats, let him impart one to him who hath none; and he who hath meat, let him do likewise.'"[13] The similarity of these verses to certain socialist principles is only apparent since there is no discussion of a society and its relations but only of a man and his soul. Religion calls for giving and a revolution for taking. The external result may in certain cases be identical, but the internal one is completely different.

The road claimed by religion is too difficult and is only for the devoted. When the Qur'ān says: "God places on no soul a burden greater than it can bear,"[14] it is clearly aiming at Christianity. All pure religions have known two ways or two programs. In Buddhism, there is the "Mahayana," "the great road," severe and difficult, reserved for the elite, and the "Hinayana," "the small road," easier and less severe, reserved for the common people.[15] A similar moral division can be found in Christianity: the priesthood and the orders versus the ordinary life of lay people, and celibacy for the clergy versus marriage for ordinary people. Celibacy is the only true solution; marriage is an obvious compromise.

---

[11]All quotes from the Gospels: Matthew 6:31, Matthew 5:29, and Matthew 5:28.

[12]Paul: I Cor. 1:19.

[13]Luke: 3:10

[14]The Qur'ān 2:286.

[15]Daisetz Teitaro Suzuki: *Studies in the Lankavatara Sutra, One of the Most Important Texts of Mahayana Buddhism, in Which Almost All Its Principal Tenets Are presented, Including the Teaching of Zen* (London: G. Routledge & Sons, Ltd., 1972); and Bhikkhu Buddhadasa, *Toward the Truth: Hinayana Buddhism*, ed. Donald K. Swearer (Philadelphia: Westminster Press, 1971).

This powerful inner dynamism, accompanied by unheard-of renunciation, is entirely personal and is always connected with the rejection of every social activity. Being a priori against the use of violence, Christianity and religion in general could not directly influence anything that might improve man's social position. Social changes are not initiated through prayer and ethics but through force backed by ideas or interest. Here is the source of the accusation — historically justified but morally unjustified — that religion supports whatever status quo is reigning at that time — a state which objectively serves, regardless of "psychological opposition," the purposes of the ruling class. Christianity is not a practice in the ordinary sense of the word and must not be judged as such. The Qur'ān calls it the "announcement" (the gospels — the "annunciation") of the deepest truths of human existence. "Thou shalt love thy neighbor as thyself," "Love thine enemies, bless them that curse you," "Resist not the evil ..." — these claims go against the grain of the practical logic of man's life to such a degree that they direct us toward a search for their other and true meaning. They bring indeed the announcement of another world, as Jesus indicated: "My kingdom is not of this world."[16]

The revelation of the Gospels' clear and radical positions meant a turning point in history. Mankind was for the first time brought to a full consciousness of man's value and through that a "qualitative" rather than a "historical" progress was realized. The appearance of Jesus was therefore a milestone in world history, "a sign to the world,"[17] and the vision and hopes he proclaimed were incorporated into all human efforts from then on. Western civilization, regardless of all its deviations, delusions and doubts, bears the seal of Jesus' teachings. In the primeval conflicts of society or man, of bread or freedom, of civilization or culture, the West, bound to the Christian tradition, has always sided with the second alternative.

Acceptance and Rejection of Christ

Religion can affect the world only if it itself becomes "worldly," secular, of this world — that is, if it becomes involved in politics in the broadest sense of the word. Islam is Christianity reoriented

---

[16]John: 18:36.

[17]The Qur'ān 21:91.

toward the world. This definition shows both the similarity and difference between these two religions.

Islam includes one purely Judaic component but also many non-Judaic elements. In his classification of religions, Hegel views Islam as the direct continuation of Judaism, an idea which can be attributed to his Christian point of view.[18] Similarly, Spengler calls the Book of Job an Islamic writing.[19] In his *Patterns of Comparative Religions*, Mircea Eliade places Muhammad at the transition point between the second and third (last) period in mankind's spiritual development. The third period, which has not yet ended, started with Muhammad. The history of the human mind, according to Eliade, is a process of general secularization. In this vision, Muhammad stands on the threshold of the triumph of religion (Christianity) and the new secular age. As such, he stands at the focal point of historical balance.[20]

Setting aside the one-dimensionality of Eliade's historical vision which is unacceptable from the standpoint of this book, we point out the inevitable "middle" position of Islam and Muhammad as characteristic of this seeing. This impression persists regardless of the variety of approaches and explanations.

Jesus avoided Jerusalem because, as any other city, it was also a city of Pharisees, disputers, scribes, unbelievers, and shallow believers. Socialism does not address villagers but inhabitants of large cities. Muhammad goes to the cave of Hirā' but each time returns to the godless city of Mekkah to carry out his mission.

Notwithstanding this, what took place in Mekkah could not yet be called Islam. Islam reached its culmination in Medinah. In the cave of Hirā', Muhammad was a faster, an ascetic, a mystic, a *hanif*.[21] In Mekkah, he was a herald of religious thought; in Medinah, he became a herald of Islamic thought. The message that

---

[18]George W. F. Hegel: *Early Theological Writings*, trans. T. M. Knox and Richard Kroner (Philadelphia: University of Pennsylvania Press, 1971).

[19]Oswald Spengler: *The Decline of the West*, trans. Charles Francis Atkinson (New York: A. A. Knopf, 1926).

[20]Mircea Eliade: *Patterns in Comparative Religion*, trans. Rosemary Sheed (New York: Sheed & Ward, 1958).

[21]*Hanif* literally means "one who scorns the false creeds surrounding him and professes the true relgion."

Muhammad bore was completed and crystallized in Medinah.[22] Here — and not in Mekkah — was the "start and source of the entire Islamic social order."[23]

Muhammad had to return from the cave. If he had not returned, he would have remained a *hanif.* Since he came back, he became a preacher of Islam. That was the meeting of the inner "real" world, mysticism and reason, meditation and activity. Islam started as mysticism and ended as a state. Religion accepted the world of facts and became Islam.

Man and his soul — that is the relationship between Muhammad and Jesus of the Bible. Between the Holy Scriptures and the soul is a sameness of nature. In their essence, they contain the same mystery ... the soul and the Holy Scriptures, which mutually represent each other symbolically and mutually throw light upon each other as well."[24] Islam is the repetition of man. It has, just as man, its "divine spark," but it is also a teaching of shadows and the prose of life. It has certain aspects which the poets and the romantics might not like. The Qur'ān is a realistic, almost antiheroic book. Without man to apply it, Islam is incomprehensible and would not even exist in the true sense of the word.

Plato's ideas, Leibniz's monads and Christianity's angels signify in essence the same thing: the kingdom of the timeless, perfect, absolute, and immobile world. Islam does not really idealize this world. The angels' bow to man who "has been taught by God to know the names of all things" confirms the prevalence of life, man, and drama over immobile and eternalized perfection.

Christianity has never reached the full consciousness of one God. In fact, Christianity has only a vivid concept of the divine and not a clear idea of God. The mission of Muhammad was to make the Gospels' image of God clearer and closer to the human mind and thought. Allah is a God who corresponds to the yearning of our soul and also to certain sublime ideas of our mind. In the

---

[22]"Today I have perfected your faith and fulfilled my mercy upon you. I am satisfied that your faith be Islam," as one line from the Medinah period of the Qur'ān states.

[23]Stetano Bianco: *"Polyvalence and Flexibility in the Structure of the Islamic City"*, *WERK*. Switzerland, 9 (1976).

[24]Henri de Lubac: *The Drama of Atheist Humanism*, trans. Edith M. Riley (New York: New American Library, 1963), pp. 4-5, 211.

Gospels, God is father; in the Qur'ān, God is master. In the Gospels, God is loved; in the Qur'ān, God is respected. This particularity in the Christian understanding of God was reversed later in a series of confused pictures that compromised the original monotheism of Christianity (the Trinity, the devotion paid to the Virgin Mother, saints, and so on). Such a development is not possible in Islam. Regardless of all the historical crises it has passed through, Islam has remained "the clearest monotheistic religion."[26] Man's soul conceives of divinity only. Through the mind, divinity is transformed into the idea of the one and only God — Allah.

The Christian God is the lord of the individual world (people and souls) only, while Lucifer holds the reins of the material world.[27] This is why the Christian belief in God preconditions inward freedom, while the Islamic belief in Allah implies a demand for the outward freedom as well. The two essential dogmas of Islam (*Allahu Akbar*: God is the greatest, and the famous *al-'aqidah* — creed —, *lā ilāha illallāh*: There is no deity but Allah), are at the same time the two most revolutionary devices in Islam. Sayyid Qutb rightly holds them to be a revolution against a worldly authority which has usurped the fundamental prerogatives of divinity." According to him, they mean that "the power is to be taken away from the priests, the leaders of the tribes, the wealthy and the rulers, and returned to God." Therefore, as Qutb concludes: "'There is no deity but Allah' is abhorrent to those who are in power in any age and place."[28]

In the same manner, Christianity was unable to accept the idea of a perfect man who was still a man. From Jesus' teaching, Christians drew the conclusion of a god-man, of Jesus as the son of God. Muhammad, however, had to remain just a man because he would otherwise have been superfluous. While Muhammad gave the impression of a man and a warrior, Jesus gave the impression of an angel. The same applied to the women in the Qur'ān who — unlike Martha and Mary of the Gospel — appear exclusively in their natural function, namely as spouses and mothers. Therefore, the Christian attack on Muhammad's "too human nature" is actually

---

[26]Le Bon: n.p.d.

[27]Several Christian legends inform us of Lucifer's almighty power.

[28]Sayyid Qutb: *Islam and Universal Peace* (Indianapolis: American Trust Publications, 1977). Sayyid Qutb: *Social Justice in Islam*, trans. John B. Hardie (New York: Octagon Books, 1970).

a misunderstanding. The Qur'ān itself stresses that Muhammad is only a man[29] and paraphrased all future attacks on him: "What sort of an apostle is this, who eats food and walks through the streets..."[30]

A mere comparison of the vocabulary used in the Gospels and the Qur'ān leads us to several obvious conclusions. In the Gospels, certain words appear very frequently: blessed, holy, angel, eternal life, heaven, pharisee, sin, love, repentance, forgiveness, mystery, body (as the bearer of sin), soul, purification, salvation, and so on. In the Qur'ān, the same terms are based on an image of the world, the foreground of which is now occupied by entirely definite and realistic terms such as: reason, health, cleanliness, strength, buying, contract, pledge, writing, weapons, battle position, force, struggle, trade, fruit, decisiveness, caution, punishment, justice, profit, revenge, hunt, medicine, interest, and so on.

Islam knows no specifically "religious" literature in the European sense of the word, just as it knows no pure secular literature. Every Islamic thinker is a theologian,[31] just as every true Islamic movement is also a political movement.

Similar conclusions can be drawn from the comparison between a mosque and a church. A mosque is a place for people, while a church is "God's temple." In the mosque, an atmosphere of rationality prevails; in a church, it is an atmosphere of mysticism. The mosque is always the focus of activity, close to the market, at the heart of the settlement,[32] while the church seems too "elevated" for a similar position. The architecture of the church tends to stress ceremonious silence, darkness, height, a hint of the "other world." "The truth is that in entering a Gothic cathedral, people leave all the earthly cares outside, as if they were entering another world."[33] In a mosque, people are supposed to discuss certain very "earthly" worries after prayer. This is the difference.

---

[29]The Qur'ān 17-93, 18:110 and 40:6.

[30]The Qur'ān 25:7.

[31]Ernest Bloch adds the characteristic remark that "almost all Arabic theologians were also doctors." Ernst Bloch, *Natural Law and Human Dignity* (Beograd: n.p., n.d.), p. 58. A line from philosophy to theology to law to medicine can be traced.

[32]St. Bernard demanded that churches and monasteries be built as far from cities as possible. Kenneth Clark, *Civilization: A Personal View* (London: British Broadcasting Corporation, 1962).

[33]Ibid.

Compare the Christian principle of the Pope's infallibility to the infallibility of the Islamic *ijmā'*: "My people cannot agree upon an error" as related from Muhammad. The New Testament turns to man; the Qur'ān turns to the people. Thus, the principle of the people, the whole, the community emerges. Nothing here is chance. The former is entirely in harmony with the spirit of Christian elitism and its hierarchical, sacral, monastic principle similar to Buddhism. The latter has a certain secular connotation and refers to the people as an expression of a higher, common mind. Islam does not recognize the elite in terms of monks and saints, nor are there two programs, one for the chosen and the other for the ordinary people. This is an announcement of a democratic principle.[34]

The Gospels and the Qur'ān — as distinguished from the Old Testament — declare the principle of a spiritual community. However, while the Gospels remain categorical, Islam recognizes nations and itself becomes a new dimension above them — *ummah* — that is, a supernationality of all Muslims.[35] Moreover, the Qur'ān cautiously re-affirms the principle of kinship and blood, which Jesus had entirely rejected.[36]

The conditions under which Islam came into being can also help us to understand it more fully as a teaching of the unity of faith and politics. At that time, the Arabs were a vital and potent people, filled with both merchant-warring and religious-metaphysical traditions. Their Ka'bah had been not only a religious but also a trading center for centuries. The natural surroundings they inhabited did not allow them to ignore the importance of the economic factor in life. This was not the fertile Galilee, the cradle of Christianity, where one could sustain oneself with little effort. Life could be maintained here only through hard pains such as long caravan trips or hard work for every foot of fertile land or gallon of water. At the same time, the desert stimulated and sustained a powerful and deep religious feeling. These two contradictory facts, under permanent influence of which the genius and the instinct of the Arabic people were brought up, predestined this nation for Islam as a heaven-and-earth teaching. The Gospels could say: "Live like the lilies in the field,"

---

[34]A proposal to introduce a collective management instead of the solitary papal institution, made at the Second Vatican Council, failed since the idea was completely opposed to the very nature of Christianity.

[35]The Qur'ān 49:13.

[36]The Qur'ān 3:6 and 4:1. Also, compare the Qur'ān 49:10 and Matthew 12:47-49.

but the Qur'ān had to say: "God has given you the day so that you may scatter and find for yourself food and God-granted gifts."[37]

According to the Qur'ān — and not the Gospels — God created man to be master of the earth.[38] Man could attain supremacy over nature and the world only through knowledge and work, therefore through science and action. With this fact, as with its focus on law and justice, Islam proved that it wanted not only culture but also civilization.[39]

Islam's attitude toward civilization is evidenced in its relation to literacy as one of the most powerful levers of civilization. The art of writing is mentioned in the first revealed section of the Qur'ān.[40] Writing is inwardly alien to religion. The Gospels remained as an oral tradition for a long time, and — as far as we know — were only written down an entire generation after Jesus. Conversely, Muhammad used to dictate parts of the Qur'ān to his scribe immediately after their revelation, a practice that would have been quite disliked by Jesus, and which would have been more akin to the blamed Pharisees.[41]

The Qur'ān's insistence on the right to struggle against evil and oppression[42] is not religious in the strict sense of the word. The principles of nonviolence and nonresistance are closer to religion. Those principles of pure religion appear in the same form both in Jesus' teachings and in Indian religious thought with the direct continuation of the Indian variant being Gandhi's *satyagraha*, a method of fighting through nonviolence and civil disobedience. When the Qur'ān approves of or even orders struggle instead of suffering and obedience,[44] it is not a religious or a moral code but rather a sociopolitical one. Muhammad was a warrior. A pedantic chronicle noted that he had nine swords, three spears, seven cuirasses,

---

[37]Compare Matthew 6:28 to the Qur'ān 62:10.

[38]The Qur'ān 2:30.

[39]Islam is the only religion which created its own integral law.

[40]The Qur'ān 96:4-5.

[41]Moses also used writing, which completely complies with his place and mission in history (Numbers 33:2, Romans 10:5).

[42]The Qur'ān 42:39.

[43]Mohandas Karamchand Gandhi: "Satyagraha in South Africa," *Mahatma Gandhi at Work*, ed. C. F. Andrews (New York: The Macmillan Company, 1931); and Erik Homberger-Erikson: *Gandhi's Truth on the Origins of Militant Nonviolence* (New York: Norton, 1969).

[44]The Qur'ān 2:216, 22:39, 60:2, 8-9, 61:10-11, and so on.

three shields, and other weapons. In this respect, Muhammad resembles Moses, "the fighting prophet."[45]

The prohibition of alcohol in Islam primarily has a social character since alcohol is firstly a social evil. Religion in general can have nothing against alcohol. Certain religions have even used artificial stimulants to some degree to help ecstacy — the darkness of the cathedral and the odor of incense belong here as well. Christians see nothing wrong with the symbolical transformation of wine into Christ's blood during the eucharist. Here, there is not a vestige of the Islamic teaching that wine is a great sin and therefore prohibited (*haram*). When Islam forbids alcohol, it functions as a science, not as a religion.

The unique feature of Islam as a unity is, however, torn asunder by some who emphasize its religious component at the expense of its other component: unity. Islam is reduced to religion and mysticism. As soon as activity weakens, as soon as we neglect our "share in this world"[46] and cease to be in harmony with it, the Islamic state becomes like any other state, and the religion in Islam begins to affect as any other: the state becomes a naked power serving only itself, while religion begins to pull society toward passivity and backwardness. The kings, emirs, godless scientists, clergy, dervish orders, mysticism, drunken poets — all of these simply constitute an external aspect of the inner break according to the well-known Christian formula: render unto God that which is God's and unto Caesar that which is Caesar's.[47] The mystic philosophy at its base is certainly the most typical form of that deviation, which could be called the "Christianization" of Islam — a relapse within Islam from Muhammad back to Jesus.[48]

There is another, opposite danger too, but the general impression prevails that the "materialism" of Islam — that is the sum of

---

[45]We find many other parallels between Moses and Muhammad, or between Judaism and Islam. Such parallels between Judaism and Christianity do not exist. In a certain sense, the two latter teachings are in a thesis-antithesis position. This fact could explain the phenomenon of anti-Semitism in most Christian countries, a feeling entirely unknown among the Muslim peoples.

[46]The Qur'ān 2:177.

[47]Matthew 22:21.

[48]It goes without saying that we have in mind here the wrong practices of some dervish orders whose devotions ended in passiveness and retirement from active life. However, if deep religiousness is in question, we can say that every Muslim is a *sufi* and that Muhammad was one before anybody else.

the natural and social elements inherent to it — make the Islamic world impervious to other extreme materialistic teachings which are constantly spreading from Europe. In prerevolutionary Russia, its Don Quixote-esque Christianity was unable to face the realism of the leftist teachings. The lack or failure of Marxist revolutions in Muslim countries is not accidental. Islam has its own form of Marxism. The Qur'ān kept somewhat of the coarse realism of the Old Testament, while Marxism in Europe is a compensation for the Judaic component which Catholic and Orthodox Christianity pushed out entirely.[49] Rational Protestantism proved itself more resistant to revolutionary challenge. From this viewpoint, the Protestant form of Christianity is closer to Islam than the Catholic one.

As a result of historical reasons and political confrontations between Christianity and Islam, their kinship has very often been overlooked. That Islam accepts the Bible as a holy book and Jesus as God's messenger has been ignored. This fact, if we draw all the necessary conclusions from it, could direct the relations of these two great world religions to an entirely new dimension in the future.[50]

---

[49]Points in common between the Old Testament and the Qur'ān can be found in those verses which denounce unworthy holders of power and wealth. The Qur'ān thunders against "arrogant leaders" (7:75), "sinful aristocracy" (6:123), "dignitaries" (7:59), "godless chiefs" (11:27), "profuse wealth" (34:34), and so on. This is, of course, an expression of the social engagement which is characteristic of both Judaism and Islam.

[50]"And say: 'We believe that which has been spoken unto us and which has been spoken unto you; for God is one God; and it is to Him that we bow'" (The Qur'ān 29:40). Or: "Say: 'O people of the Book, come to common terms as between us and you ..." (The Qur'ān 3:64), and so on.

Chapter 8

ISLAM AND RELIGION

Salah (prayer) is not only an expression of the Islamic view of the world; it is also a reflection of how Islam wants to order it.

ISLAM AND RELIGION

Bipolarity of the Five Pillars of Islam

Salāh (Islamic prayer) is not only an expression of the Islamic view of the world; it is also a reflection of how Islam wants to order the world. *Salāh* announces two things: first, there are two original human aims; and second, these aims, no matter how logically separated, can be united in human life since there are no prayers without cleanliness and no spiritual efforts without the accompanying physical and social efforts. *Salāh* is the most perfect illustration of that which we call the "bipolar unity" of Islam. Owing to its simplicity, *salāh* reduces this quality to an abstraction and becomes the formula or the "cipher" of Islam.

Salāh is useless without ablution, while pure prayer can go along with the "holy uncleanliness" found in certain monastic orders in Christianity and Hinduism. According to the feeling of these orders — a feeling which is authentically religious — the disregard and active neglect of the body can even reinforce the spiritual component in prayer. This logic starts from the premise that the prayer, due to its underlying principle, will be truer if "cleansed" from physical additions. The less the physical is present, the more the spiritual is stressed.[1]

---

[1]Among clerical authorities who brought this aspect of prayer to the extreme, the most decisive was certainly the Apostle Jacob. The extent to which such deliberate physical neglect could go is illustrated in the following lines on the views of cleanliness held

Wudū' (ablution) and the movements constitute the rational side of *salāh*. Because of them, *salāh* is not only a prayer but a discipline and a hygiene as well; it is not only a mysticism but also a practicality. There is something military indeed in that morning washing with cold water and in the prayer in close formation. When a Persian advance scout, prior to the battle of Qādisiyyah, saw Muslim warriors lined up for their morning *salāh*, he said to his officer: "Look at the Muslim army going through its military routine."[2] The external movements of *salāh* are simple to a certain degree but involves almost all parts of one's body. Five prayers during the day with a washing (or bathing), the first of which must be done before sunrise and the last one at night, are indeed effective devices against comfort and wantonness.

If we now focus upon this "rational" aspect of *salāh*, we see that it is not one-sided. The duality is repeated: ablution is hygiene, but hygiene is "not only a knowledge but also a virtue."[3] In hygiene, Islam identified something which belongs inwardly to it, which is "methodologically" Islamic. The result: Islam raised hygiene to the level of an idea and organically bound it to prayer, while the Qur'ān — unexpectedly from the point of view of a religion — states: "God loves those who keep themselves pure and clean."[4] The statement that physical cleanliness is one aspect of faith could only appear in Islam. In all other known religions, the body is "out of grace."[5]

Tarawīh, a prayer connected to the fast of Ramadān, clearly has a health-oriented, medical intention. This is also possible only in Islam.

The fact that *salāh* is connected to a definite time of day and a geographical direction (the Ka'bah) means that a prayer is bound — contrary to religious logic — to nature and its movements. The times of *salāh*, as well as fasting and *hajj* (pilgrimage), are dependent

---

in the early Middle Ages: "Cleanliness was viewed with abhorrence. ... Saints, male and female, would boast that water had never touched their feet except when they had to cross rivers." Russel: *The History of Western Philosophy* (London: n.p., 1946), p.371.

[2]As stated by Risler in *La civilization arabe*, p. 35.

[3]Jean Jacques Rousseau: *Emile*, trans. Barbara Foxley (London: Dent, 1955).

[4]The Qur'ān 2:222.

[5]Let us remember here that the public baths built by Roman civilization disappeared with the ascent of Christianity. Moreover, the Church closed down baths and built monasteries. Islam, on the contrary, built baths near its mosques. There is almost no mosque in the world without a fountain at least. None of this is accidental.

upon certain astronomical facts. Certainly, it sounds more religious that "piety is not that you turn your faces toward the East or the West ...,"[6] but in Islam, the Islamic concept of prayer prevails — one which includes equally the physical (natural) elements in the end. In this way, *salāh* belongs to our space-time world. The fast development of astronomy in the first centuries of Islam was heavily influenced, if not conditioned, by this need for a sufficiently accurate definition of space and time. We have many reasons to believe that this development was Islam's intention.

This aspect of *salāh* (call it worldly, practical, or natural) highly recommended another quality: the social one. *Salāh* is not only a gathering of people for a common prayer but also for personal immediate contacts, and as such, it is in direct opposition to negative individualism and separation. Life segregates people; mosques bring them together again and mixes them. It is an everyday school of harmony, equality, community, and good will.

This social tendency of *salāh* (the process of the socialization of prayer) is completed by the *jumu'ah*. *Jumu'ah* (Friday prayer) is a nearly urban or "political" *salāh*. It is held on holidays, in the central mosque, by a state functionary. The *khutbah*, (the speech before Friday prayer) its crucial part, is primarily a political message. Christians would claim that this implies a negation of prayer — a conclusion typical for the Christian way of thinking but not justified from the point of view of Islam.

The metamorphosis of religion in Islam is also clearly evident in the example of *zakāh*. In the early period of Islam (the Mekkan period), *zakāh* was voluntary giving to the poor, a kind of alms. When the Medinan community was established — (the historical moment at which a purely spiritual community was turned into a state), Muhammad began to treat *zakāh* as a legal obligation, a tax to be paid by the rich to the poor — as far as we know, the first tax in history. By adding a component of force to the Christian institution of alms, Islam created *zakāh*, "the obligatory charity" as Risler named it. The same logic which had turned prayer into *salāh* now turned alms into *zakāh*, and in the final result, religion into Islam.

With the proclamation of *zakāh*, Islam began to take on the contours of a social movement. It no longer functioned only as a religion. *Zakāh* only took on its true weight with the formation of the

---

[6]The Qur'ān 2:177.

Medinan political community. A certain indication of this character of *zakāh* is the fact that it is mentioned in the Qur'ān eight times in the Mekkan suras, and twenty-two times in the Medinan suras.

Zakāh is a response to a phenomenon which by itself is not one-sided. Misery is not only a social issue. Its cause is not only the privation but also the evil in human souls. Deprivation is its external side, and sin is its internal side. How else can we explain the existence of misery in affluent societies? In the second half of the twentieth century, one-third of mankind is chronically undernourished. Is that owing to a lack of goods or to a lack of feelings? Every solution to the problem of misery must include the confession of guilt and, in addition, must serve as a penitence. Every social solution must include a human solution. It should not only change economic relations but also the relations between man and man. It should bring about the just distribution of goods as well as proper upbringing, love, and sympathy.

Poverty is a problem, but it is also a sin. It is not solved only through a shift of the ownership of goods but also through personal striving, aim, and good will. Nothing would be done in the true sense of the word if the ownership of this world's goods changed, but hatred, exploitation, and subjugation remain in man's soul. This is the reason for the failure of Christian religious revolts and socialist revolutions. "For two thousand years, the sum of evil in the world has not lessened. Not a single empire, divine or revolutionary, has attained its end."[7] Religious revolts were too religious and social revolutions too social. Religion felt that it would be more religious if it rejected politics and violence, while socialism held as its main duty to convince its adepts that violence is the only way, whereas charity is just a deception. Man needs a religion which is politics and politics which are ethics, or charity which can become a social obligation, a tax. Thus we come to the definition of *zakāh*.

People are mirrored in *zakāh*. It depends on them whether it will be a tax or a voluntary giving from man to man. *Zakāh* demands money chests and hearts to be opened. *Zakāh* is a great river of goods flowing from heart to heart, from man to man. *Zakāh* eliminates poverty among the poor and indifference among the rich. It reduces material differences between people and brings

---

[7]Albert Camus: *l'Homme révolté* (Paris: Gallimard, 1951).

them closer to each other.[8]

The goal of Islam is not to eliminate riches but to eliminate misery. What is misery? It is a shortage of the things which are indispensable for a normal life, having less than the necessary minimum for life, being below "the minimum living standard." "The minimum living standard" is a natural and historical category and represents the sum of goods that is necessary for a man and his family to satisfy their physical and social needs. It follows that society is not bound to reduce everyone to the same level, but first of all to give every man the said minimum standard. Islamic social measures are limited to the elimination of misery and do not extend to the equalization of property, the moral and economic justification of which is dubious.

Every settled society, in addition to moral and humane criteria, rules by the imperative of survival. Islamic society, to be so, must be maximally humane and maximally efficient. It is not Islamic if humane regards threaten its stability, and vice versa, if exaggerated emphasis on aspiration to efficiency and power allow the violation of the essential principles of freedom, human rights, and humanism. The constitution of an Islamic society is determined by the coalescence of these two opposite conditions.

Theological considerations concerning *zakāh* are usually limited to how much of what to give. Except for the institution of *zakāh*, the very principle of solidarity is more important than percentages and figures. The principle according to which the higher part of society is obliged to financially help the poorer part is of crucial importance. Doubtless, one day when the true Islamic order is established, it will strive to fulfill the very intention of this principle, whether income level and population statistics are overstepped or not. Also, the goal of this principle will be attained only when the richer part of society will give to the poorer part according to the needs of the latter. Since *zakāh* is the right of the poor,[9] it will be,

---

[8]Of course, direct social intrvention by the state might be the most efficient way to realize social justice, but social institutions with their faceless manner and with the spreading of all-pervading indifference undermine the very foundations upon which a healthy and happy community rests.

[9]The Qur'ān 70:24-25.

if necessary, provided by force.[10]

According to some authors, there are eighty-two places in the Qur'ān where the obligation or suggestion of giving is mentioned. Due to this persistent Islamic teaching on giving, a quiet revolution took place in Muslim societies through the institution of *waqf. Waqf,* by its widespread character and importance, has no parallel in non-Islamic societies. There is almost no Muslim country where big properties have not been given as *waqf* to serve the common welfare. *Waqf* is not mentioned in the Qur'ān, but it did not appear by chance. It emerged as the result of a spirit of mutual assistance and as a consequence of *zakāh's* educational function. This humane practice offers the hope that certain important social goals can be attained without violence. The *waqf* or material goods in the service of ethical aims prove that great changes can be brought about in the field of economics without the intervention of material interest. In this regard, *waqf* is the opposite of the so-called "natural laws of economics." It is an anomaly from the viewpoint of political economy, but with its duality ("economic category with a soul") it is a typical Islamic practice.

Can *zakāh* negatively influence the people's efforts to improve their condition through their own work? Some critics believe so. First of all, there are so many troubles which cannot be solved through personal efforts: natural deficiencies, invalidity, natural disasters, and so on. In this regard, *zakāh* does not differ from any other type of subventions which all civilized and certain uncivilized societies know. In the USA 1965 budget, for example, a billion dollars was set aside for "assistance to poor Americans."[11] Nobody feared that this notable sum of money would negatively influence the

---

[10]We mention here for comparison the interesting idea of "negative taxation" as proposed by the American economist Milton Friedman, the Nobel Prize winner for Economic Science in 1976. According to this idea, financial departments would pay a "negative tax" to all who earn an insufficient amount. "Poverty in America would have disappeared long ago if social funds had been steered to those who truly need them instead of being wasted on inefficient and extremely expensive social services." See Milton Friedman and Wilbur Joseph Cohen, *Social Security: Universal or Selective?* (Washington: American Enterprise Institute for Public Research, 1972). *Zakāh* remains what it is, but Friedman's "negative tax" reminds us strongly of *zakāh*.

[11]This category consisted of American citizens with an income below $2,000.00 per year. It has been calculated that at that time, there were about 35 million Americans in this category.

energy of the people of the most enterprising nation in the world.[12]

This detailed analysis of *salāh* and *zakāh*, the best known practices of Islam, has proved their inner dualism, but if observed externally, their different function within the structure of Islam is also evident. In that focus, *salāh* is seen as a spiritual and *zakāh* as a social component. *Salāh* is directed toward man and *zakāh* toward the world; *salāh* has a personal and *zakāh* a social character; *salāh* is an instrument of upbringing and *zakāh* a component of the social order. Almost all Islamic thinkers agree on a certain dependence between *salāh* as a personal prayer and *zakāh* as a social attitude in harmony with *salāh*. This opinion even led to the conclusion that *salāh*, if not strictly followed by *zakāh*, has no use.

The union of *salāh* and *zakāh* is confirmed by the Qur'ān which constantly stresses their interdependence. 'Abdullah ibn-Mas'ūd noted that Muhammad once said: "It is ordered to you to perform *salāh* and give *zakāh*; the one who does not give *zakāh* has nothing from *salāh*." This premise can be explained only as a claim against parting faith from doings and man from the world — a claim that is Islamic in its very essence. Abu-Bakr, the first caliph, used the same logic when he decided to use force against a tribe which had refused to give *zakāh*. It is alleged that he said on this occasion: "I swear, I will fight against anyone who differs between *salāh* and *zakāh*.

The Qur'ān's very frequent formula "perform *salāh* and give *zakāh*" is only a specific form of another, more frequent and more general "bipolar" formula "believe and do good deeds," which can be considered as the fundamental form of the Qur'ān's religious, moral, and social commandments.[13] This formula defines the two irreplaceable pillars upon which the whole of Islam rests. It would

---

[12]Professor Lester Turrow from the Massachusetts Institute of Technology has even proved the contrary. He states that there are no conflicts between social giving and economic efficiency and that social programs can be as economically productive as socially just. Refuting the thesis that extensive social giving would threaten tthe economic balance of the nation since it could "spoil the people," Professor Turrow even states that the nations with the least gap between the rich and the poor are one by one overtaking the United States: Sweden, Switzerland, Denmark, Norway, and soon West Germany. Here as well, the "third" combined way has proved to be the closest to man and therefore the most efficient as well.

[13]An important verse of the Qur'ān (2:277) points to this connection "Those who believe and do righteous deeds perform *salāh* and give *zakāh* will have their reward with their Lord. On them there shall be no fear or grief."

be appropriate to look at it as the first and the highest form of Islam The whole of Islam is under the sign of this bipolar unity.

Shahādah (the profession of faith by which one becomes a Muslim) is made before witnesses because of the double meaning of that act. By this profession, one is entering a spiritual community, an act for which witnesses are not necessary, but he/she is also entering a sociopolitical community, which implies legal — not only moral — obligations. To join a religion no witness is necessary since this is a relationship between man and God. Moreover, in this case, the intention or the inner decision is quite sufficient. Joining in the presence of others holds an element of publicity, unnecessary from the point of view of religion.

There is a similar side, no doubt, to the Islamic fast during the month of Ramadān. Muslims have always held it as a manifestation of the community's spirit, and this is why they react so strongly to public violations of this duty. Since fasting is not solely an issue of faith in Islam, it is not only a personal matter of the individual but also a social obligation. Such an interpretation of a religious norm is incomprehensible in any other religion. The Islamic fast which is the union of asceticism and joy — and even pleasure in certain cases — is the most natural and most radical educational measure that has ever been put into practice. It is equally present in the king's palace and the peasant's hut, in a philosopher's home and a worker's home. Its greatest advantage is that it is really practiced.

Then, what about *hajj* (the pilgrimage to the Ka'bah in Mekkah), known as the fifth pillar of Islam? Is it a religious rite, a trade fair, a political gathering, or all in one? It is clearly a religious rite, but one "à l'Islam," all in one.

The bipolarity of Islam is evident in many other ways. Listen to this line from the Qur'ān: "Your atonement for a false oath shall be either to feed ten of the poor with simple food that you and your family are used to eating, or to dress them in simple clothes, or to give a slave his freedom. If that is beyond your means, then fast for three days."[14] Thus, useful, social acts in the outside world are preferred to purely spiritual acts, the latter being implemented as a replacement only when the former are impossible. In the previously

---

[14]The Qur'ān 5:92. Also, Muhammad once said: "If you witness an evil, remove it by hand. If that is not possible, condemn it by word, or at least in thought, but this last is the weakest faith."

mentioned Qur'ānic quote, the fast is such penitence — a spiritual act of penitence, atonement, and prayer.

The Old Testament prescribes retaliation, the New Testament forgiveness. See how the Qur'ān makes a "molecule" from these "atoms": "The recompense for an injury is an injury equal thereto in degree; but if a person forgives and makes reconciliation, his reward is from God."[15] Sometimes the synthesis is almost mechanical: "We prescribed in the Torah a life for a life, an eye for an eye, a nose for a nose, an ear for an ear, a tooth for a tooth, and wounds equal for equal. But if any one remits the retaliation by way of charity, it is an act of atonement for himself,"[16] or: "O believer, do not forbid yourself the good and pure things God has granted you, but commit no excess; God does not love those given to excess."[17] Islam is not a religion which forbids man the "fruits of the earth," or one which always teaches that there are more and more forbidden things. Islam does not anathematize the earth. Quite the contrary: if one has no water, earth can be used for ablution. The symbolics of *tayammum* (ablution without water) can have this meaning only.

Some Islamic postulates are religious only in title, form, or origin. Nevertheless, they are Islamic in the best sense of the word. This clearly applies to the order for cleanliness and the prohibition of alcohol. Similar orders are not religious for the simple reason that they spring from a care for the exterior, physical, or social life. They are not even part of culture. They attain their complete meaning within civilization. The great crowded cities of today are incomprehensible without a certain degree of personal and public hygiene, while alcoholism has proved to be the greatest trouble in the era of technology and urbanization.

The logic of the preceding considerations will direct us to a well-founded thought, namely that Islam naturally tends to an integration of art and technology. This type of synthesis is most consistently realized in architecture. In fact, out of the great arts, Islam has the most understanding of architecture since it is the least "pure" art or because it is a "general art."[18] Pure art stresses the individual too much, while the spiritual stresses the other side of man. In this

---

[15]The Qur'ān 42:40.

[16]The Qur'ān 5:48.

[17]The Qur'ān 5:90.

[18]Kenneth Clark even calls it a "social art which helps people to live a richer life." Kenneth Clark, *civilization*, p. 242.

way, it is in opposition to the concept of balance on which Islam insists. Architecture is concerned, interested, functional, and an answer to human needs as distinguished from music.

It is this "double" character of architecture which predetermined it as a typical Islamic art. Just like Islam, it also has a mind and a body.[19] The outstanding achievements of Islam in architecture are not accidental. They are premeditated.

The sources of Islam are also marked by the same dualism. There are two basic sources: the Qur'ān and Ahādith, each of them representing inspiration and experience, eternity and time, thought and practice, idea and life. Islam is less a way of thinking, more a way of living. All the interpretations of the Qur'ān indicate that without ahādith, and therefore without a life, it is not quite comprehensible. Only through the interpretation of a life (that of Muhammad) does Islam display itself as a practical philosophy, as an overall scheme of life. If we include in our analysis the third source of Islam — that of *ijmā'* — we remain in the same position. *Ijmā'* is the consensus (unanimous, according to Imam Shafi'i, and a majority, according to at-Tabari and ar-Razi) of scholars on certain *shar'i* (legal issues). Islam would not be what it is if it did not combine an elitist principle with number and quantification. In *ijmā'*, there is at the same time a qualitative (aristocratic, elitist) and a quantitative (democratic) aspect.

The city of Mekkah and the cave of Hirā' can be included in this order of "duality," for they represent in the very emergence of Islam the oppositeness between the real and the inner world, between activity and meditation. In Islam's two-phase development, first in Mekkah, then in Medinah — two periods whose different spirit and meaning are registered by every history on Islam — the same contradiction (or paradoxical unity) is encountered, but now in terms of

---

[19]Duality is reflected in its name as well: archi-tecture litrally means more than a "tecture" (ordinary building with mere practical functions) either by its dimensions, its style, or its elevated purpose. This is why an absolutely functional architecture is not possible; it would be a contradiction in terms, for architecture cannot be reduced to mere function without losing its meaning. On the other hand, so-called "pure architecture," a functionless architecture, does not exist. In this respect, it is indicative that almost all great Renaissance architects were artists (painters or sculptors), and that, on the other hand, the greatest English architect, Christopher Wren, was first a mathematician and astronomer. "Wren's buildings show us that mathematics, measurements, observing — all that makes science — did not prove unfriendly to architecture." Ibid., p. 212. Architecture is a strange "mixture" of art and science.

faith and politics, a community of faith versus community of interests.

Finally, the greatest figure of Islam is the *shaheed*, who is a fighter in God's way," a saint and a warrior in one person. What was broken down in Christianity into the monastic and the chivalrous principles is united here into the figure of the *shaheed*. This is a unity of mind and blood, two principles which belong to two different orders of things.

Religion Turned Toward Nature

The Qur'ān steadily continues to repeat its two-sided demand, giving it new and newer forms: now it is a demand for joining meditation with observation. One is religion, the other is science, or rather the promise of a science.

The Qur'ān does not include, nor should it include, ready-made scientific truths. Instead, it implies an essential scientific position, a concern for the outside world which is unusual for a religion. The Qur'ān points to so many facts in nature and calls on man to respond to them. The command for science (for "reading") now does not appear to be against God, but is actually issued in the name of God: "Read, in the name of the Lord ..."[20] Man observes, searches, and perceives not the self-made nature but a world which is God's masterpiece. This is why this observation is not objective, indifferent, or free of desire. It is the mixture of scientific curiosity and religious admiration. Many of the descriptions of nature in the Qur'ān, sometimes very poetic, are the best illustrations of this tendency. Let us listen to some of them:

Behold! In the creation
of the heavens and the earth;
in the alteration
of the night and the day;
in the sailing of the ships
through the ocean
for the profit of mankind;
in the rain which God
sends down from the skies,

---

[20]The Qur'ān 96:1.

and the life which He gives therewith
to an earth that is dead;
in the beasts of all kinds
that He scatters
through the earth;
in the change of the winds,
and the clouds which they
trail like their slaves
betweent the sky and the earth;
(here) indeed are signs
for a people that are wise.[21]

It is God Who causes
the seed grain
and the date-stone
to split and sprout.
He causes the living
to issue from the dead,
and He is the One
to cause the dead
to issue from the living.
That is God: then how
are you deluded
away from the truth?
He it is Who cleaves
the daybreak (from the dark):
He makes the night
for rest and tranquility,
and the sun and moon
for the reckoning (of time):
Such is the judgment
and ordering of (Him),
the Exalted in Power,
the Omniscient.
It is He Who makes
the stars (as beacons) for you,
that you may guide yourselves,
with their help, through the dark spaces
of land and sea:
We detail Our signs

---

[21]The Qur'ān 2:164.

for people who know.
It is He Who has
produced you
from a single person:
Here is a place of sojourn
and a place of departure':
We detail Our signs
for people who understand.
It is He Who sends down
rain from the skies:
with it we produce
vegetation of all kinds:
From some We produce
green (crops), out of which
We produce grain,
heaped up (at harvest);
out of the date palm
and its sheaths (or spathes)
(come) clusters of dates
hanging low and near:
and (then there are) gardens
of grapes, and olives,
and pomegranates,
each similar (in kind)
yet different (in variety):
when they begin to bear fruit,
feast your eyes with the fruit
and the ripeness thereof.
Behold! In these things
there are signs for people
who believe.[22]

It is He Who sends down
rain from the sky:
from it you drink,
and out of it (grows)
the vegetation on which
you feed your cattle.
With it He produces
for you corn, olives,

---

[22]The Qur'ān 6:95-99.

date palms, grapes,
and every kind of fruit:
Verily in this is a sign
for those who give thought.
He has made subject to you
the night and the day;
the sun and the moon;
and the stars are in subjection
by His command: verily
in this are signs
for men who are wise.
And the things on this earth
which He has multiplied
in varying colors (and qualities):
Verily in this is a sign
for men who celebrate
the praises of God (in gratitude).
It is He Who has made
the sea subject, that you
may eat thereof flesh
that is fresh and tender,
and that you may extract
therefrom ornaments to wear;
and you see the ships
therein that plough the waves,
that you may seek (thus)
of the bounty of God
and that you may be grateful.[23]

And God sends down rain
from the skies, and gives therewith
life to the earth after its death:
Verily in this is a sign
for those who listen.
And verily in cattle (too)
Will you find an instructive sign.
From what is within their bodies,
between excretions and blood,
We produce, for your drink,
milk, pure and agreeable

[23]The Qur'ān 16:10-14.

to those who drink it.
And from the fruit
of the date palm and the vine,
you get out wholesome drink
and food: behold, in this
also is a sign
for those who are wise.
And thy Lord taught the bee
to build its cells in hills,
on trees, and in (men's) habitations.
Then to eat of all
the produce (of the earth),
and find with skill the spacious
paths of its Lord: there issues
from within their bodies
a drink of varying colors,
wherein is healing for men:
Verily in this is a sign
for those who give thought.[24]

It is He Who created
the night and the day,
and the sun and the moon:
All (the celestial bodies)
swim along, each in its
rounded course.[25]

How many populations have We
destroyed, which were given
to wrongdoing? They tumbled down
on their roofs. And how many
wells are lying idle and neglected,
and castles lofty and well-built?
Do they not travel
through the land, so that
their hearts (and minds)
may thus learn wisdom
and their ears may
thus learn to hear?
Truly it is not their eyes

---

[24]The Qur'ān 16:65-69.
[25]The Qur'ān 21:33.

that are blind, but their
hearts which are
in thier breasts.[26]
Do they not look
at the earth — how many
noble things of all kinds
We have produced therein?[27]

Do they not travel
through the earth and see
what was the end
of those before them?
They were superior to them
in strength: they tilled
the soil and populated it
in greater numbers than these
have done: there came to them
their apostles with clear (signs),
(which they rejected, to their
own destruction): it was not
God who wronged them, but
they wronged their own souls.[28]

Do they not look
at the sky above them? —
how We have made it
and adorned it,
and there are no
flaws in it?
And the earth —
We have spread it out,
and set thereon mountains
standing firm, and produced
therein every kind of
beautiful growth (in pairs)
to be observed
and commemorated
by every devotee
turning (to God).

---

[26]The Qur'ān 22:45-46.
[27]The Qur'ān 26:7.
[28]The Qur'ān 30:9.

And We send down
from the sky rain
charged with blessing,
and We produce therewith
gardens and grain for harvests;
and tall (and stately)
palm-trees, with shoots
of fruit-stalks, piled
one over another —
as sustenance for
(God's servants) —
and We give (new) life
therewith to land that is
dead: thus will be
the Resurrecton.[29]

Do they not look
at the camels,
how they are made? —
and at the sky,
how it is raised high? —
and at the mountains,
how they ae fixed firm? —
and at the earth,
how it is spread out?[30]

Have you watched the seed
which you sow in the ground?
...
the water you drink?
...
the fire you light?[31]

In these verses, turned entirely toward nature, we find a complete acceptance of the world, a total lack of any sort of conflict with nature. In Islam, matter is lent to so many beautiful and noble things, as is the case with the body in *salah* and the estate in *zakah*. The material world is not Satan's kindgom; the body is not the seat of sin. Even the world to come, the object of man's

---

[29]The Qur'ān 50:6-11.
[30]The Qur'ān 88:17-20.
[31]The Qur'ān 56:63-71.

greatest hopes, is portrayed in the Qur'ān in the colors of this world. In this fact, Christians see a sensuality which is incongruent with their own religion. In fact, this only demonstrates that the material world is not inwardly alien to Islam.

Certain verses of the Qur'ān awaken intellectual curiosity and give impetus to the exploratory mind: "We made from water every living thing."[32] or "The same water waters them (fruit trees) and yet they differ in taste. There are signs here for those who possess reason."[33]

This last verse is particularly "provocative" to the intellect. It states a problem which lies at the base of all chemistry. The result: it was the Muslims who finally put an end to the endless dispute about substantial issues which obsessed Christianity and turned toward chemistry (alchemy). This was a turn from mystical philosophy to rational science.

A common element of all the cited passages of the Qur'ān is the command of observation, the activity by means of which all man's power over the world and nature started.

An investigation into the basis of the West's power proves that it does not lie mainly in their armies or economics. This is only the external appearance of things. The basis of its power lies in the observation and the experimental method of thinking which Western civilization inherited from Bacon.[34] Jean Fourastie writes: "Observation of nature, society, and people is the first stage in the basic education given to all children of the Western world. ... An interest in the outside world is opposed to the interest of the Brahman and Buddhist philosophers who turned from the outer to the inner world. ... It is useless to think that a people could join the route of progress if it has not adopted the principles of experimental thinking of Galileo, Pascal, Newton, and Claude Bernard. The precondition for every economic and social progress is a change in the intellectual viewpoint, a transition from the abstract to the concrete, from the rational to the experimental, from stagnation to innovation."[35]

---

[32]The Qur'ān 21:30.

[33]The Qur'ān 5:4.

[34]That is, after Bacon received it from the Muslims — see Chapter XI of this book.

[35]Jean Fourastie: *The Civilization of Tomorrow* (Zagreb: n.p., n.d.), pp. 47-48. Fourastie was more specifically referring here to the experimental ideas set forth in Maurice A. Finocchiaro, *Galileo and the Art of Reasoning: Rhetorical Foundations of Logic and Scientific Method* (Dordrecht, Holland: D. Reidel Publishing Company,

It is impossible to carry out Islam in practice on a primitive level of consciousness. *salah* can only be correctly performed if the orientation in time and space is correct. In *salah*, people turn toward Mekkah, orienting themselves in terms of space. The prayer is made at a time defined by astronomical facts. The act has to be performed at an exactly determined set time of year — that is, at a certain position of the earth in its orbit around the sun. *Zakah* requires statistics, evidence, and accounting. *Hajj*, the pilgrimage, is connected to travel and the acquaintance with many facts that only a long journey calls for. Simply put, leaving everything else aside, the Muslim community, by practicing nothing but these four pillars of Islam, has to reach a minimal level of civilization. One cannot be a Muslim and yet remain in a state of barbarity.

This tendency was intentional, no doubt. An argumental history of Islamic science could show how the development of all scientific fields in the first centuries of Islam started with efforts to realize the orders of Islam as strictly as possible.

This was certainly most evident in astronomy. In John Gunther's *History of the Natural Sciences*, we find facts which confirm the very vivacious activity of the Islamic world in that field.

In the valley of the Euphrates, Islam came across a well-developed astrology which had been gathering important knowledge about celestial phenomena for almost 3,000 years. However, since beliefs of any tie between human destiny and the stars were foreign to Islam, its monotheism and its rationalism had to transform this astrology into astronomy. Speaking of the Baghdad school of astronomy, named after the famous observatory near Baghdad, Sédillot says the following: "What was typical for the Baghdad Astronomy School from the very beginning was its scientific spirit: to move from the known into the unknown and never to accept as proved that which could not be verified through observation." Khayyam's calendar approaches the accuracy of the Gregorian calendar we use today.[36] The Toledo tables, the probable author of which is Ibrahim

---

1976); Blaise Pascal, *Oeuvres complètes*, ed. Leon Brunschvieg and Pierre Boutroux (Paris: hachette et Cie., 1965); Sir Isaac Newton, *Works*, ed. Alexander Dyce, vol. 3: *Remarks Upon a Discourse of Free Thinking* (New York: AMS Press, 1966); and Claude Bernard, *An Introduction to the Study of Experimental Medicine*, trans. Henry Copley Green (New York: Dover Publications, 1957).

[36]Llewelyn Powys: "Omar Khayyam," *Rats in the Sacristy* (Freeport, New York: Books for Libraries Press, Inc., 1967), p. 125.

az-Zarkali, considered the movements of the planets and were for a long time the basis of European astronomy. Al-Biruni set forth the hypothesis that the earth, and not the sky, rotates around its axis. Ibn-Bajjah claimed that the planets' orbits are possibly elliptical and not circular.

This lively interest in astronomy and the natural sciences during the first centuries of Islam was a direct consequence of the Qur'ān. Religion turned toward nature initiated a great chapter in the development of science, one of the most brilliant in history.

This tendency of integrating religion and science — an Islamic tendency in the best sense of the world — can be seen in the simultaneous construction of mosques and schools. The first order to build schools near the mosques dates back to the second caliph 'Umar ibn-al-Khattab. This order was repeated by Caliph Haroun al-Rashid (786-808). The parting of mosques from schools came about much later, through the creation of Nizamiyyah schools, but the school programs continued to be based on the principle of "bipolar unity."

The mosque has never, through out its history, been only a place of worship. In the first centuries of Islam, according to Risler, any meeting place where honest people gathered "be it a school, a club, or market," was considered a mosque.[37]

This tendency resulted in a phenomenon known only in the Islamic cultural circle: the mosque-school, a unique construction with a double function which has no adequate name in European languages. At most, we find it in French in the form of the mechanical compound "mosque-école."[38] This characteristic building is the material or technical equivalent of that primeval Islamic postulate of the unity of religion and science with which the very revelation of the Qur'ān started: "Read, in the name of your Lord... ."[39]

The same concept was reflected in all programs offered by these schools. The famous Baghdad Nizamiyyah was for a long time an

---

[37]Risler: *La civilization: arabe*, p. 128. In an excellent article by Stefano Bianco in the magazine "Werk" (Switzerland, September 1976) the aforementioned phenomenon is considered in terms of the polyvalence of Islamic space as the title of the article indicates: "The Polyvalence and Flexibility in the Structure of the Islamic City."
[38]There is historical evidence that the first mosque, Masjid an-Nabi, which was built by Muhammad himself, was a school at the same time (it was called Suffah).
[39]The Qur'ān 96:1.

archetype of the Islamic school. To the Europeans, it was a "high religious school." Actually, its program included what we would call theology — Qur'ānic commentary (*tafsir*), hadith, morality (*akhlāq*), and articles of faith (*'aqa'id*), but it also put an equal emphasis on law, philosophy, literature, mathematics, astronomy, and the basic facts of medicine as an integral part of its program.[40] The Nizamiyyah served as a model for many similar schools and became the most frequent type of school in all large Islamic cities.

This is why schools in the Islamic world cannot be classified according to the European criterion of secular versus spiritual. Such institutions were considered by all Muslims to be only natural, as they stemmed directly from the spirit of Islam. The same attitude has been maintained up to the present day, and wherever it is different, it can be attributed to foreign influence. The original state always corresponds to the basic Islamic concept of the unity of religion and science. Cairo's al-Azhar, the largest and one of the oldest Islamic schools (founded in 972) referred to both as a mosque and as a university, was in the beginning a school and became a theological school only at the time of deepest decadence. By the 1961 Reform, al-Azhar had reinstated its original integral character with the founding of a medical and technological faculty within its complex. In Pakistan, the state entrusted the imams with mass literacy courses, a measure which is essentially correct, although one pursued with insufficient energy. A similar example can be found in Iran, where educated soldiers perform their military service by teaching illiterate people to read and write and where mosques serve as school buildings.

The mosque-school is one of those symbols to which nothing can be added and from which nothing can be subtracted.

Islam's orientation toward the external world endowed it with a special realism in its conception of man. Acceptance of nature in general implied the acceptance of human nature. Rejection of this world, which also implies the rejection of the human body, is found in every religion. Islam is the realization of the impossible objective of forcing Christianity to acknowledge the reality of the world. Some verses from the Qur'ān sound unlikely from the standpoint of pure religion (for example, those concerning the acceptance of pleasures, sexual love, struggle, hygiene). This is a most

---

[40]See Risler.

decisive fact in the history of religions and in the history of the human mind in general. It has marked the appearance of "the religion of the two worlds," of the all-encompassing system of human life, of the cognition that man has no need to reject religion for the sake of science or to renounce the struggle for a better life for the sake of religion. Islam's far-reaching importance lies in the fact that it has not overlooked the existence of suffering and the fight against suffering which is the crux of human history.

While affirming the greatness and dignity of man in general, Islam is very realisic, almost "anitheroic" when dealing with man as an individual. Islam never strives to nurse properties which are not rooted in human nature. It does not attempt to make us angels, as this is impossible. It tends to make us what we are: human. Although it knows a kind of asceticism, Islam has never tried to destroy life, health, intellect, sociability, or desires for happiness and pleasure. A certain degree of asceticism is here only to counterbalance our instincts or to provide a balance between body and soul, between animalistic and ethical urges. Through ablution, prayer, fasting, *jama'ah*, activity, observation, struggle, and mediation, Islam carries on nature's work of shaping man. There is no room for opposition to nature. The continuity is maintained even when objectives do not coincide.

It is just this attitude of a religion which has caused misunderstandings that have lasted until this very day.

Some attacked Islam for its ostensible sensuality, backing their claims with quotes from the Qur'ān and examples from Muhammad's life. We must clearly and openly say: yes, Islam pleads for a natural life and against asceticism, for richness and against poverty, for man's power over nature not only on this planet but if possible also in the universe. Yet, to understand Islam properly, we should look at these ideas of nature, richness, politics, science, power, knowledge, and joy in a somewhat different way than the people of Western civilization do.

Islam requires that man takeover all responsibility; it does not impose the ideal of poverty, asceticism, and sufferance.[41] It does not forbid man to taste "the salt of the earth and of the large salty sea."[42]

---

[41]"There is no monasticism in Islam," Muhammad (pbuh).

[42]André Gide: *Fruits of the Earth*, trans. Dorothy Bussy (London: Secker and Warburg, 1962).

It postulates for man a complete and full life.[43] This life is charted by two coordinates: one is the natural desire for happiness and power; the other is moral perfection, "the permanent creation of oneself." These desires contradict and exclude each other in logic only; in real life, they have come together in innumerable ways in our own life and before our eyes. Such a possibility has only been given to man, and man — this controversial being — can be defined by it.

The Gospels condemn instincts and speak only about the soul. The Qur'ān brings them back, for they are true and real, although not so noble. The Qur'ān mentions them with understanding, not with blame. The angels' bow to man[44] implied the superiority of the human over the angelic, in the same way that a drama is more truthful than the sublimity of an idyll. Men are not gentle and graceful beings solely oriented toward good. They are physical, coarse, contradictory, stretched between desires and temptations. In an unnatural wish to make them sinless and infallible, we suddenly realize that we have obtained bloodless, sentimental, and false personalities incapable of both good and evil. Separating them from mother earth, we separate them from life, and where there is no life, there is no virtue either.

Freud proved that sexuality cannot be destroyed but only repressed; the repressed sexual urge brings about even more troubles. However sublime the Christian postulate for chastity and restraint is, the Islamic idea of a controlled and moderate sexual life suits man better as it recognizes the issue. In this area, Islam is not primarily religion. All arguments supporting sexual life are rational and practical, not religious.

The question we are discussing is the problem of man's harmony with himself, a harmony between his ideals and his natural, physical, social, and intellectual desires. Conflicts in this basic area are an important source of neuroses; another source is the donflict between man and his surroundings.

The Qur'ān rarely addresses the individual. It more frequently addresses the people, and when it does, sometimes as citizens only. Man as a member of society is a child of this world, and only

---

[43] "O believers, do not keep yourselves from the good things that God has given you, but commit no excess. For God does not love those given to excess" (The Qur'ān 5:9].

[44] The Qur'ān 2:34.

as a personality is he an inhabitant of heaven. That which he shares with other people, and not his specific individual qualities, makes him a social being. If the individual and the society are shaped independently, according to different models and ideals, a conflict between the individual and the society is inevitable. Emphasizing justice instead of evangelic love as its supreme order,[45] Islam evidently wanted the education of the Muslim as a man and as a citizen to be identical, for jsutice is both a personal and a social virtue ("a political virtue" as Aristotle called it).[46] This is why we can rightly expect that a Muslim, due to the balance of physical and moral requirements, will be in better harmony with his surroundings than any other type of man. Christian teaching, like any other idealistic teaching, leads to disappointment and insecurity because of an evident contradiction between desires and reality, between theory and practice.[47]

Neuroses and deformations of the Western man are partly the consequence of inner conflicts between the Christian ideal of man and society's political models which develop separately and independently from Christian ideals. This is a situation where the church takes care of the souls and the state governs the bodies according to the postulate: render unto God that which is God's, and render unto Caesar that which is Caesar's.[48] Western man has been allowed to be a Christian in his private life and to be a Machiavellian in his public and business dealings. Those who are not able to solve or endure this conflict become victims of neuroses. On the other hand, all those who have come to know the Muslim world have had a unanimous impression of a harmony between man and society, of an integration of the individual into the social fabric, of a cohesion which is not artificial, political or legal, but interior, organic. The fact exists, in spite of the poverty and backwardness that reign in that region.

Muhammad, upone whom be peace, blamed the extreme positions: "I am indignant with two things: the ignorant who is devout

---

[45]The Qur'ān 4:135, 5:9, 45, 6:152, 7:28, 84 and so on.

[46]Aristotle: *Politics*, trans. H. Rackham (Cambridge, Masachusetts: Harvard University Press, 1959). St. Thomas Aquinas considers justice a "supreme celestial virtue." See Thomas Aquinas: *Summa Theologia* (Cambridge, London: Blackfriars, 1964), II, 191. Love, evidently, is not quite "in scale" with this world.

[47]Karen Horney: *New Ways in Psychoanalysis*, (New York: W. W. Norton & Co., Inc., 1939).

[48]Matthew: 22:21.

and the scholar who does not believe."[49] No doubt, Muhammad was indignant with many other "two things": the believers who are powerless and the rulers who do not believe; the pure soul in a dirty body and the corrupted soul in a well-groomed body; justice without power and power that is tyrannical. He did not mind wealth and abundance, but he was decisively for richness in virtue and almost certainly against bare virtue, powerless and unprotected. He ranks the struggle for a better life and against tyranny, ignorance, illness, misery, and dirtiness on the same level as moral virtues. Muslims are not saints, even when making prayer and fasting. They are ordinary people, men and women, dreaming about love and the delights of life, though still human to the core, sharing the real life and always returning to it. They do not retire to caves far from society, nor do they neglect themselves; they do not give themselves up to the mercy of their enemies, neither do they reject "the good things that God has allowed them to enjoy."[50] They do not consider inner freedom sufficient — every believer enjoys this kind of freedom. They want the physical freedom as well and do not agree to be slaves. Though they believe this life on earth is not the only life, they still do not want to resign from it. The Qur'ān addresses the true children of the earth "who serenely and cheerfully tread upon it, without violence, but seeking the Lord's favors."

Islam can be defined as a requirement to live both the physical and the spiritual life, in the external and internal world, or, as the Qur'ān puts it, to live an internal life "without forgetting one's part in the temporal world."[51] Starting from that definition, we could say that all people, or most of them, are potential Muslims.[52] This is the probable meaning of the assertion (attributed to Muhammad) that every child is born as a Muslim, but then his parents or circumstances turn him into something else. Man cannot be a Christian, for "God does not charge anyone with a burden he cannot carry."[53] Still, man cannot exist as a mere biological fact, as a member of a society — he cannot exist without Jesus. man cannot live either according to Jesus or against him. All of man's fate on

---

[49]This was quoted by Ralph Waldo Emerson in *The Conduct of Life, Nature, and Other Essays* (New York: E. P. Dutton & Co., 1915).
[50]The Qur'ān 5:90.
[51]The Qur'ān 28:77.
[52]"If that is Islam, then all of us are living in Islam," as stated by Goethe. The Qur'ān also makes a similar statement.
[53]The Qur'ān 2:286.

earth takes place between these two contradictory facts. Islam, on the other hand, suits man because it recognizes the duality of his nature.[54] Any different answer would stress only one side of human nature, thereby hindering the full sweep of human forces or bringing about their inner conflicts. That is why man is the most obvious argument of Islam.

Islam and Life

Dualism is not a supreme human philosophy; it is the supreme form of life. Poetry is in principle a matter of the heart, but the greatest poets — Homer, Firdausi, Dante, Shakespeare, Goethe — have combined in their poems reason and feelings, science and beauty. Poetry pertains to the individual, not to the society, even though Homer's poems helped form the Greek nation, and Whittier's angry poems helped abolish slavery in America. Mathematics pertains to the intellect, but "a good mathematician must be a poet too."[55] All top-level physicists and astronomers were in a sense mystics as well: Copernicus, Newton, Keppler, Einstein, Oppenheimer. Punishment, although a repressive measure, can also work as a powerful moral factor. If it is just, it has an educational value both for the guilty and for other people. Fear is the start of morality, just as fear of God is the start of love for God. Sport, though merely a physical activity, evidently has a powerful educational value. Plato, one of the greatest minds of all times, got his name from his broad shoulders. The strong body nursed a most noble spirit. Body and soul, heart and brain, science and religion, physics and philosophy meet at points which mark the peaks of life. Naked intellect or pure inspiration are a sure sign of decadence. So, the secular principle can help the sacral one, cleanliness of the body can serve the purity of the soul, and *salah* can be the supreme form of human prayer.

Let us consider some more phenomena from the same perspective. What is the aim of the so-called "natural education"? Rousseau gives a characteristic answer: "The aim is to bring together that which is considered difficult to be joined, but which all great men have succeeded in doing: physical and mental powers, the intellect

---

[54]The Qur'ān 30:30.
[55]Weierstrass, n.p.d.

of a philosopher and the strength of an athlete."[56]

Speaking of education, Montaigne says: "In order to strengthen the child's spirit, we must strengthen his muscles,"[57] and Rousseau asserts that Locke, Fleury, and De Crusa also agree on the point, while he himself repeatedly comes back to this subject: "The body must be strong in order to be able to obey the mind: a good servant must be strong. Excesses give rise to passions which eventually weaken our body, and the other way around: tortures of the body and fasting have the same result but for opposite reasons. The weaker the body is, the more it commands. The stronger it is, the more obedient it is. All sensual passions are housed in weak bodies: the less they can satisfy them, the more suffering they incur."[58]

Taken in principle, force has nothing to do with morality; however, in real life, there is no justice without force. Justice is the unity of the concepts of equity and power. Have not political movements gotten rid of so much of the injustice tolerated for centuries by the church and religion? The ideas of *égalité, liberté,* and *fraternité* came from religion, but as a reality (if they are reality), they were materialized through revolution — that is, politics and violence. The impotence of religion to carry out in practice even a part of the great ideals it preaches compromises its demands before the humble and the oppressed. Violence and politics, on the contrary, have been justified to a certain extent, for they created the means needed for realizing the great ideas which religion had discovered or inspired but could not manage to translate into reality.

Let us take human work. It has, at first glance, two aspects: first, the very activity, which is human and nonutilitarian, and second, the result of that activity, a product, which is motivated by usefulness. Religion is concerned with the first aspect, civilization with the second.

Religion has determined man's destiny on earth with the saying: "In the sweat of your brow you shall eat your own bread,"[59] while science and materialism promise an earthly kingdom without work, where machines will increasingly replace man's work, and where

---

[56]Rousseau: *Emile.*

[57]Michel de Montaigne: *The Education of Children,* trans. Lizzie E. Rector (New York: D. Appleton, 1899).

[58]Rousseau: *Emile.*

[59]Genesis: 3:19.

working days will become shorter and shorter. Religion requires work for work's sake as the means against sin because "the mind of an idle man is Satan's dwelling" and because its objective is not "production and reproduction of material life." Civilization, on the contrary, is concerned with the results of work, or more accurately, with production. The Marxist writer Henri Lefèbvre finds it necessary to emphasize that work, according to Marxism, is "a productive factor not an ethical one."[60] The cult of work in Europe is originally Protestant and not socialist, as is usually thought. Religion wants all to work, regardless of the resutls. Civilization, on the contrary, has in mind only the result, and it is trying to avoid work as much as possible by hiring others to work: slaves in ancient times, machines in modern times.

In this overview, work is analyzed, broken down. As a whole, as a useful activity, as a unity, work has both a moral and an economic side. It is a factor against evil and passions, just as it is a factor against poverty. In this regard, work is a typical Islamic phenomenon.

The parallelism of the useful and the ethical can be clearly seen in a phenomenon which concerns both the natural and social life of man. It is a question of the prevention or the permanent limitation of incest during the evolution of the human family. The attitudes of science and ethics coincide here perfectly.

The prohibition of marriage between close relatives — which has a universal importance because it is found in all parts of the world and at all times — is a good example of something that could be termed "natural" Islam. Life itself seems to have found its Islamic path.[61]

Is the prohibition of incest purely moral, or is it motivated by biological reasons? A simple answer cannot be given. The biological reasons are beyond doubt. The famous Russian biologist Timiriazev wrote: "There is much evidence to prove that the parents'

---

[60]Henri Lefebvre: paper read at the Geneva International Encounters.

[61]It is curious how primitive people found simple but efficient proceedings against unconscious breaches,of this prohibition. With the Pygmies of Africa or the Lutochtons of Australia, each family belongs to a totem group which in turn consists of several interconnected families. A number of closely related totem groups belong to a certain marital class whose symbol is a plant or an animal. When a young man decides to marry, he can only choose his bride from a different class, symbolized by a different plant or animal.

close kinship affects their children's health. There is no need to try proving this again nowadays because a whole series of experiments have shown this to be a natural law which concerns not only man but also animals and plants; it is a law which applies to the entire organic world." On the other hand, the prohibition of incest is very old, a fact which should bring us to the conclusion that it is based on moral concerns. The fact remains, however, that throughout history and even in our own times, incest has been regarded as morally wrong and has therefore been prohibited. In any case, it is a perfect example of the harmony between ethics and science, a principle representative of the essence of what we call the Islamic approach.

If we observe some interesting phenomena which have accompanied the development of medical science, we can perceive the "dualism" of its nature. Medicine has never been either in the past or in the present time, a pure science. It has been wisdom, ethics, and a spiritual discipline at the same time. Recently, some illnesses have been discovered where no organic deformations could be identified. The disturbances felt by the patient were closely related to his psychic life. Psychosomatic medicine, a recent medical branch which studies the mutual interaction of the body and psyche, considers ulcers, bronchial asthma, obesity, diabetes, migraine headaches, and some rheumatic disturbances to be primarily of a psychological origin. Investigations have shown that these and other illnesses are due to psychic conflicts or stresses and that the accompanying organic changes are of a secondary nature. These changes are sometimes completely absent.

This is why a true treatment cannot be reduced to physio-chemical therapy or surgery, that is, to mechanical intervention and operation. Contemporary medicine is becoming more and more conscious of the deficiency of "industrialized medicine" because, in reality, there is no sickness, there are only sick persons. Medicine is not concerned with phenomena but with people, or better, with personalities. The same cause does not necessarily lead here to the same consequence, nor are the "same" illnesses and treatments identical for two different men. This is why we must believe that there are particles of truth in old stories about healing by means of relics, prayers, sacrifices, fasting, and beliefs. This tendency has been maintained until today. In certain Paris hospitals, musico-therapy is applied,[63] for illness is not just a physical state or a physiochemical

[63]Yehudi Menuhin is the chairman of the Committee for Musico-Therapy.

or physiological disturbance. As opposed to alchemy or astrology (which turned into chemistry and astronomy, i.e., into science), medicine will always fluctuate between the two poles, for while chemistry and astronomy have matter as their object, medicine's "object" is life, or more accurately, human life. Medicine — like everything that directly concerns humans — will have to realize the integration of science and religion.

If we continue to consider things from this point of view, we notice that every art implies a craft. Nobody can deny the difference between art and craft nor ignore what they have in common. From a statute of a Paris painters and sculptors' guild dating from 1391, we can establish that there were no differences between this and any other tradesmen's guild statute. Here we find provisions concerning the training, apprenticeship, opening of a workshop, and so on. Two opposite tendencies can always be observed in this regard: first, art was (and had to be) separated from craft; second, this separation has never been complete — art and craft always maintain some common features. A human work is never completely mechanical, nor is it ever exclusively creative. There is no craft which does not imply creation, and there is no art which does not imply technique. The same bipolarity can be observed on other planes too: there is the artist and the art dealer, the writer and the publisher, the architect and the investor, and so on.

The history of music proves the interdependence of technique and idea. The greatest musicians (Beethoven, Bach, Mozart) were also concerned with the problems of musical technique and the organization of the orchestra. Beethoven's symphonies, the climax of Western music, cannot be imagined without those considerable improvements in musical technique which preceded them. The number of instruments was considerably increased; they were individualized and organized into groups within the whole orchestra which eventually contained as many as 150 musicians. A symphony was not possible without an orchestra as its exterior, technical basis.

Life is always a result of the mutual interaction of two independent factors. From a biological aspect, this is the unity of a physiochemical basis and a certain — let us call it the "entelechial" principle.[64] In history, this is the combined impact of the material basis

[64]Entelechy refers to a hypothetical agency that in some vitalist doctrines is considered inherent in living substances and regulates or directs the vital processes of an organism but is not discoverable by scientific investigation.

and the creative influence of the human conscious factor (the powerful personalities, leading ideas and ideals, and so on). The historical situation is in every moment a result of these two essentially independent forces.

The human influence on the course of history depends on the level of willpower and consciousness. The greater the spiritual strength of the partakers in historical events, the greater is their independence from external laws. The conditionality here is in reverse proportion to the activity of the subject. In principle, man is completely free, and external laws have no power over him. He has managed with his willpower to resist illnesses and dangers. Man, if he found himself among lions, would be lost, but this evident law does nto apply to a lion tamer. History is a continuing story about small groups of decisive, courageous, and clever people who have left an indelible stamp on the course of historical events and managed to change their flow.

The power of objective circumstances increases to the same degree as the individual factor decreases, as it becomes more and more inert — that is, as the subject becomes less of a man and more of an object. We have power over nature, and over history as well, if we have power over ourselves. This is Islam's attitude toward history.

Such an essentially Islamic view of historical movements can efficiently explain the flow of history and also determine the share of people in historical events; their power over historical events, and the limits of that power; the distinction between what man *can* do and what he *must* do as a subject of historical occurrences. This attitude explains the creative influence of ideals on historical reality and the changes of this reality through man's will and energy. On the other hand, it also explains the role of objective factors, the necessity of relying on facts. It rejects both historical determinism and any empty idealism not rooted in reality. Facts and ideas, and so reality and man, assume in this concept their proper measure.

Chapter 9

THE ISLAMIC NATURE OF LAW

The true laws of a society are only those which, besides the threat of punishment, oblige the conscience of the citizens, too.

THE ISLAMIC NATURE OF LAW

Two Aspects of Law

If the system of law is defined as human interest sanctioned as a right, then both religion and socialism are unfit for the law. Religion does not understand interests, and socialism does not understand rights.

No law can be based on interest only. Neither can it be based on the so-called "common interest" or the "state reason" because the common interest and the innate right of the so-called individual usually oppose each other. If man is not a person and is only a member of society, as is the case in socialism, then he has *a priori* no absolute and natural rights — he has only the "rights," bestowed upon him by the state. Beyond that, a member of a society has no other rights.

Rights are inalienable only if they are original and not the will of a king, or a parliament, or of a social class — that is, if they are given by nature or by God and were established only with the creation of man. Rights are an aspect of human dignity, and being so, they transcend time, conditions and history, and reach to the act of creation. Here lies the link between natural rights and religion, and the divergence between natural rights and materialism.

In *The Jewish Question* (1844), Marx writes: "So-called human rights, *droits de l'homme*, as distinguished from *droits du citoyen*, are nothing but the rights of a member of the middle class, i.e., those of an egoistic man, separated from other men and society."

Another writer of the materialistic school, Jeremy Bentham, wrote about human rights with disdain: "Human rights are nonsense, and natural human rights are nonsense squared." In one writing, Bentham calls the French Declaration of Human Rights a "metaphysical work," which in a sense it is. The search for the origin of the tricolor: freedom, equality, and brotherhood (*liberté, égalité, fraternité*) in Europe leads us to Rousseau and to the American Declaration of Independence in 1776. Jellinek declares that the Declaration of Human Rights is the consequence of the Reformation, not of the revolution.[1]

Ernest Bloch, who tries to reconcile Marxism and natural human rights, is obliged to conclude: "It cannot be accepted that man is free and equal by birth. There are no innate human rights; they are all obtained or have to be obtained by struggle."[2]

From this point of view, history is not a conflict between rights but a conflict between different interests. That is the meaning of "class struggle." The class that emerges victorious in this struggle proclaims its interest (its will) as law. Therefore, the Marxists say: "Law is the will of the ruling class transformed into legal regulations." Accordingly, there is no right and wrong, justice and injustice. The question is only which interest comes out as the winner in this struggle.[3]

If that is the case, then it is only the stronger who will have rights. Nevertheless by nature, every law is the total opposite: the right of the weaker for the strong do not need any law. Law has always been a way for the weak to oppose the strong, in the same way as the liberty of opinion and belief is primarily the right to have a different opinion and a different belief. A law which gives the citizen "the right" to applaud and to glorify the ruling clique would not be a law but cynicism. The touchstone of the legality of any social system is the way it treats its opponents and minorities. The

---

[1]Jellinek: *Die Erklarung der Menschenrechte*, 1904.

[2]Ernest Bloch: *Natural Law and Human Dignity* (Belgrade: n.p., 1977) p.178.

[3]One of those definitions of "the law" reads: "The law is the collection of the rules expressing the will of the ruling class. ... The application of these rules is done by the force of the state, with the aim to solidify, to strengthen, and to develop the social relationships and conditions corresponding to the will and profit of the ruling class. Vishinsky: *The Main Tasks of the Science of Soviet Socialistic Law*, 1938. The author of this definition, as the main state prosecutor during the purges of 1936-1939 in the USSR, had a good opportunity to show where such a definition leads to.

power of the strong is a fact, not the law. The law starts where the limitation of this power begins and where it has taken the stand of the weak as opposed to the benefit of the strong. This is why every people fight for a constitution, and every king tries to get rid of it.

Bloch rightly says that "every dictatorship is the suspension of law." That also applies to dictatorships of the proletariat. After all, is it not the proletarian dictatorship "a reign unlimited by law and based on violence" (Lenin)? Has not practice proved that the dictatorship of the proletariat has been transformed into a dictatorship of the secretariat? The statement that law is the will of the ruling class is the negation of the law's essence. The definition according to which "law is the measure of politics" (Lenin) or that "the law conscience is a part of the political conscience"[4] has the same meaning. No doubt, this negation of the law has its parallel in the denunciation of religion — that is, a direct result of materialistic philosophy. How could the power of the strong be limited except by religious principles? For what sake should a nation tolerate a minority that it could easily exterminate or divest of its property? What principles did the white immigrants in America violate when they almost completely exterminated the native population? If law is the will of the ruling class, it had a right to do so for it was stronger and historically more progressive, in a word, it was the "ruling class." What principles did the capitalists violate during the time that Marx called the period of primary capital accumulation? If law is the will of the ruling class, the capitalists — because they were the ruling class — did no violence but the law. That would mean that the workers who resisted were breaking the law, for they were working against that monstrous "will of the ruling class," or rather were working against a limiting principle of this will — that is, an independent principle.[5] The examination of the nature of this principle puts us in front of the same problems as when searching

---

[4]Vishinsky: *The Law of the Soviet State*, trans. Hugh W. Babb (New York; The Macmillan Company, 1948). Also, see Karl Marx's position on the subject (introduction, ibid., p.37): "Society does not rest on law. That is the phantasy of the jurists. On the contrary, law — in contrast to the arbitrariness of the separate individualism — must rest on society, must be an expression of society's general interests and needs, as they emerge from a given material means of production."

[5]A clear proof of this law is the fact that even the slave-holder's Roman law had to declare the principle of man's freedom: "Ab initio omnes homines liberi nascebantur" ("From the very beginning all men were born free"). Without this, it would not be a law, but the will of the ruling class.

for the essence of life, art, or freedom.

The true laws of a society are only those which, besides the threat of punishment, oblige the conscience of the citizens, too. Every system of law is such, or at least it pretends to be so. In practice, proletarian dictatorship tends to be a democracy. Any law defined as the will of the ruling class ceases to be only the "will," for it inevitably becomes "justice," "righteousness," or in a word law. This "duality" cannot be avoided; in fact, it is an imitation of the original dualism of the law.

If this dualism were to be destroyed, law would disappear. In the first case, law reduces itself to its subject — that is, interest, power, politics, to the *utilitas* of Roman law; in the second case, it sublimates itself to an abstract idea of righteousness or to moral appeal. In both cases, it ceases to be law.

Accordingly, law cannot be based on one principle only. Neither Christianity nor materialism can produce a system of law. Law, as seen by Christians, is an illusory attempt at bringing this world into order, an attempt inevitably bound to fail in the end. Jesus came to restore love and not the justice of the Old Testament. Nevertheless, love does not belong to this world; it is heavenly virtue.[6] Jesus did not recognize the need for judges,[7] while Hugo Grotius cuts the former connection between natural law and the "Sermon of the Mount" because of "its higher degree of holiness."

Law is objective, involved in politics and society, totally facing this world. But at the same time, it includes norms and ethics and tries to bring into this world the principle of justice — that is, a moral principle, which means something being not "of this world." As such, law is a "bipolar unity" — like man and Islam.

Law cannot be established only by religion or materialism, nor can it be established contrary to them. Without Christian emphasis on the value of man's personality — his intention, righteousness, natural human rights, and so forth — there is no law. On the other hand, without admitting the value and importance of this world and without interests and power — without that which Judaism emphasized — law will have no meaning. Without the Christian

---

[6]St. Thomas Aquinas: *Basic Writings of Saint Thomas Aquinas*, "Summa Theologia," II, 1, 91. ed. Anton C. Pegis (New York: Random House, 1945).
[7]Luke 12: 13-15

approach, it would not be possible and without the Jewish approach, it would not be necessary. From the said premises, it follows that law is Islamic by nature.

Historically speaking, law is a phenomenon of the mature stage in the life of a culture. It emerges in the time of balance between religious and people's socio-political aspirations. This is a time when religious feelings are still strong and are capable of influencing the people's life, but are already limited to a great extent by the rational utilitarian reasons of the coming civilization. Besides man, whose value was confirmed and established by religion, society also emerges as an independent reality. At that moment, they are two equal values. Their balance (Islamic balance) is a prerequisite to creating and developing a complete system of the law.

This situation can be observed in the emergence of the three most famous law systems in history: the Roman, the Islamic, and the European.

The first phase of Roman law, known as the time of the civil law (period of the Kingdom and the first three centuries of the Republic), is characterized by a complete identity between law and religion, between *ius* and *fas*. Civil rule (*ius*) has the nature of the religious norm (*fas*), and vice versa. Later, these principles are separated from each other. Nevertheless, Roman civilization and Roman political thinking had to be permeated by stoical moral and religious philosophy in order to enable the further development of its law. The Roman empiric principle of *utilitas* joined the stoical idealistic idea of *lex universalis*[8] for neither Roman civilization nor the Stoical philosophy could create the Roman legal system by itself.[9]

In Islam, we find a kind of "personal unity" between law and theology. Almost every great "religious" thinker of Islam has written books on jurisprudence.[10] It is difficult for Europeans to

---

[8]The best parts of Roman law were undoubtedly created under Stoical influence, for example, the following: "Juris preecepta sunt heac: honeste vivere, alterum non leadere, suum cuuique tribuere" ("These are the rules of the law: to live honestly, not to offend anyone, to give everybody what is due to him").

[9]Roman jurists came into contact with Stoical natural law about 150 B.C., when Panetius, one of the most famous Stoics of his time, was in Rome. Cicero's works are by far the best result of this synthesis. On the impact of Stoicism on Roman law, see Barth's *Die Stoa*, p. 120 ff.

[10]For example, the well-known Imam Abu Yusuf wrote on finance (*Kitab al-Kharaj*) and another great "religious" writer, Ash-Sha'bāni, wrote on war law.

distinguish between law and theology in these works. Islam does not recognize this separation. In a sense, law is a natural product of Islam. Alfred V. Karmer writes: "The Arabs [Muslims] are the only people during the early Middle ages who, in developing the science of law, achieved significant results. These results, in their grandiosity, stand immediately with the works of the Romans, the lawmakers of the world."

In European history, the development of law starts along with the overcoming of the Church and continues up to the appearance of socialist theories and socialism in European science. These few centuries, when elements of European culture and European civilization coexist, is the period of great European charters and codes. This dualism — in essence Islamic dualism — is reflected very clearly in the great juridical opus of Hugo Grotius, the central personality of European juridical thinking. At the end of the Reformation, he summed up the teachings of Catholic and Protestant juridical writers, and proved how law is, at the same time, dependent upon and independent from ethics and religion. Later, because of this dualism, some writers (such as Werner and Ahrens) tried to prove that the distinction made between law and morality was a great achievement of Grotius, while the others (such as Kirchmann) tried to prove the opposite. With the claim that God is the ultimate source of law, Grotius confirmed his belief in the mutual relation between law and religion.

The independence of law cannot be destroyed even in the most politically extreme Marxist state. Regardless of very clear theoretical views, in practice it is not possible to completely identify law with the will of the state — there always remains an insurmountable distance. Socialism and an independent, developed, and free juridical system are mutually exclusive.[11] Every law needs distance and standards. Socialism requires immediateness, objectiveness, and direct action. In socialism, which applies physical (or biological) habits of thinking to social life, there is no room for law since law is the opposite of physics, not recognizing "should" but only "is."[12]

---

[11]Still in 1978, 30 years after the People's Republic of China was founded, it had neither a civil nor a criminal legal code. It was considered for a long time to be a "forbidden zone" to complete the laws, according to a statement of the well-known Chinese jurist Han Yi Tung at a conference in 1978.

[12]Jevengenij Pasukanis, the best-known Soviet law theorist between the two world wars who disappeared in Stalin's purges, wrote that: "... there is no proletarian law, and consequently there is no socialist law." See his *Allegemeine Rechtslebre und Mar-*

The poor reputation of courts in poeple's democracies is the result of the ideological attitude toward law which, in spite of all pressures, remains in a sense natural law and not the will of the ruling class. Courts, as the executors of law, must share the bad position of law in general and be in "disfavor" (this is also true with the legal profession). Every government of this type tries to degrade law to the rank of politics, and courts to the rank of secretariats; but, as it never completely succeeds in this, it usually ignores the courts and, when necessary, uses direct prosecution by the police, the administrative authorities, and concentration camps — that is, the extra-judicial means. The state and the government are the expression of physical power, the courts and law of moral power. To recognize that the moral power of the courts and law can balance the physical power of the state means to recognize the supremacy of an idea over things and mind over matter. The principle of court independence is not compatible with the system of an atheistic state.[13]

The consistent part of the said situation is the disrespect of their own laws, and the "production" of an inflationary number of regulations.[14] Such is the consequence of "direct action" — that is, the attempt to replace law by political action, or simply by political regulations, letters, messages, and even speeches of leaders which become more important than the constitution and laws, for example, the *Quotations of Chairman Mao*. In all states of this type, we meet the large power of the executive authorities at the expense of the elected bodies and the police at the expense of the courts and the legal profession. These kinds of states are trying to make courts obedient tools in the hands of the administrative authorities, but they are never completely successful. Law can be curbed or subdued to some extent but, like man, it cannot be destroyed or reduced to nothing.

---

xismus, 1929, p. 33. Compare this statement with the "similar" Christian negation of the law by Rudolf Sohm: "The Law of the Church stands in opposition to and contradicts the very nature of the Church." See his *The Law of the Church*.

[13]It has to be noted that the principle of permanency of a judge (lifetime appointment for judges), which is a condition of the judges' true independence, is usually, in the socialist states substituted for the opposite principle, that of re-election (appointment of judges for a limited period). This system makes judges directly dependent upon the government. Judges are permanently worrying about being on "good terms" with those who re-appoint them.

[14]In the USSR during 1937-1974, about 370 laws were passed but, at the same time, the executive authorities (different ministries), produced over 700,000 regulations (sub-law precepts).

All men believe in the soul and act accordingly, even if they do not always speak up. If somebody has committed a murder and admits it, but insists that he did it unintentionally, what follows then with the prosecutor, the defense, the witnesses, the experts, and the court? Why do they deliver learned speeches, analyze every detail, and so on, when the very deed has been admitted to and its consequences are evident? All their efforts are not concerned with external objective facts, but with an inner problem: that of intention. It is not a question of what actually happened, but what happened in the heart of the murderer. Even when we examine the facts, we do so only to find out the state of the soul — that is, the intention. Moreover, everyone involved in the case spontaneously believes that the intention is more important than the consequences. That means that everyone, maybe unconsciously, prefers the soul to the facts. A worker who, unintentionally, causes a mine disaster in which hundreds of miners are killed, will be less responsible and less punished, than a man who kills an old woman in order to rob her. Does not this "illogical" sentence reveal that there is a soul, and that we really judge not what happened in the world, but what happened in the heart of the criminal?

Man's judgment strives to imitate God's judgment. The more we consider one's intention in the judgment, the more we come nearer to that of God. "But there is no blame on you, if you make a mistake therein; what counts is the intention of your hearts."[15] By accepting the intention, even in the smallest degree, we admit the existence of God and thus reject materialism. Starting from the inverse logic, materialistic philosophy arrived at the negation of responsibility — that is, of justice and injustice, and to the affirmation of an opposite principle, that of the *defense sociale*. Both lines of this development were completely justifiable.

Punishment and Social Defense

Whether punishment is justifiable or not has been a controversial issue. Two different positions in this regard can be stated. The first says that the use of punishment is justified because of the free choice that every man has; the second says that punishment is useless because the criminal act was predetermined. That being the case,

---

[15]The Qur'ān 33:5.

there is no place for punishment, but for the defense of the society, *defence sociale* — that is, the measures undertaken by society to protect itself from the guiltless doer.

The dilemma of punishment — social defense — is as old as criminal law. Its discussion could give a new perspective to some questions that this book addresses.

As early as the Hammurabi Code, the oldest law book so far, we find the ideas of *dolus* and punishment. On the other hand, Van Der Made has demonstrated that the idea of social defense existed among the ancient Greeks.[16]

Individualists believe that man is responsible for his misdeeds. Positivists think that society and circumstances — that is, something out of man's control, is responsible. According to the first school, man is an acting subject, a free and responsible person; the second says that man is a thing among things, a biological fact liable to the inevitable laws of nature and unable to obtain his freedom from them. The one standpoint is based on the belief that man can choose to be either good or bad; the other implies that man is neither good nor bad, for circumstances determine his behavior. Positivists do not believe in the existence of a free person who can choose independently and who is responsible.

Practice proves that it is wrong to suppose that either of the two schools is more tolerant or more rigorous than the other. That depends on many other circumstances.

Starting from the principle of social defense, we can arrive at different conclusions. We can think that rigorous punishment is not justifiable because crime is a result of circumstances, and thus any kind of punishment would be senseless. Still, it is possible to consider the interests of society and the concern to prevent their encroachment as decisive, and so come to punishments which are very severe and completely unjust. The history of criminal law has shown that the principle of personal guilt has not only sometimes resulted in extremely severe punishments — such as the Inquisition — but also in a very humane interpretation of the law. Even on an emotional issue like capital punishment, adherents of both sides are

---

[16]Van Der Made: "Contribution a l'Etude de l'Historie de la defense sociale," *Revue de Crimonologie et de Droit penal*, 1949-50, p. 944.

represented.[17] Capital punishment can be both justified and condemned from both positions. According to individualists, it would be a sanction against a free man who has committed a grave crime. To advocates of social defense, it would mean the "dismounting" of a defective part of society. In the first case it would get a humane explanation, and in the second a mechanical, inhumane one. In these explanations, we see a philosophical or metaphysical background, which in the first case reminds us of a "prologue in heaven," and in the second case of Darwin and evolution. One thing is sure: individualism will always include the ideas of retaliation, never as punishment. The aim of these measures, according to Ancel, is to "*neutralize*"[18] the delinquent. The term "neutralize," borrowed from physics, means rendering a criminal ineffective either by eliminating or putting him aside, or by medical treatment or re-education.

Generally speaking, the difference between a punishment and a measure of defense is that the first aims at justice and personality, the other at interest and society. Punishment is in proportion to guilt, while the measure of defense depends on the degree of the social (that is, objective) danger of the perpetrator, on how dangerous the criminal is from the viewpoint of society.

It is therefore possible to presume, in the case of social defense, a large derogation from one's rights without any guilt of the doer. The measures of social defense can take very severe and unjust forms in the case of protection or general prevention. Measures of this kinds have been used in some countries against political dissidents. A drastic example is Stalin's "purges," in which, according to some data, up to 10 million persons were "wiped out." Let us pay attention, as a purge is not a punishment but a "purgation" of the society from unwanted elements. Both "neutralization" and "purge" are mechanical procedures and mechanical terms. On the contrary, punishment is a moral idea appearing first in ancient religious books as God's punishment, which proves the terminological and the historical connection between religion and the theory of punishment.

---

[17]For example, M. Grave, a Swiss lawyer, an active protagonist of the social defense movement, is advocating the reintroduction of capital punishment in Switzerland.

[18]In theory, however, there is no exception to the said rule. The idealists, like Kant and Hegel, advocated almost literally "a tooth for a tooth ...," and the materialistic Holback refused absolutely the principle of the retaliation in criminal law. See Holback's *System de la Nature*.

Behind the legislation, implying punishment, lies idealistic philosophy, and behind those based on the principle of social defense, stands positivism.

Punishment goes along with the legal process, while the measure of social defense goes with treatment. A trial is a drama dealing with the exciting and exalted question of freedom, responsibility, and justice. The trial has always been tied to a fixed ceremony, which reminds us of drama or a rite.[19] On the contrary, the measure of social defense is a question of purpose and is decided by a doctor, psychologist, sociologist, or the administration, but never by a judge. Apart from exception, in practice the measure of protection is an integral part of the general manipulation with human beings in utopia. In utopia, there are no courts and no trials because there is no freedom and no responsibility, as there is neither ethics nor law.

Therefore we punish a free man, but we protect ourselves from a member of society. The member of society is neither guilty nor responsible; he can only be useful or harmful. This is not a question of choice but of fact, and the facts are senseless. Humanism in not necessarily mercy. Epictetus says: "You pity the lame and the blind, why not the evildoers too? They are evil against their will."[20] This is an example of mercy but not of humanism or religion. Humanism is the affirmation of man as a free and responsible being. Nothing degrades man more than the proclamation of irresponsibility. Man is responsible, animals and things are not. Here lies the difference between Stoicism and religion. Stoicism puts mercy and forgiveness in the foreground, while religion puts responsibility.[21] The "*defence sociale*" is basically inhumane, even if it absolves the man. On the contrary, the theory of guilt is humane, even when it pronounces severe sentences. Punishment is the human right of the criminal, and any derogation from it is connected with a derogation from other human rights. Hegel consistently stated that only punishment, as retaliation, is in harmony with the

---

[19]Ernest Bloch has shown that drama has two origins: the court and the mystery, (E. Bloch, ibid., p. 238) Benjamin has demonstrated that the famous three unities of tragedy (place, time, action) can also be traced back to the courts (Benjamin, Ursprung des Deutschen Trauerspiels, 1928, p.111).

[20]The Qur'ān 23:116, 23:116 and so on.

[21]An example of the predomination of the principle of moral guilt is the present Italian Criminal Code. The opposite examples are the penal codes of the Scandinavian countries, especially Iceland's new penal code.

human dignity of the criminal, and that it must not have another aim such as prevention or the like. Responsibility, as an aspect of human dignity, has its moral — that is, other worldly meaning. The responsibility of man on earth toward other men exists only because it exists in its absolute sense in eternity, toward God. All legislations are a pale attempt to imitate God's judgment of the earth.

The category of responsibility, and therefore of judgment and punishment, has no place in the inventory of materialism.

The purpose of punishment is not the prevention, protection, improvement, compensation, or even the re-education of the criminal. The purpose of punishment has nothing in common with this world. Its aim is to re-establish the moral balance which was put out of order by the committed crime. The punishment is a "negation" (Hegel), a *remedium peccati*. Though this definition sounds somewhat lifeless, it will always preserve its original meaning and importance. Punishment will remain a retaliation or a moral answer to an immoral act, even if it is in practice useless. On the contrary, the measure of defense is always motivated by usefulness, by the protection of the greater interest, sacrificing the lesser one, or by the subordination of the individual's interest to the interest of the society. Punishment aims at a moral effect, while the measure of defense aims at the social interest.

The ideas of retaliation and punishment have their origin in the religious view that crime provokes the anger of God. Regardless of all later limitations and corrections, this idea will always remain a consistent part of the conception of criminal justice. In some instances, instead of God's anger, the violated moral order is referred to, which really is nothing but a terminological difference, because God is the creator and protector of the moral order.

The preceding considerations are only the theoretical aspects of the question. From the point of view of this book, two facts are important. First, that the theory of moral guilt has to be followed by the theory of social defense as its opposite equivalent. Second, in practice, all actual legislation, regardless of their philosophy, never make "pure" laws. In any of the actual laws, we find the presence of a principle disavowed in theory. So, there is no penal law based completely on the principle of guilt, in the same way as there is no penal law based completely on the principle of social defense. In fact, we can only talk about a lesser or greater preponderance of one of these principles.[22]

Even the modern social defense movement, which in the nineteenth century started from extreme positions, passed through an unavoidable evolution. Marc Ancel, one of the protagonists of the movement, writes: "Between the two wars in the legislature, at last the middle way (media via) between the classical doctrine of guilt-revenge and the doctrine of social defense triumphed."[23]

And further: "However, does it mean that the idea of social defense must necessarily include the rejection of all compulsory procedures and, in the end, the rejection of punishment as such? Do we now have to finally decide between criminal law and social defense? Many active social supporters of social defense, on the contrary, think that criminal law and social defense have to be united into a new perspective."[24]

The L'Union International de droit penal, which was founded in 1889, and was in the beginning the great pleader for social defense, now speaks about the necessity of synthesizing these two doctrines. In 1914, the Union proclaimed that it "now represents both doctrines." In the theory of law, revolution resulted in the so-called "relative theory of punishment," and in practical legislation it appeared under a new formula of "protective punishment," a form of the "bipolar unity" in the field of law. In practice, the "third way" triumphed in the end.

Islam, as religion, started from the principle of retaliation but, as the religion "Islamized," it accepted some elements of social defense. Basically, this is the same development — based on the "liability to this world" — which created *salah* from prayer, *zakah* from *alms*, and an *ummah* (spiritual-political community) from a spiritual congregation. Islamic criminal law recognized a special system of education for minors, which is very similar to today's conception — that is, the principle of the free proof trial, and some aspects of the sociological understanding of delinquency and delinquent.

Marc Ancel says: "Islamic law of the 14th century accepted the principle of the irresponsibility of a child under 7 years of age,[25] and

---

[22]See note 21 above.

[23]Ancel: *La defense sociale nouvelle* (Paris: n.p., 1954).

[24]Ancel: ibid.

[25]This notion was inherent in Islam from the beginning and not a fourteenth century phenomenon.

ordered only the measure of re-education for minors from 7 years to the age of puberty. These proceedings did not have the character of punishment. To deal with delinquents who have come of age, a system was formed, in which some aspects can be regarded as social defense. With the exception of the five grave crimes defined in the Qur'ān, the courts were given a free hand with some crimes, and they were obliged to take into consideration the crime as such, the conditions under which it was committed, and the character of the criminal."[26]

---

[26]For more about this subject, see Said Mustapha El-Said Bey: "La notion de responsabilite penal"; Travaux de la Semaine international de droit musulman (Paris: n.p., 1951), and L. Milliot: *Introduction a l'Etude de droit musulman* (Paris: n.p., 1953).

Chapter 10

IDEAS AND REALITY

A religion which wants to replace free thinking with mysticism, scientific truth with dogmas, and social actions with ceremonies must inevitably clash with science.

IDEAS AND REALITY

Prefatory Notes

Both religion and utopia get deformed when they enter life: they exist in their consistent form only in books. In practice, religion gets "naturalized" by admitting something from the animal part of man's nature. On the other hand, utopia becomes "humanized" and takes on some moral features. The deformation of both Christianity and materialism brings them nearer to man, to the animal-human figure of man. The one is a descent from the divine; the other is an ascension from the animal. In both cases, it is a motion toward the human.

Some well-known occurrences in the history of Christianity are only different forms of the unavoidable deformation of religion when faced with life. The instances are numerous: the institutionalization of religion (the establishment of the church organization and hierarchy); the approval of marriage (instead of chastity); the recognition of work; the new attitude toward property, power, education, knowledge (contrary to the evangelical "blessed are the poor in spirit..."); the acceptance of force and violence (the Inquisition) and so on. The searching for a possible coexistence with Marxism in our day belongs here as well.

In practice, Marxism or materialism display similar "reciprocal" deviations: Acceptance of certain humanistic principles of the French Revolution (even if as a matter of form only), such as the rights of man and citizens and of some "prejudices" from the cultural inheritance of the past (such as personal freedom, freedom of thought, sanctity of mail, and privacy); moral incentives as reward for work (contrary to the claim that man is only motivated by interest); the crucial role of politics (that is, the subjective and conscious factor); the personality cult of the leaders; presenting its own laws as "objective and just," (the opposite of the definition of law as the will of the ruling class); acceptance of marriage, family, property, and the state (contrary to the classic doctrines of Marxism); adherence to the principle of guilt in criminal law; proclamation of heroes; maintenance of the idea of brotherhood and patriotism (brotherly help, brotherly parties, patriotic wars and so on — are not brotherhood and patriotism bourgeois illusion?); calls to live and work for the glory of the socialistic fatherlands; ideological and theoretical dogmatism (do "eternal truths" exist?), and so on.

Although religion in its essence is a call to man to live only for the other world, people have always connected religion with their everyday hopes and aspirations — they actually desired Islam. In the first days of Christianity, the public means (*agape*) had an important part in the spreading of the new religion. This also happened with the "prayer or absolution of sins" which often changed to a demand of an absolution of debts. Tertuillian even had to intervene to reaffirm the original meaning of this prayer. Many movements during the Middle Ages were at the same time spiritual and social, and it is difficult to explain their nature in a one-sided way. Certain social movement of today refer to the texts of the holy scripture. The preceding facts confirm the general view of Islam that pure religion and pure politics exist as ideas only. In real life, we find only blends of their components. In some cases, it is even impossible to separate them from each other.

Jesus and Christianity

When discussing the question of the feasibility of pure religion in the world, a crucial example cannot be overlooked, namely the historical failure of Christianity.

To explain Christianity and to understand its historical development, we have to distinguish the life of Jesus from the history of Christianity. From the very beginning, Jesus was on one side, while Christianity was on the other. As time has passed, this difference has been transformed into the difference between the divine and the human. This fact could also explain the emergence of the dogma of Jesus as the son of God. In the Christian myth about the god-man lies the silent admission that pure Christianity is not possible in real life. "The last Christian died on the cross."[1]

Some authors believe that the failure of Christianity is the main motive of Cervantes' famous *Don Quixote* (The Black Gospel), with Don Quixote as a caricature of Jesus. Jesus blamed his first successor Peter for "not thinking about the divine, but the human," even though Peter was "the cornerstone on which the Church has been built." By this saying, Jesus, before anyone else, predicted the future development of Christianity — Christianity as church: parting from Jesus.

The historical process through which Christianity was transformed from Jesus' teachings (pure religion) into an ideology, church and organization, is one of the most dramatic events in world history. After almost three centuries of persecution, which represents the most persistent struggle between religion and paganism, the Greco-Roman empire began to accept the new state of things. In 311, Emperor Galerious promulgated a decree of tolerance toward Christianity and not long after that Emperor Constantine recognized the new faith. By making a strong organization from a spiritual community and giving the Church political power, Emperor Constantine took a decisive historical step toward the deformation of Christianity. During the fourth century, the synod confirmed the church doctrine and the liturgy became more colorful with ceremonial rites, borrowed from pagan religions. The cult of saints and of the Virgin Mary appeared at this time. In the beginning of the 5th century, Emperor Theodosious II proclaimed Christianity the state religion, and in 435 issued an edict against pagans. After this came the establishment of a clergy, and the title of metropolitan appears. "Christianity has made a synthesis of the two types of clergymen which were known in ancient society: the hellenistic and the oriental. The first is an elected magistrate and God's servant, and the second is dedicated to mysteries, a true intermediary."[2] Most of the New Testament was written down during the end of the second century, and the Cross, as the symbol of Christianity, was finally accepted in Nicaea in 325. A strong discipline in interpreting religion and the

---

[1]Fredrich W. Nietzsche: *The Anti Christ.* Nietzsche also observed: "My brethren, believe me, he [Jesus] died too soon; himself would have retracted his doctrine had he lived to my age. He was noble enough to be able to thus to retract." See George Burman's *Fredrich Nietzsche* (New York: The Macmillan Company, 1931) p.214.
[2]Lucien Henri: *The Origin of Religion.*

religious texts was introduced. The bishop tookover the spiritual function and became the absolute authority on religious matters. He was paid by the Church. Baptism and the Eucharist were introduced. Bishops, who met in synods (meetings similar to present-day parliaments), decided the doctrines, teachings, and many other things related to the faith. The formation of the Church was mainly completed.

All great and sincere Christians — no matter when they lived — maintained that Jesus' teachings could not become science in the true sense of the word.[3] "Personal faith results from ecstacy, theology from mathematics," and the Church turned Christianity into a systematic teaching, similar to mathematics or biology.[4] Barth, the Catholic theologian, writes in his Dogmatica: "Dogmatic is a science by which the Church, depending on the level of the knowledge it has, explains to itself the contents of its teachings. It is a critical discipline ..." As if the idea of love and brotherhood could become a subject of scientific analysis without ceasing to be what it is. The spiritual wandering of Christianity began in this way. The endless discussion about dogmas and holy secrets moved the focus of Jesus' teachings from moral essence to scholasticism. On the basis of theology as science, the Church organization was founded, with all its erudition, ceremonial, hierarchy, richness, and the tragic errors and mistakes. On the contrary, we find that the monastic orders resulting from true religious inspiration always emerged outside the Church organization.[5]

The opposite in question was not only the difference between the idea and the real, its different aspects concerned the very essence. The father of Christianity was Jesus; the father of the Church was Paul (or Augustine). The first brought Christian ethics,

---

[3]Gardini explains: "There does not exist a system of moral values, or a religious attitude, or a life program which could be separated from Christ's personality and of which it could be said: This is Christianity. Christianity is He himself. A doctrine is Christian only if it is coming out of His mouth. The personality of Christ in its historical unity and eternal brightness is the only category that decided the essence, activity and teaching of Christianity." The Essence of Christianity.

[4]Bertrand Russel maintains that theology had mathematics as its model. Such was the case in ancient Greece, in the Middle Ages, and in Europe up to Kant. Bertrand Russell, ibid., p. 56.

[5]St. Francis of Assisi was a layman without theological education. The Church officially rejected his main vow — that of poverty.

the second Christian theology. Even the hesitation of the Church between Plato and Aristotle, which characterized Church thinking throughout the Middle Ages, was a result of the same contradiction. Jesus' teaching as a religion is nearer to Plato, and the Christian theology to Aristotle. In his *History of Ethics*, Jodl writes: "In relation to practical life, the teachings of the first Christians, as expressed in the Gospels, were different from the later Church teachings (starting from Paul's theology) and also from all the world around, whether Jewish or pagan." And further: "Christianity, as an ethical religion in all times, has been searched for and found in the Gospels: Christianity as a mystery, as a religion of salvation — in the Epistles." The Church always has referred to Paul and the Epistles; faith and morality always to Jesus and the Gospels. With Paul, the simple and sublime history of Jesus ends, and the history of the institutionalized religion starts. As distinguished from the Gospels, Paul recognizes property, work, economy, ranks, marriage, obedience, inequality, and even slavery. Jesus and the Gospels are on one side, and the Church and theology on the other. The first is idea, the second is reality.

Marx and Marxism

Marxism is consistent in theory but not necessarily so in practice. Marxism claims that man is a product of his environment, both as a biological and as a social being; that his social being determines his conscience and not vice versa; that one's opinions and beliefs reflect one's social position; that historical events result not from ideas or men's intentional acts but from objective facts independent of men; that history is subject to merciless historical determinism. Slavery was not abolished because of moral reasons, but because it no longer suited economic needs and interests. Feudalism was not removed because somebody wanted it to be, but as a consequence of the development of production — that is, material and objective facts beyond the influence of man. The development of capitalism is only a function of economic needs, production forces, and so on, and has nothing to do with theories that are written by philosophers, economists, jurists, and moralists.

It is also logical to assume that the establishment of a socialist system does not depend on political parties, desires, or ideas but only on the development of production forces. A social revolution emerges when technical developments and the army of industrial workers outgrow the existing relations to such a degree that the balance is changed and the inevitable overthrow is perceived. Such is the explanation in all Marxist schoolbooks.

In real life — as the believers do not rely much on God's intervention — atheists also do not believe very much in the "natural development of events." They leave nothing to these "objective factors" but try to manage people and events. Where communist ideology does not appear "naturally," it is imported. So we find communist rule even where a working class does not exist. Those who claim that personalities have no part in the course of history create infallible leaders — "gods, by a head greater than other men," whose wisdom we have to thank for everything — from victories on the battlefield to the revolutionary developments in linguistics. According to the Marxist schedule, the following turn of events is to be expected: develop industry and the working class and the political party will emerge. In reality this turn is usually reversed. Thus, in some underdeveloped countries, communist governments decide to build up industry and with it the working class — that is, the being is created by consciousness, history by politics, and the base by the superstructure. Nothing from Marx's scheme remains but the political power of the Communist Party, and even it does not consist of workers but of socially heterogeneous elements.[6]

According to Marx, development is gradual and inexorable, and cannot be interrupted or subdued. Still, Marxists try to impose the same recipe for social and economic order on all countries, ignoring the fact that the existing economic and social developments in one country are on quite different levels than the other. The program of the American Communist Party, for example, is not essentially different from the program of the communist parties in Costa Rica or Indonesia. There are over 80 parties in the world today, working under very different economic and social conditions, form a tribal country in Africa to the most developed capitalistic country in

---

[6]The well-known Marxist postulate about the relation of "base" and the "superstructure" reads: "In the social reproduction of their life, people enter certain necessary relations which are independent of their will, i.e., in production relations corresponding to the developmental degree of their material productive forces. The entireness of these relations makes an economic social superstructure with which the different forms of the social consciousness correspond. The process of social, political and spiritual life in general is conditioned by the way of production in material life. The social being of the people is not defined by their consciousness, but on the contrary, their consciousness is defined by their social being." Karl Marx: *Zur Kritik der Politischen Okonomie*, Preface.

Europe. Nevertheless, all of them propagate almost the same economic and socio-political models: collective ownership of the means of production, collectivization of agriculture, a one-party political system, a monopoly on ideas and politics, and so on. If the teachings about "the base" and "the superstructure" are correct, how is it possible to build the same superstructure on different bases? How is it possible to implement socialism on all these different socio-economic bases if the premises of historical materialism are correct?

The incoherence of the materialistic interpretations of historical events can be easily proved by analyzing any period in history. Nevertheless, there is somewhat of a historical irony in the fact that even the appearance of the communist movements and states in the first half of this century is an evident rebuttal of the materialistic theory. Communist overthrows did not happen where — according to the theory — they should have. The history of communist overthrows is a series of unexplainable anomalies from the point of view of historical materialism. Communist movements were successful not where the objective conditions existed, but rather where subjective factors were present: a strong political party or intervention from outside.

It is clear that Marxism, as a theory, has to adopt historical determinism, but as a living practice has to reject it. Both facts are indicative for the subject we are discussing. Every materialistic theory is based on the first; any living phenomenon on the second. The break up is inevitable. Engels admitted in his letter to Conrad Smith (May 8, 1890) that if the Marxist theory of economics is literally applied, "sometimes incredible nonsense occurs." He disputes Paul Barth's claim that Marxists reject all influences of consciousness on economy.[7] Engels recommended a "not too strict use of the theory of conditions." He wrote about "the reverse influence of the ideas on the base," which he immediately removed by saying: "Their general dependence is on economic conditions." After all, there remains only a characteristic vacillation and withdrawal of materialism when confronted with the obvious facts of life. Marxism had to admit many of these facts at the expense of its consistency. Positivistic thinkers refuse to accept Marxism as science, saying that it contains a lot of idea, political, ethical, and even mythical elements. Still, positivism remained literature, and Marxism tried to

---

[7]Barth: *History of Philosophy from Hegel and His Followers to Marx and Hartman.*

conquer the world. That was possible only because Marxism never was — and never became — consistent materialism.

The teaching on alienation, which belongs to Karl Marx's early works, is in its essence idealistic. Its origin should probably be sought for in Hegel's philosophy, as this man has a great impact on Marx. The theory of alienation — maybe because of its idealistic character — was treated with silence for a long time. Marx's *Economic and Philosophic Manuscripts*, which contained this theory, was published around 1930: (80 years after *The Communist Manifesto* and 60 years after the first volume of *Das Kapital*), even though it had been written in 1844. In his book *Thesis on Feuerbach*, written at the same time as the aforementioned work, we find the same spirit of diffuse materialism. Both works, strongly influenced by humanistic ideas, are typical of the young Marx. Only the works from his later period should be considered as truly Marxist. These are, above all, *Das Kapital* and *Zur Kritik der Politischen Okonomie*, especially the preface to the *Kritik*, in which Marx gave a summary of the materialistic conception of history.

When Marxism had to be implemented in practical life, new nonmaterialistic and non-Marxist elements had to be incorporated. In some respects, even Marx would hardly be able to identify his teachings in many present-day socialist countries. There is a symptomatic fact to be noted here: The Protestant countries which, through the Reformation, freed themselves from Catholic romanticism and mysticism, have remained largely immune to Marxism. But in neo-Latin nations and underdeveloped countries, communist ideas have been very successful. Protestant countries rejected communism for the same reasons as they rejected Catholicism. We therefore come to the paradoxical conclusion that communism gets its strength from the same sources as Catholicism and mysticism do.

From the strict viewpoint of historical materialism, we cannot speak about just or unjust social relations because that is possible only in practice. According to such a viewpoint, there are no just or unjust but only tenable (untenable) relations. Let us notice that "justness" is a moral term, and that "tenableness" is a physical, mechanical term. As long as capitalism is in harmony with its technical base (or the production forces in Marxist terms), the system is going to maintain itself, and it is at the same time a justified system as well. The moral principles are not decisive, only the objective factors are. It follows that all the evils of the capitalistic system were necessary and justified until it was congruent to the production forces. Or, as Marx clearly said: "As long as a system of production is necessary, the exploitation of man by man is also necessary."

That is the theoretical aspect of things. What about in practice?

Even the Marxists themselves do not strictly adhere to this brilliant definition, as it makes any human action useless. Clever and logical definitions have their place in schoolbooks but, in practice, all of us use conceptions that are less strict but nearer to men and life. In practice, Marxists, especially their political leaders, use the term "exploitation" exclusively in its moral, human meaning. Exploitation ceased to be a "way of using the work of others" — that is, an economical or technical operation in the production process. In Marx's *Das Katpital* as well ("The Work Day"), exploitation is clearly portrayed in terms of good and evil. The exploiter becomes personified evil, and the exploited victim the personification of the good and the just (let us remember "The Union of the Righteous" which preceded Marx's "The Union of Communists" — a trace has also remained in the name). When giving examples of the exploitation of workers, Marx is full of unconcealed accusations, like the Old Testament prophets who thundered against wicked deeds and injustice. Still, the attitudes of the religious reformers are easily understood because they believe that evil can be avoided. To condemn an evil deed is to recognize that it is the result of man's free choice. Otherwise, the condemnation would be meaningless. The condemnation of a necessary exploitation is a contradiction. However, the fact that we do condemn exploitation, and that even Marx does so, proves that the relations between people can never be reduced to naked economic terms.[8] Condemning the "necessary" exploitation, Marx is right but not consistent.

Therefore, even the most famous materialistic thinker was not a consistent materialist, nor could he be. We wonder how pure was the materialism or atheism of Lenin himself, if his favorite author,

---

[8]To the wife of his friend Kugelmann, who was having difficulty understanding what she was reading, Marx suggested that she read *Das Kapital* beginning with the eighth chapter ("The Work Day"). This part of Marx's most important work has in main countries been published separately. The said chapter is closer to people, because it implies a moral, not a historical or objective approach. The drama is much more complex than any mathematical, abstract formula, but still most people will understand any drama quicker than mathematics. That is the case with "The Work Day."

according to his own statement, was Tolstoy. It seems that the strength of Marxism comes mainly from inconsistency — that is, from the presence of moral and idealistic elements, from which Marx could not escape. Marxism wanted to be a science, but it was also a messianic appeal for hope, justice, and humanism.[9] Contrary to his wish and aim, Marx regarded capitalists and workers not only as functions but as moral characters, the living symbols of good and evil. One is an oppressor, the other is the oppressed, and that classification engages people morally. Through contact between workers and capitalists, European man again experiences the primeval Jewish antagonism between the just and the unjust.

One cannot be a true atheist and materialist even if he wished to be so with all his heart.

Marriage

Marriage, an institution as old as humankind, is a good example of the conflict between ideas and reality, or between ideas and Islam.

Pure religion demands chastity; materialism principally permits complete sexual freedom. But both teachings, when confronted with many problems during their implementation, are moving toward the institution of marriage as a middle solution.

In original Christianity, there is no place for marriage. Jesus called for complete chastity: "You were told not to commit adultery, and I say to you: 'Everyone of you who looks at a woman with desire has already committed adultery in his heart.'"[10] These words can only mean that according to Jesus' teachings, man has to strive for complete chastity. Tolstoy concludes: "Those who believe that the marriage ceremony relieves them from the obligation of chastity, so as to enable them to reach a higher level of purity, are wrong ..." Saint Paul recommends in one of his epistles: "Unmarried people worry about God, how to please God; married people worry about this world, how to please his wife."[11] In general, Christianity looks at marriage as a necessary evil, as an unavoidable

---

[9]Bertrand Russell has made a similar remark: "Marx proclaimed himself an atheist, but he retained a cosmic optimism which can only be justified by theism." Bertrand Russell, ibid., p. 754.a

[10]Mark 5:27.28.

[11]Corinthians 7:38.

reduction of perfection. "It is good for man not to touch a woman, but to avoid prostitution, man should have a woman, and a woman a man."[12] In this epistle, we feel the clear Christian principles weakening and moving closer to reality. It is a kind of compromise. From the Christian point of view, marriage is not a solution based on principle but one forced by practice ("...to avoid prostitution" — St. Paul).

Materialism also rejects marriage but for quite different reasons: "Individual marriage is seen as the subjugation of one sex under the other. ..." Or:

> The first class hostility appeared with the development of the antagonism between man and woman because of individual marriage. ... With the transfer of the means of production into common ownership, the single family ceases to be the economic unity of society. Private housekeeping is transformed into a social industry. The care and education of the children becomes a public affair; society looks after all children alike, whether they are legitimate or not. This removes the anxiety about the consequences, which today is the most essential social-moral as well as economic factor that prevents a girl from giving herself completely to the man she loves. Would not that suffice to bring about the gradual growth of unrestrained sexual intercourse, and with it a more tolerant public in regards to a virgin's honor and a woman's shame?[13]

There is a clear relation between the Christian view of the world and its claim of chastity.[14] In the West, some writers of materialistic orientation see that as a connection between reactionary social systems and sexual repression. The theories of Wilhelm Reich, Trotsky and of the so-called "Frankfurt School" belong here. Herbert Marcuse maintains that capitalism suppresses sexuality in order

---

[12]Corinthians 1-2.

[13]Engels: *The Origin of Family, Private Property and the State*

[14]This claim assumed in some cases more extreme forms. In Christianity, there has always existed a tendency toward castration. Origen performed castration on himself to purify his body. The followers of the Christian sect of Valeriani in Arabia castrated not only themselves, but also everyone who passed through their territory. Castration was known among other religions too. The Church only forbade castration at the end of the 19th century.

to use one's sexual energy in other fields.

Celibacy (the vow of chastity) is neither based directly on God's commandments, nor it is found in early Church tradition.[15] Nevertheless, celibacy [in the sense of not being married] is a natural part of materialism. In the last Vatican Council, an attempt to abolish celibacy was easily rejected. In reality, of course, neither of these principles can be consistently realized. Celibacy is the practice of a small number of selected people, while in the USSR, after much negative experience with sexual freedom, the institution of marriage was reinstated.

The return to the institution of marriage is also present in both cases, but from a different starting point: Christianity from the demand of complete chastity, and materialism from the demand of complete sexual freedom. By so doing, Christianity turns marriage into a sacrament, while materialism turns it into a contract, in some cases even a formal and ceremonious contract (the development of the marriage law in the USSR is very indicative of such a practice). Still, the distance between the Catholic and the civil marriage remains great, mainly because of the question of divorce. A marriage which is a sacrament must not be dissolved since it would then be turned into an agreement. Likewise, an absolutely indissoluble marriage would completely lose its character of being a contract by becoming a holy thing which no positivist is ready to accept.

Islamic marriage untied these two types of marriages. From the European point of view, Islamic marriage is both a religious and a civil marriage. It is at the same time a contractual and a ceremonial religious act. It is performed by a "clergyman" and a government official but both in one person. An Islamic marriage can be dissolved because it is a contract, but divorce is only allowable for permissible reasons. Prophet Muhammad considered it "the most hated of all permitted things" — which is an expression of religious and moral thinking. Marriage is therefore a typical Islamic institution. Marriage, as it is in Islam, is a solution aiming to answer the problem of how to reconcile one's spiritual desires and one's physical needs; of how to save chastity without rejecting love, and of how to put in order the sexual love of an animal which can become a man but not an angel. This aim is in its essence Islamic.

Marriage is comparable with justice. They are ideas of a

---

[15]It was introduced by the Church Council of 1139.

coarser structure which nevertheless will provide more purity and righteousness than their Christian equivalents: chastity and universal love.

Tolstoy obviously perceived these facts but drew different conclusions form them. He writes:

> Since in pure Christian teachings there is no base for the institution of marriage, the people of our Christian world do not know how to relate to it. They feel that this institution is not Christian in its essence, but they do not see Christ's ideal — sexual abstention — because it is hidden behind the present doctrine.
> From it comes a phenomenon which at first glance looks strange: among the nations which have lower religious teachings than Christianity, but who have clear sexual standards, the faithfulness between spouses and the family are much stronger than among so-called Christians. Among peoples who have lower religious teachings than Christianity, there exits norms for concubinage, polygamy and polyandry, but there is no such promiscuity, concubinage, polygamy and polyandry reigning among Christians under the cover of feigned monogamy.[16]

Two Kinds of Superstitions

If what we say is correct, then two kinds of "superstitions" are to be found: the first, science trying to explain man's inner life; and the other, religion trying to explain natural phenomena.

When explaining the world of spirit, science analyzes it objectively by turning it into an object, into a thing. when explaining nature, religion personalizes it — that is, turning it into nonnature. We are faced with misconceptions of the same kind, but in a "reciprocal," reversed relation.

Primitive religions with their magicians and taboos are close to superstition; they can hardly be distinguished from it. In fact, their religions reflect man's inner disharmony. They emerge from the two basic preoccupations of early mankind: first, the spiritual, when

---

[16]Tolstoy: *The Road to Life.*

man becomes aware of himself as a human being as distinct and different from the surrounding nature; and second, the physical, his need to survive in a hostile world full of danger. Primitive religious conscience, under the pressure of the instinct to survive, turns to this world for its aim becomes more natural (successful hunting, rich harvest, protection from a hostile nature, sickness, wild animals, and so on), while the methods and means remain religious (i.e., magic, sacrifices, spiritual dances, songs, and symbols). Primitive religion is religious conscience oriented in the same direction, outward, toward life's needs, instead of inward, toward spiritual desire. Since it can achieve nothing in the real world, primitive religion leaves the impression of man's weakness and delusion.

Accordingly, a religion which wants to replace free thinking with mysticism, scientific truth with dogmas, and social actions with ceremonies must inevitably clash with science. On the contrary, true religion is compatible with science — a kind of theism known by many great scientists. Moreover, science can help religion in suppressing superstition. If separated, religion pulls toward backwardness, and science toward atheism.

However, science also has its own superstitions, when it leaves the field of nature. Infallible on the matters related to the inorganic world (physics, astronomy, and so on), man's intelligence is nevertheless uncertain and awkward in the field of life. Using its methods of analysis and quantification in the field of life, science has necessarily come to the negation of some important life and spiritual phenomena, reducing them to their outside manifestations. So, the sociology of religion missed the very essence of religion, biology missed life, psychology missed the soul, anthropology missed man's personality, and history missed its inner human meaning.[17]

Dialectical and historical materialism offer many striking examples of the failure of scientific methods in the field of life and history. For instance, "religion is the opiate of the masses," law is "the will of the ruling class," the abolition of slavery is seen as being in the "interest of developing capitalism," Kant and Goethe are

---

[17]The development of psychology is very instructive in this regard. Behaviorism, which represents the ultimate stage of this development, declares the "expulsion of the soul from psychology" and the formation of a "psychology without soul." The logical result will be seeing man as "beyond freedom and dignity." Just such a book by a representative of behaviorism can be found in many book stores. See B. F. Skinner's *Beyond Freedom and Dignity* (New York: Alfred A. Knopf, 1971).

"defenders of the capitalistic system," and the philosophy of the absurd is a "reflection of the crisis of the capitalist system," and so on. One Marxist writer said Satre's philosophy about fear and death is nothing but an expression of the crisis of a system of production.[18]

Balzac, the great French writer, also made his contribution to this kind of error when he added to his famous novel a less-than-famous preface. In this, he tried to analyze a human being by using scientific and positivistic methods. Balzac's preface is an appropriate example of the failure of the scientific method to deal with man's inner life. The truth about human beings, which the author of the *Human Comedy* so truthfully and lively described in his novel, has little to do with the intellectual explanations of their destinies in the preface.

When science describes a work of art, it reduces it to a psychological phenomenon. For science, the artist is a victim of a psychosis. Stekal, a psychoanalyst, has stated that this research has convinced him that there is no difference between a poet and a neurotic. From the scientific point of view, an artistic creation is best analyzed by another science: psychoanalysis. The result of this investigation is the paradoxical assertion that there is a congruence between creation and neurosis.[19]

From the rationalistic viewpoint, no objection to artificial towns or military barracks is possible: "If we build honestly, a cathedral must not be different from a factory," Mies van der Rohe, an ideologist of functionalism, draws a logical but absurd conclusion.

Biological science concluded that a man is really an animal, that an animal is really a thing, and that life is in the end mechanics — nonlife. In ethics, a similar development resulted: reason concluded that morality is only a refined, "enlightened" from of selfishness — that is, morality is the negation of morality. Psychoanalysis has abolished the distinctions between artistic creation and sickness. So, scientific research in the human field ended with a series of negations: intelligence first denied the existence of God and then, according to a style of descending gradation, it denied man, then life, and at last came to the conclusion that everything is only a play and reciprocal interaction of molecular forces. Intelligence could find nothing else in the world but itself: mechanism and causality.

---

[18]Lucien Goldman, in the magazine "Art," writing about existentialism.
[19]See Dr. V. Jerotic: *Sickness and Creation* (Belgrade: n.p., 1976).

Chapter 11

"THE THIRD WAY" OUTSIDE ISLAM

Both the European religion and its atheism will have a radical and exclusive nature.

increasing call for social democracy. Protestant countries have found in social democracy the solution which traditionally Catholic countries try to find in the "historical compromise." Social democracy, which in Europe means a compromise between liberalism and social interventionism, between the European Christian tradition and Marxism, has been advancing throughout the postwar period and all over the world.* After comparing the election results just after World War II with those 25 or 30 days later, we can see an increase in the number of social democracy votes in nearly all countries having free elections. The increase is 22 percent in Sweden, 36 percent in Denmark, 54 percent in Holland, 27 percent in Norway, over 100 percent in West Germany and as much as 34.8 percent in Malta. In England it is only 5 percent, but we must bear in mind the fact that the process started here much earlier, and that England reached a state of balance before any other European country. Social democracy is a "stable compound," it is a form of social and political balance in Europe.

Mexico and Venezuela, two countries that are very close to social democracy, are at the same time the two most stable countries in the usually unstable area of South America. Development in Japan has not led to polarization but to a strengthening of the center. The term "middle road" is more and more frequently heard in political debates in Mexico and Japan. The social-democratic meeting in 1976 in Caracas was called "historical" mainly for the relation of its conclusions, but more so for the feeling that it might be the first step toward formulating a new doctrine. The statement made by the Mexican spokesman Gonzales Sos explained what kind of doctrine it would be: "There are three great political options in the present world — capitalism, communism, and social democracy — and Mexico has to choose among them."

The internal tension of the socialist countries is not primarily connected with socialism as an economic problem. The most serious opposition concerns the problem of human rights. Everywhere, [illegible] asking for a kind of Christianity with a social

---

* The ideological or purely [illegible] side of this world does not see the situation in this light. Moscow's magazine "The Communist" of July 1979 declares that the "middle road" [illegible]. According to this magazine, no alternatives in the form of a "third road" is possible. There are only two antagonistic socio-political systems and the polarizing process is not fading; on the contrary, it is strengthening [illegible] countries will sooner or later cling to either the capitalist or the socialist [illegible]

"THE THIRD WAY" OUTSIDE ISLAM

The Anglo-Saxon World

Europe built up its basic outlooks through the rude school of the Middle Ages. Despite its coming of age, these childhood experiences have never faded from the European mind. Religious or nonreligious, Europe will always think within the Christian alternatives: either Kingdom of God or Kingdom on Earth. Europe will either bitterly deny science or religion. No religious movement in Europe will be able to adopt a social program. Both the European religion and its atheism will have a radical and exclusive nature.

A part of the Western world, however, owing to its geographical position and its history, has remained free from the direct influence of medieval Christianity as well as the complex of this powerful age. This part of the world has been looking for and has found a middle road, bearing from the *outside some resemblance* to the third way of Islam. The country we have in mind is England, but also, to a certain extent, the Anglo-Saxon world in general.[1]

The foreword to the first official English translation of the Bible begins with the following words: "The wisdom of the Anglican Church from the very beginning of its public liturgy was to follow the middle course between the two extremes." This attitude seems to

---

[1]Later on, we will see that the diluted form of this phenomenon appears in many countries belonging to reformed types of Christianity.

have become the first law of English religious and practical life.

Christianity divided the history of the Western world into two entirely separate and opposed periods: the Middle Ages and the New Era, which corresponds to the two alternatives: religion and science, or the church and the state. This historical scheme is not valid for England, at least not in the sense that it has been in continental Europe.

That is why England's experience of European history must be considered separately. Europe without England had only two ages: the age of the church and the age of the state. Historically speaking, Europe's middle, "Islamic," age can be found only in England. Democracy in Europe — this blend of secular and metaphysical principles — is an English invention. Nietzsche, the man who belonged to Europe more than anyone else, expressed the distinction between the English and the European mind through his famous question: "How to save Europe from England and England from democracy?"

From the viewpoint of a philosophy of history, the emergence of England and the Anglo-Saxon spirit in the history of the West corresponds to the emergence of Islam in the history of the East. Here is the meaning of Spengler's parallel between Prophet Muhammad and Cromwell,[2] the two personalities who appear as "contemporary" in his vision of world history. The united English church and state, as well as the English world power, started with Cromwell. The united Islamic religion and state, as well as Islamic world power, started with Muhammad. Both were puritan believers and founders of large empires. This seems to be quite normal for the Islamic and Anglo-Saxon mind, but quite strange to the European mind. Louis the Pious wrecked the Franconian state; in the Islamic world, on the other hands, every kind of political and social progress always started with a religious revival. As soon as the European state had grown strong, it began to call for primacy — in the same way as the church had done a few centuries before. It was "the second Canossa" (the first one was in 1077 when Henry IV submitted to Pope Gregory VII). The Inquisition, which spread throughout Europe, never spread to England. Thus, neither England nor Islam experienced a

---

[2]Spengler: *The Decline of the West*, trans. Charles Francis Atkinson (New York: Alfred A. Knopf ,1926) pp. 211-213.

Canossa or the Inquisition. The English reformation destroyed — by an inherent logic — both extremes: the papal and the royal predominance. For fifteenth and sixteenth century Europe, England seemed to be revolutionary. To the mind of present-day Europe, it is conservative. The word "conservative" in England is an appeal to "conserve" the authentic English spirit, which means the middle road in the broadest sense of the word.

This dualism of the English way of life will be better understood if we recall that it was Roger Bacon who was the founder and forerunner of England's later spiritual progress. From the very beginning, he set the entire structure of English philosophical thought on two separate foundations: inward experience, which leads to mystical illumination (religion), and observation, which leads to true science (*scientia experimentalise*). Though the religious components were emphasized in the same way as in Islam, Bacon remained a consistent dualist, never attempting to reduce the scientific or religious outlooks at the other's expense. He established a balance between them. This aspect of Bacon's genius is considered by most Englishmen as the most authentic expression of English thought and feeling; many even consider all subsequent English philosophy as nothing but the development of Bacon's principles of thinking. His enormous influence on the trends and ways of English philosophy and science can be explained only by this seemingly controversial approach.

There is, however, another important fact related to Bacon which has never been sufficiently studied and recognized: the father of English philosophy and science was really a student of Arabic. Bacon was strongly influenced by Islamic thinkers, particularly by Ibn Sīna, whom he considered to be the greatest philosopher since Aristotle.[3] The character of Bacon's thought and, through him, the origin of the middle way, which distinguished the whole of English thought and practice from its counterparts in continental Europe, might be explained by this fact.[4]

---

[3]Bertrand Russell: *History* ..., pp. 452-453. A similar statement is given by Karl Prant, the author of the most extensive history of logic: "Roger Bacon has taken over from the Arabs all the results in the field of natural sciences which had been attributed to him." *Geschichte der Logic*, III (Leipzig: n.p., 1972) p. 121.

[4]When trying to explain this phenomenon, it is interesting to hear Russell's explanation as well. According to him, the aversion of Englishmen to generalizing theories is a consequence of their negative experience in the Civil War. The conflict between King and Parliament in the Civil War gave Englishmen, once and for all, a love of

One proof that nothing has so far changed in this respect, and that England remains faithful to its own spirit, is the personality of another great Englishman, that of Bernard Shaw. Shaw was a poet and a politician who at the same time preached both socialist and anarcho-individualistic ideas. Someone called him "an unrepeatable unity of contradictions," aiming at his being simultaneously a satirist and a mystic, a stern social critic and an incurable idealist.

Or, let us consider the following fact. On the Continent, an empiricist, as a rule, will also be an atheist. In England, the father of empiricism, John Locke, placed the concept of God in the center of his ethical theory and supported with the ardor of a priest the recognition of the hereafter's sanctions — punishment and reward — in establishing moral principles: "If human hope is confined only to this world, if only here can we enjoy life, then it is neither strange nor illogical to look for happiness, avoiding everything that is unpleasant in this world and following everything that amuses us. If there is nothing beyond the grave, then the following conclusion is justified: let us drink and eat; let us enjoy the things that make us happy because tomorrow we will die."[5]

Moreover, the famous empiricist has detailed his own proofs for God's existence.[6] Hobbes, otherwise a positivist and materialist, undertook to prove the harmony between natural laws and the Bible ("Quod lex naturalis est lex divina").[7] This is typical of the English way of thinking. European thinkers would later unanimously declare Locke's standpoint to be untenable. However, the fact remains that his as well as Bacon's and Hobbes' controversial philosophy was the starting point of England's later intellectual and social development.

Sharp opposition of the natural to the moral, typical for the Christian approach, became more reconcilable with a number of English thinkers and was finally wiped out by Shaftesbury. For Shaftesbury, morality is a state of balance between the selfish and the unselfish emotions; this balance can be destroyed both when a selfish tendency prevails or when altruistic feelings become too exclusive (this echoes Aristotle's "reasonable ethical egoism" as well as some

---

compromise and a fear of pushing any theory to its logical conclusion, which has dominated them down to the present time" Russell:" ibid., p. 625.

[5]In his *Essay on Human Understanding*, Book II, Chapter 28, par. lo and on.

[6]Ibid., Book IV, Chapter 10: "Our Knowledge of God's Existence."

[7]John Locke: *De Cive*, Chapter IV.

verses from the Qur'ān). The English so-called "common sense philosophy" and Mill's formula for the reconciliation of the individual and the society belong here as well.

The objective of the well-known Cambridge School can most succinctly be defined as a "rationalization" of theology. Jodl, speaking of Cudworth, a prominent representative of this school, writes: "The close relation between philosophy and religion, between speculation and faith, is typical for the Cambridge School. In this context, we come to understand how the same man was able, first as a philosopher, to emphasize so strongly the rational essence of the moral, sufficient unto itself, and then, as a preacher, to point out equally strongly the necessity of religious sublimation. Thus there is a philosophy which satisfies religious needs, and a religion which corresponds with reason and permeates us with a warm and bracing feeling. This was a point upon which all the people of the Cambridge School agreed."[8]

The English mind has surpassed itself in creating the theory of the so-called utilitarian morality. This "circle quadrature" is a typical creation of the English eclectic mind. In literature, it is referred to as "the English morals of utilitarity." Moreover, this theory assumes in its later developments a certain theological tint and appears as a new trend under the name of "theological utilitarianism." This is where Buttler, with his assertion that "conscience and egoism," if properly understood, take the same path to happiness, belongs. Hartley's simultaneously held materialistic psychology and concept of God and belief in immortality belong here as, to a certain extent, do the ideas of Warburton, Pali and Richard Price. Pali's idea of God's will about the welfare of human beings, based on the observation of nature, is a purely Islamic method and recalls certain sayings from the Qur'ān.[9]

In this pleiad of thinkers of "the middle way," a particularly prominent name seems to be that of Adam Smith. The nature of his works is literally expressed by the fact that he wrote two books with apparently contradictory but very similar, contents, namely: *The Theory of Moral Sentiments* and *An Inquiry into the Nature and Causes of the Wealth of Nations*, the latter being one of the most influential books of the 18th century. The first book, dealing with

---

[8]Frederick Jodl: *The History of Ethics*, p. 145.
[9]Pali: *Natural Theology*.

ethics, took as its starting point the principle of sympathy; the second, covering social economy, took for its leading idea the principle of egoism. This makes us think that the books were essentially contradictory, but this would not be true because Smith, a professor at Glasgow University, taught ethics, economics and politics as the component parts of an integral course on philosophy. Moreover, in his works, Smith explicitly pointed to the connections between ethics and the wealth of nations. In his *Theory of Moral Sentiments*, we come across the following lines: "Both egoism and moral feelings are facts. In the universal economy of God's project, both of them have been taken into account. Man is a unity. He cannot be in his economic life something different than that."

Totomianc reports some impressions concerning the contradictions inherent in the various parts of Smith's works; Europeans have the same impression of the Qur'ān and Islam. Smith's as well as Hume's aversion to clericalism and religious organization inevitably brings the associations of similar attitudes within Islam.

Spencer's Education might very well have been written by a Muslim; his teachings are typically English when he claims that morals are essentially a state of harmony between the individual and society, and that there are two simultaneous trends of development which coincide, whether true or not: an increasing individualization and an increasing interdependence at the same time.

While in Catholic France the implacable struggle between the spiritualistic and the positivistic school is still continuing, in English ethics the idea of balance between the principle of welfare and the principle of conscience is dominant. Mill's ideas on economy, his insistence on the reconciliation of the individual and social principle, as well as his opinion that wealth has a certain moral importance, have something in common with *zakah* and the Qur'ān. Here, we must also mention a trend known as neo-idealism which appeared in England in the second half of the 19th century (through the works of Martin, Bradley, Green and others), after the predominance of empiricism, and which is also in harmony with the preceding English model.

I would like to quote here a rather long passage on English political life written by Crossman , a contemporary English writer with a socialist orientation. After emphasizing that any simplified assertion about English political life is quite sure to be false, Crossman writes:

> Unlike the utilitarian theorists, the Victorian business man based his politics upon a foundation of religion. He detested the oligarchy not only for its defense of the landlord, but also for its flagrant disregard of moral principle ... the intellectual energy of the victorian age was directed not to a critique of Utilitarian economics but to theological speculation.
>
> It was Darwin's *Origin of Species* not Marx's *Capital* which really disturbed the British middle classes; the Oxford Movement and the Ritualistic controversy into which the activity of its ablest minds were thrown. Gladstone genuinely felt that politics was a second best in comparison with taking orders. The enormous moral stability and self-confidence of 19th-century England can only be understood if we give proper weight to this religious faith. ... The abolition of slavery, the revival of missionary crusade, the attack on child labour, the spread of public education, and dozens of other movements sprang not from a political faith but from the Christian conscience of the community. ... Most of the great 19th-century movements of reform were derived from this source, and only after they had fired the popular imagination did they become part of the programme of politicians. ... It is only on this background of religious convictions and social reforms that a true portrait of British political ideas can be painted.[10]

In another place Crossman continues: "British democracy was connected closely with the struggle for religious freedom. So, the religious motive in its primeval Christian form was harnessed for the sake of democracy, and the triumph of liberalism led to a religious renewal in Victorian England. ... That was possible nowhere else but America ... since progress, people and democracy were for the German and Italian liberals only the subject of the secular cult. Devoted Catholics hold that there is no bridge over the gap dividing belief in Christ and belief in progress, and devoted liberals that clerical domination has nothing in common with democracy and liberty."[11]

English socialism is also of a special kind. On the continent,

---

[10]Crossman: *The Government and the Governed* (New York: Pica Press, 1969) pp. 155-158.

[11]Ibid.

socialism appears closely connected with materialistic and atheistic philosophy, while "from the labor speakers' platforms in England, one can hear as many quotations from the Bible as from the church pulpit of the country," wrote an amazed French newspaper reporter.

Beyond doubt, an authentic English example of the joining of opposites was offered by Bertrand Russell when he said: "The problem of a durable and satisfactory social order can only be solved by combining the solidity of the Roman Empire with the idealism of St. Augustine's City of God."[12] Likewise, in answering the question if ideas help create the world or if it is the other way around, he said: "For my part, I believe that the truth lies between these two extremes. Between ideas and practical life, as everywhere else, there is a reciprocal interaction."[13]

The spiritual sources of American pragmatism are easily recognizable in such outlooks. Its dualism, its acceptance of both religion and science, "provided they prove their practical value," and its postulate that life experience ought to be taken as a criterion for truth is a typical Anglo-Saxon philosophy, and at the same time completely non-European. William James presented the essence of that philosophy in his major work *Pragmatism*. We find it necessary to quote three typical fragments from this remarkable book:

> Most of us expect good things on both sides of the line. Facts are good, give us also a lot of facts; principles are good, give us then a great number of principles, too. The world is beyond doubt a unity if considered in one way, but it is also multiple if considered in another way. It is one and a multitude at the same time. We shall accept, therefore, a kind of pluralistic monism. Everything is determined of course, but our will is free: a kind of determinism of free will would be the most appropriate philosophy. Evil of individual entities cannot be denied, but the whole cannot be evil; and in this way, practical pessimism can be linked with metaphysical optimism.[14]

---

[12]Russell: *History* ... p. 505.

[13]Ibid., p. 620.

[14]William James: Pragmatism (Cambridge: Harvard University Press, 1978) p. 16. Also, note the following: "To rationalists this describes a tramp and vagrant world, adrift in space, with neither elephant nor tor-

James displays here the natural human inclination toward dualism, a form of natural Islam. He called his own philosophy "the new name for some old ways of thinking."[15] James continues: "And then, what philosophy is offered to you when you are in trouble? You find empirical philosophy which is not religious enough, and religious philosophy which is not empirical enough for what you need."[16] Or somewhat further: "Your dilemma is the following one: you find these two systems to which you are aspiring to be hopelessly separated. You find empiricism, but also inhumanity and unreligiousness; or you find rationalistic philosophy which can even call itself religious, but which refrains from any definite contact with real facts, and joys and sorrow."[17]

Bertrand Russell gave a very acceptable formula for understanding pragmatism by underlining two basic philosophical tendencies of its founder: "There were two sides to William James' philosophical interest: one scientific, the other religious. On the scientific side, the study of medicine had given his thoughts a tendency toward materialism, which, however, was held in check by his religious emotions."[18] Let us recall here that English thought, as well as American, started from the same two premises found in Roger Bacon seven centuries earlier. In the meantime, Europe has passed a complete semi-circle, starting from St. Thomas Aquinas at one pole, and ending with Lenin at another.

We cannot surely say what kind of impression pragmatism made on the European mind, but we presume it raised a sort of aversion. From the European point of view, pragmatism is illogical, heterogeneous, inconsistent — qualifications which Europeans usually attribute to Islam.[19] But, pragmatism is the first great American

---

toise to plant the sole of its foot upon. It is a set of stars hurled into heaven without even a centre of gravity to pull against. In other spheres of life it is true that we have got used to living in a state of relative insecurity. The authority of 'the State,' and that of an aboslute 'moral law,' have resolved themselves into expediencies, and holy church has resolved itself into 'meeting-houses.' Not so as yet within the philosophic class-rooms. A universe with such as us contributing to create its truth, a world delivered to our opportunisms and our private judgments! ... Such a world would not be respectable, philosophically. It is a trunk without a tag, a dog without a collar, in the eyes of most professors of philosophy." p.125.

[15]In the subtitle of his work *Pragmatism*.

[16]Ibid., p. 17.

[17]Ibid., p. 19.

[18]Russell: *History* ... p. 774.

[19]One author claims that "pragmatism is the consistent part of the Islamic trad-

philosophical system, one which Europe was *a priori* incapable of creating. It is certain that this pragmatic philosophy was either a stimulus for, or an expression of, or both, the extraordinary vitality and energy of the American people.

This parallelism between English and Islamic minds can be followed through a series of symptomatic facts which deserve to be dealt with separately. The English revolution of 1688 was not very radical. In Russell's opinion, it was the most moderate and, at the same time, the most successful of all revolutions. A lot of occurrences of British political history were never brought to their ultimate conclusions, to their pure forms, but froze in the middle of the road. In England, revolt against the monarchy has not resulted in its abolition, but some elements of the aristocratic system continued to coexist side by side with democratic institutions. In England, the word "minister" has both religious and political connotations — state official and priest. We meet with a similar dualism of terms in Islamic terminology. Contrary to most European states, England introduced a kind of tax on behalf of the poor which recalls the Islamic *zakah*. A similar mind, when facing practical life, was bound to come up with similar solutions.

In the future, it is to be expected that Europe will accept all the consequences of science, including its extremely inhumane results, while England and America will most probably stop at halfway, pragmatic attitudes. For in Europe, congruent to the Christian position, religion is religion and science is science, while in England the supreme judge will always be practice — that is, life.

"Historical Compromise" and Social Democracy

Tendencies toward the "third way" can be found in other parts of the world, though different from England where they exist also in theory — at the levels of thought and feelings. While in Europe, they appear only as a practical necessity, not as a matter of belief. This phenomenon has different manifestations in Catholic and Protestant countries. The ideological polarization is more evident in countries where Catholic influence has historically been stronger. Here, the movement toward a middle way is hard, dramatic, and

---

ition." Dragosh Kalaich in the article "Actuality of Islam", Delo, Belgrade, No. 7, 1978, p. 62.

uncertain. These countries have in a sense become incapable of the "third road." Italy, France, Spain, and Portugal have been or still are examples of sharply polarized societies. Public opinion is here uncompromisingly divided between the Christian (rightist) and the Marxist (leftist) parties and movements. The center is either quite limited or has even been entirely destroyed. The two most famous dogmatisms in history — Catholicism and Communism — have met here, face to face, exhausted through a confrontation in which there can be no winner. Just before its civil war, Spain was a typical example of such a situation. In the 1936 elections, Spain's leftist parties got 51.90 percent, the rightist ones 43.24 percent, and the center only 4.86 percent of all votes.[20] Today's Italy has almost reached "the Spanish proportion" of total polarization. The situation in France is similar.

The inner disintegration of the two dogmatisms is seen in a series of symptoms. One of these is the dialogue between Marxists and Catholics, cautiously instigated in the middle of the sixties.[21]

These dialogues are typical of the European state of mind and of relations on the ideological front between Marxism and religion which has lasted for over a century without a stop or mutual concession. They are a symptom of the failure to organize life on only one principle. Marxists were forced to back down from their classical formula that religion is the "opiate of the masses," and Catholics admitted that the Marxist goal is developing a more just social order.

In the course of one of these Marxist-Catholic dialogues, organized by the Paulus Gesellschaft Society, the following paper was presented: "The Christian Love of Mankind and Marxist Humanism." At the Salzburg meeting, the well-known Marxist writer Roger Garaudy [now a Muslim] said: "The birth of Christianity brought with it for the first time in history an appeal for a community without boundaries, for a totality encompassing all totalities. ... The glorification of love, the concept through which man creates and

---

[20]While writing these lines, Spain is getting ready for its first free elections. Some think that the Spanish people will now choose the center for the first time in their history. If that happens, both rightist and leftist dogmatists will be in a position to learn something.

[21]As far as I know, the first such dialogue was held in Salzburg in 1965 on the initiative of liberal Catholic theologians from West Germany. Soon this became common.

recognizes himself only with the help of others and in others, is the most dignified image that man ever created of himself and of the purpose of life." Palmiro Togliati, leader of the Italian Communist Party, emphasized the need for Marxism to change its attitude toward religion and called for Marxists to face this necessity as soon as possible. In the papal encyclical letters "Pacem in Terris" and "Populorum Progressio," we come across some ideas completely new for the Catholic church: a recognition of the primacy of social over private ownership, the right of intervention by public authority in the economy, the right to agrarian reform and nationalization for the benefit of the community, a support of workers' participation in the management of their firms, and so on.[22]

The Twenty-Second Church Council (the Second Vatican Council) removed the traditionalists' tendencies to condemn Marxism. Judging from relevant reports, this Council admitted that the extremely spiritual Christian position was untenable. Said Cardin Chardin: "In my opinion, the world will adapt to Christian hopes only if Christianity adapts to the hopes of the world. Only in this way will it be possible to divinize it." Is this not a way of "Islamizing" Christianity?

The tendencies are most often interlaced and interwoven, as certain recent symptoms in French developments prove. Not long ago (1977) the Permanent Council of the French Episcopate published a special communication entitled "Marxism, Man and Christian Faith." The French bishops asserted here the failure of the social politics of liberalism and admitted that "Marxism includes a part of truth which we do not ignore." Only a year ago George Marchais, leader of the French Communist Party, declared in his "Lyon Appeal": "Our goal is to make the Communists and the Christians acknowledge each other and follow the same path of respect toward their own originality, standing side by side in the campaign for building a more humane society." The phenomenon in question can be observed with dramatic clarity in Italy. After years of irreconcilable confrontation, the Italian Communist Party decided to take a logical, although unexpected, step: to call for a "historical compromise." If our considerations are correct, this appeal is not just a tactical move

---

[22]Pope Paul II recently made the statement on the occasion of his visit to the USA in 1979 that the "systematic threat to man's rights is connected with the distribution of material goods." Anyone familiar with the true nature of Christianity can estimate what a turn this statement implies.

with temporary goals; it is a sincere proposal arising from the consciousness that there is no other way out. The appeal was addressed to Christians and could not have been addressed to anyone else. After the accounts were made and arguments settled, all others gradually disappeared, leaving only *two* forces on the scene: Looking from the outside, those are Christian democracy and communism, or from the inside, religion and materialism. Italy is an experiment for the future of a large part of the world.[23]

The so-called "Eurocommunism" is an expression of the typical tendency of those polarized societies in European Catholic countries — Italy, France, Spain. The phenomenon is new, but it is already quite clear that it equals communism minus dictatorship plus democracy: a breakthrough from the extreme left (walled within a barrier of dogmas) toward the center.[24] Under the pressure of reality, communism leaves its dogmatic position and accepts the essentially idealistic ideas of freedom and pluralism. That has given Eurocommunism a clear meaning of compromise.

The difference between Eurocommunism and the "historical compromise" is that in the first case we are dealing with a corrected or modified communism, and in the second with communism and Christianity as two equal forces.[25]

The "middle road" in other, mostly Protestant countries, manifests itself in the increasing influence of the centrist parties in those nations's political life. These countries reject pure Christian as well as pure communist governments and show a permanent tendency toward middle solutions. This trend is especially reflected in the

---

[23]In the Italian Communist Party Statute, we come across a definition which would have been unimaginable some time earlier: Party members can be "all those who accept the Party programs, regardless of their religious and philosophical beliefs" (Article 2 of the Statue of ICP). Although the Italian Communist Party is not the only one that changed its attitude on religion, most parties still support a kind of militant atheism. This is the case especially in backward, less civilized countries. Evolution is nevertheless evident and must be continued.

[24]The same meaning seems to apply to the abandonment of the "Cultural Revolution" in China following Mao Tse Tung's death. This occurrence, the most persistent and far-reaching attempt so far at materializing a utopia, evidently proved to be a failure. China could hardly bear to "stand on one leg," i.e., to keep on this ultra-leftist position for ten years. What followed was an inevitable return to a more natural state. If we use the usual terminology (right-left), we are now witnessing a movement from the left toward the center in China.

[25]A number of European communist parties have wiped out the term "dictatorship of the proletariat" from all party documents.

increasing call for social democracy. Protestant countries have found in social democracy the solution which traditionally Catholic societies try to find in the "historical compromise." Social democracy, which in Europe means a compromise between liberalism and social intervention, between the European Christian tradition and Marxism, has been advancing throughout the postwar period and all over the world.[26] After comparing the election results just after World War II with those 25 or 30 days later, we can see an increase in the number of social-democracy votes in nearly all countries having free elections. The increase is 22 percent in Sweden, 36 percent in Denmark, 54 percent in Holland, 27 percent in Norway, over 100 percent in West Germany and as much as 34.8 percent in Malta. In England it is only 5 percent, but we must bear in mind the fact that the process started here much earlier, and that England reached a state of balance before any other European country. Social democracy is a "stable compound," it is a form of social and political balance in Europe.

Mexico and Venezuela, two countries that are very close to social democracy, are at the same time the two most stable countries in the usually unstable area of South America. Development in Japan has not led to polarization but to a strengthening of the center. The term "middle road" is more and more frequently heard in political debates in Mexico and Japan. The social-democrats' meeting in 1976 in Caracas was called "historical" mainly for the relevance of its conclusions, but more so for the feeling that it might be the first step toward formulating a new doctrine. The statement made by the Mexican spokesman Gonzales Sos explained what kind of doctrine it would be: "There are three great political options in the present world — capitalism, communism, and social democracy — and Mexico has to choose among them."

The internal tension of the socialist countries is not primarily concerned with socialism as an economic problem. The most serious opposition concerns the problem of human rights. Everywhere, people seem to be asking for a kind of Christianity with a social

---

[26]The ideologically more fanatical part of this world does not see the situation in this light. Moscow's magazine "The Communist" of July 1979 declares that the "middle road" is objectively impossible. According to this magazine, no alternatives in the form of a "third theory" is possible. There are only two antagonistic socio-political systems, and the polarization process is not fading; on the contrary, it is strengthening so that all countries will sooner or later cling to either the capitalist or the socialist system.

program, or for a kind of socialism without atheism and dictatorship — "socialism with a human face."[27] In China, for example, after Mao Tse Tung's death, censorship was gradually and cautiously removed from Beethoven's and Shakespeare's works (although unwillingly and without conviction) just as it had been removed from Dostoevski, Chagal, and Kafka in the USSR. Demands for freedom will be voiced more and more loudly in the Eastern European countries. No matter how slow, things are moving in that direction. The trend is quite obvious.

The crisis in capitalist countries, on the other hand, has been accompanied by a requirement for more intense social intervention, which sometimes implies certain limitations on freedom. For practical reason, American firms are being drawn toward socialization, while Soviet economic firms are being pushed away from rigid centralism. Professor Wiedenbaum called the contemporary American corporations "half-nationalized," bearing in mind their large dependence on the state. The meeting of prominent political and public workers form the USA, Europe, and Japan held in 1975 in Kyoto (the so-called "Trilaterial Committee") was concerned with the problem of "excessive democracy: in the highly developed capitalist countries. The report resulting from this meeting, *The Crisis of Democracy*, advocated a "moderate democracy" and pointed to a need for certain corrective measures concerning the exaggerated freedom of the press. The paper supported the ideas of economic planning and claimed a more efficient management. That is probably not a complete general plan of a new public policy, but it is a sure hint of a new ideological climate.

While all these phenomena may be symptomatic, they are not Islam nor do they lead to it for they are forced, inconsistent and defective. Islam implies a conscious rejection of the one-sided religious or social postulate, a willing acceptance of the "bipolar principle." Nevertheless, the preceding hesitations, deviations, and inevitable compromises represent a victory of life and human reality over one-sided and exclusive ideologies, and by this an indirect victory of the Islamic conception.

---

[27]That is what Maurice Diverger called "the inevitable process of liberalization in the East and socialization in the West" in his Introduction a la polique, Gallimard, Paris 1970, p. 367. Actually, the Western way of life is not sufficiently social, just as the Eastern way is not sufficiently free.

religious or social postulate, a willing acceptance of the "bipolar principle." Nevertheless, the preceding hesitations, deviations, and inevitable compromises represent a victory of life and human reality over one-sided and exclusive ideologies, and by this an indirect victory of the Islamic conception.

SUPPLEMENT: SUBMISSION TO GOD

Nature has determinism, man has destiny. The acceptance of this destiny is the supreme and final idea of Islam.

SUPPLEMENT: SUBMISSION TO GOD

Nature has determinism, man has destiny. The acceptance of this destiny is the supreme and final idea of Islam.

Destiny — does it exist and what form does it take? Let us look at our own lives and see what has remained of our most precious plans and the dreams of our youth? Do we not come helplessly into the world faced with our own personality, with higher or lower intelligence, with attractive or repulsive looks, with an athletic or dwarfish stature, in a king's place or in a beggar's hut, in a tumultuous or peaceful time, under the reign of a tyrant or a noble prince, and generally in geographical and historical circumstances about which we have not been consulted? How limited is what we call our will, how tremendous and unlimited is our destiny!

Man has been cast down upon this world and made dependent on many facts over which he has no power. His life is influenced by both very remote and very near factors. During the Allied invasion of Europe in 1944, there was, for a moment, a general disturbance in radio communications which could have been fatal for the operations under way. Many years later, the disturbance was explained as a huge explosion in the Andromeda constellation, several million light years away form our planet. One type of catastrophic earthquake on the earth is due to changes on the sun's surface. As our knowledge of the world grows, so does our realization that we will never be complete masters of our fate. Even supposing the greatest possible progress of science, the amount of factors under our control will always be insignificant compared to the amount of those beyond it. Man is not proportional to the world. He and his lifetime are not the measuring units of the pace of things. This is the cause of man's eternal insecurity, which is psychologically reflected in pessimism, revolt, despair, apathy, or in submission to God's will.

Islam arranges the world by means of upbringing, education, and laws. That is its narrower scope; submission to God is the broader one.

Individual justice can never be fully satisfied within the conditions of existence. We can follow all Islamic rules which, in their ultimate result, should provide us with the "happiness in both worlds"; moreover, we can follow all other norms, medical, social and moral but, because of the terrific entanglement of destinies, desires and accidents, we can still suffer in body and soul. What can console a mother who has lost her only son? Is there any solace for a man who has been disabled in an accident?

We ought to become conscious of our human condition. We are immersed in situation. I can work to change my situation, but there are situations which are essentially unchangeable, even when their appearance takes a new look, and when their victorious power is veiled: I must die; I must suffer; I must fight; I am a victim of chance; I get inevitably entangled in guilt. These basic conditions of our existence are reffered to as "the border situations."[1] Sure, "man is bound to improve everything that can be improved in this world. After that, children will still go on dying unjustly even in the most perfect of societies. Man, at best, can only give himself the task of reducing arithmetically the sufferings of this world. Still, injustice and pain will continue and, however limited, they will never cease to be blasphemy."[2]

---

[1]Karl Jaspers: *An Introduction to Philosophy*, vol 2, trans. E.B.Ashton (Chicago: The University of Chicago, 1970). Also, see the following on boundary situations: "Death and suffering are boundary situations that exist for me without any action of mine. At a glance I see them exhibit features of existence. Struggle and guilt, on the other hand , are boundary situations only as I help to bring them about; they are my own active doing. But they are boundary situations, because in fact I cannot be without bringing them upon myself. There is no way in which I might hold back, since by merely existing I take part in their constitution. In any attempt to avoid them I shall prove either to be constituting these two situations in another form or to be destroying myself. I deal with death and suffering existentially, in a boundary situation that I see; struggle and guilt I must inevitably create before, placed in them as boundary situations, I can become existentially aware of them and adopt them, no matter how." p.197.

[2]Albert Camus: *L'Homme révolté* (Paris: Gallimard, 1951).

Submission to God or revolt — these are two different answers to the same dilemma.

In submission to God, there is some of every (human) wisdom except one: shallow optimism. Submission is the story of human destiny, and that is why it is inevitably permeated with pessimism: for "every destiny is tragic and dramatic if we come down to its bottom."[3]

Recognition of destiny is a moving reply to the great human theme of inevitable suffering. It is the recognition of life as it is and a conscious decision to bear and to endure. In this point, Islam differs radically from the superficial idealism and optimism of European philosophy and its naive story about "the best of all possible worlds." Submission to God is a mellow light coming from beyond pessimism.

As a result of one's recognition of his impotence and insecurity, submission to God itself becomes a new potency and a new security. Belief in God and His providence offers a feeling of security which cannot be made up for with anything else. Submission to God does not imply passivity as many people wrongly believe. In fact, "all heroic races have believed in destiny."[4] Obedience to God excludes obedience to man. It is a new relation between man and God and, therefore, between man and man.

It is also a freedom which is attained by following through with one's own destiny. Our involvement and our struggle are human and reasonable and have the token of moderation and serenity only through the belief that the ultimate result is not in our hands. It is up to us to work, the rest is in the hands of God.

Therefore, to properly understand our position in the world means to submit to God, to find peace, not to start making a more positive effort to encompass and to overcome everything, but rather a negative effort to accept the place and the time of our birth, the place and the time that are our destiny and God's will. Submission to God is the only human and dignified way out of the unsolvable senselessness of life, a way out without revolt, despair, nihilism, or suicide. It is a heroic feeling not of a hero, but of an ordinary man who has done his duty and accepted his destiny.

---

[3]Gasset: n.p.d.
[4]Emerson: n.p.d.

Islam does not get its name from its laws, orders, or prohibitions, nor from the efforts of the body and soul it claims, but from something that encompasses and surmounts all that: from a moment of cognition, from the strength of the soul to face the times, from the readiness to endure everything that an existence can offer, from the truth of submission to God. Submission to God, thy name is Islam!

APPENDIX

TABLE OF THE OPPOSITES

The three columns of this table present the religious (R), the Islamic (I), and the materialistic (M) views of the world, each of them starting from Spirit, Man, and Matter, respectively. All concepts, ideas, or phenomena within a column are congruous and belong inwardly to each other (vertical line). Furthermore, each of them has its inverse equivalent in the opposite column (horizontal line).

The views of the world occur as entireties. For example, The belief that matter — and not the conscience — is the primeval base of the world (materialistic view of the world) is always followed or accompanied by a number of ideas, beliefs, and opinions appropriate to it. Therefore, a materialist will as a rule prefer society to man and be enthusiastic about Darwin, public education instead of the family education, and progress instead of humanism. He will see historical movement — and human behavior as well — as subjected to inevitable laws beyond human will and intentions. He will also advocate social rights and social security at the expense of human rights and freedom, and so on. By following this analysis, he will find an inward connection between evolution theories and denial of human rights, or between atheism and Stalin's purges, and so on. Similar inward connections between seemingly distant phenomena can also be found in the column presenting the religious view of the world.

The table is obviously too rigid and brief, something which is unavoidable.

COLUMN "R"	COLUMN "I"	COLUMN "M"
Spirit	**Man**	**Matter**
Conscience		Being
Soul		Body
Subject		Object
"Ding an sich" (Kant)		Phenomena
"Being by Itself" L'être en Soi		"Being for Itself" L'être pour soi
Organic		Mechanic
Poiesis (Aristotle)		Mimesis (Aristotle)
Concrete – Unique		Abstract – General
Genus – Symbol		Category – Number
Quality		Quantity
Religion – Art		Science

Prayer	Salah	Production
		Hygiene
Charity	**Zakah**	Tax / "Expropriation of Expropriators"
Value Judgments – Ethics		Logic Judgments – Mathematics
"Critique of the Practical Reason"		Critique of the Pure Reason
Consciousness – Ideal – Idea – Sin		Need – Interest – Fact – Damage
Meditation – Inspiration – Intuition		Observation – Intelligence – Experience
Holy Secret		Problem
Drama – Moral Questions – Metaphysics		Political Economy – Social Problems – Physics
Monastery – Temple – Art Gallery	**Mosque – School**	School – Laboratory
Morals	**Law – Shari'ah**	Power
Love – Nonviolence	**Justice – Jihad**	Class Struggle / Violence in Use of Interest
Monk – Saint	**Shahīd (martyr)**	Knight – Political Fighter – Hero
Style		Function
Aesthetical Shaping		Technical Perfection
Creation		Evolution
Man Created by God		Man, Product of Nature
"Prologue in Heaven" / Humanization of the Human		Living Matter – Animal – Man Superman
Michelangelo		Darwin
Moral Drama / Struggle for Salvation		Struggle for Survival – Natural Selection / Reproduction of the Material Life
Animism – Personalism		**Reism – Chosism**
Christian Personalism		Historical Materialism
Heroic Explanation of History		Materialistic Explanation of History
History Made by Geniuses		"History Does Not Walk on Its Head" (Marx)
Gradual Development of Absolute Spirit		Progress of the Production Means
Triumph of the Idea of Freedom		The Classless Society
Doomsday		**Entropy**
People Led by Ideas, Ideals		People Led by Needs, Interests
Ascetism – Upbringing		Drill – Education
Classical / Grammar Education		Technological / Exact Education
Might over Self		Might over Nature
"Destroy the Wishes"		"Create the New Wishes"
"Doings Are Judged by Intentions"		"Doings Are Judged by Consequences"
Principle of Guilt / Punishment	**Protective Punishment**	Social Defense Principle / Measure / Purge

Culture	**Man**	**Civilization**
Humanism		Progress
Culture – Consensus – Individualization	**Jama'ah**	Mass – Culture – Manipulation – Uniformity
Drama		Utopia
Personality		"Social Animal"
Spiritual Community	**Ummah**	Social Class
Civitas Dei	**Caliphate**	*Civitas Solis*
Liberté – Egalité – Fraternité		Class Struggle
Human Rights		Social Rights
American Bill of Rights of 1776		Soviet "The Working & Exploited People Rights Declaration" of 1918
The Humiliated and the Insulted (Dostoevski)		*The Exploited* (Marx)
Original Sin – Chastity – Celibacy		Sexual Freedom / Sexual Revolution
Marriage as a Sacrament	**Marriage**	Marriage as a Contract
Religious Cult of the Aged – Wisdom		Civilization Cult of Youth – Biopotency
Home / Mother / Family Education / The Three-Generation Family		Kindergarten /Nursery School / Tutor / Public Education / Home for Aged
Jesus	**Muhammad**	**Moses***
CHRISTIANITY	**ISLAM**	**MATERIALISM**

(*) Moses (Musa), upon whom be peace, cannot be associated with materialism, nor can Jesus be associated with pure religion (Christianity). According to the Qur'ān, they stood for Islam and were Muslims. Here, Moses stand symbolically for materialism because of his Jewish following and so does Jesus for pure religion because of his Christian following.

INDEX